MUMMY, TAKE ME HOME

David Leslie has worked for the *News of the World* since 1970. He has covered scores of major stories, including the tragedies of Zeebrugge, Piper Alpha, Lockerbie and Dunblane. He is also the author of the bestselling *Crimelord: The Licensee*, about the elusive multimillionaire gangster Tam McGraw, *The Happy Dust Gang* and *Bible John's Secret Daughter*.

Mummy, Take Me Home

A Mother's Tug-of-Love Torment

David Leslie

MAINSTREAM
PUBLISHING

EDINBURGH AND LONDON

Copyright © David Leslie, 2008
All rights reserved
The moral right of the author has been asserted

First published in Great Britain in 2008 by
MAINSTREAM PUBLISHING COMPANY (EDINBURGH) LTD
7 Albany Street
Edinburgh EH1 3UG

ISBN 9781845962296

No part of this book may be reproduced or transmitted in any form
or by any other means without permission in writing from the publisher,
except by a reviewer who wishes to quote brief passages in connection with
a review written for insertion in a magazine, newspaper or broadcast

Extracts from *The Herald* reproduced with permission of
The Herald, Glasgow © 2008 Herald & Times Group

The author has made every effort to clear all copyright permissions, but
where this has not been possible and amendments are required,
the publisher will be pleased to make any necessary
arrangements at the earliest opportunity

This book is a work of non-fiction. In some cases the names of
people have been changed to protect the privacy of others.

A catalogue record for this book is available
from the British Library

Typeset in Frutiger and Times New Roman

Printed in Great Britain by
CPI Cox and Wyman, Reading, RG1 8EX

Acknowledgements

More than a decade ago, while on a trip to the north of Scotland on behalf of the *News of the World*, I called at the home of Flora Dempster to inquire about the progress of the Jasmine case. Just weeks earlier, a Texas jury had awarded her and Morag joint custody of the child. During my visit, I was introduced to Morag and was struck by her beauty. In recent years, like everyone who knows her, I have been moved by the dreadful effect that losing her daughter has had on her. And recounting the events in detail has been at times traumatic for Morag, bringing back so many sad memories. She wanted this story told, and I am indebted to her for her courage and persistence, and for the many long hours of interviews in often difficult circumstances. Flora has been a guiding light – encouraging, cajoling, correcting and reminding. Without her, this book would not have been possible. I have been struck by the willingness of so many of those involved to gladly help, in particular Don Evans, Andrew Hathcock, May Cherry and Christine Matyear, while Terry Weeks gave me many hours from his busy schedule. I also want to thank Paul Murphy, my editor at Mainstream, for his patience and kindness.

Contents

Author's Note 9

Prologue 11

1 Spreading Wings 15

2 Breaking Up 23

3 All at Sea 31

4 The Texan 41

5 Jasmine 53

6 Flight 61

7 Sprouting Menace 75

8 Summoned 87

9 Silver Lining 97

10 Bringing Trouble 105

11 Ordeal 115

12 Raising Doubts 121

13 Changing Strategy 129

14 On the Run 135

15 Refuge 147

16 Betrayed 155

17 A Little Piece of Home 165

18 Bad Dog Defence 175

19 Good Guy, Bad Guy 187

20 Uphill Fight 195

21 Poison Pen 203

22 'The Kid Got Hurt' 213

23 Motherhood and Apple Pie 221

24 Love Lost 235

25 Downhill Journey 245

26 Last Sighting 253

27 Wrong Guys 261

Appendix 269

Author's Note

Throughout this story I have used the name 'Morag', the correct birth name of Ms Dodds, who is equally well known as 'Sarah'. Where Sarah occurs in reports, conversations or documents, I have taken the liberty, in order to maintain consistency, of changing this to Morag, a name she and her mother prefer.

Prologue

Tears streamed down the cheeks of the little girl with fair curly hair. She stared up at the strained, tense face of the young woman by her side and pleaded, 'Mummy, take me home.'

There were other two year olds on the streets of Los Angeles that mid-December afternoon. But there were no tears for them. Instead, there were rapt, happy expressions of fascination and awe at the myriad colours and toys coming to life in the windows of the giant stores that seemed to wrap around them. And there were looks of pride and pleasure on the faces of their parents as they remembered their own Christmases and thought of the delights that their children would soon be enjoying.

The pretty toddler and her slim guardian were so out of place among the hurrying shoppers. The child tried to take in the magic around her, but instead her eyes puckered in concentration and effort as she wheeled her own pushchair, her tiny hands clasped on the handles high above her head.

Hungry and weary, she ought to have been seated in it, the striped canopy guarding her from the early afternoon sun. But there was no room. It was filled not with carefully, gaily wrapped Christmas presents, but with bags, boxes, shoes, coats, books and the youngster's baubles.

At first, when her mother had said, 'Sweetheart, Mummy needs you to help. Can you try to push our things in the buggy?' the child, taught to share and help others, had looked up with light-green eyes and scanned her mother's face. 'I'm too big to be in this pushchair, Mummy,' said the little voice with an accent that caused passers-by to listen and smile.

At the start of their walk, they had sung together as if each thought that the familiar words would give the other confidence. 'There's a hole in my bucket, dear Liza, dear Liza,' began the mother, sure that this children's favourite would take her daughter's mind from the ordeal that lay ahead. 'A hole in my bucket, dear Liza, a hole.' And from beneath the hat, protecting the young one from the overhead sun, came a well-rehearsed response, the child's tiny voice struggling to plunge an octave or two lower. 'Well fix it, dear Henry, dear Henry, dear Henry, well fix it . . .' The pattern was broken by a fit of coughing.

It was the song with no end, and that was how the trek was beginning to feel. The infant's eyes were heavy, glazed over by tears, and the woman was only able to trudge slowly along, weighed down by a heavy bag strapped to her back and a suitcase in each hand. The anxiety of one intent on hiding the unease and uncertainty that had overwhelmed her thoughts for so long was evident on her face. It was the greatest fear of any mother: that of losing a child.

There were so many people who wanted to take this tiny treasure from her, to deprive her of her own daughter – none more so than the tot's father. This tanned, good-looking Texan had been a knight in shining armour to the girl with stunning looks and long blonde tresses who fell for him on a windswept oil platform far into the grey North Sea. Their passion had produced a laughing, gurgling, crying, smiling, crawling, falling bundle of joy named Jasmine.

Morag, Jasmine's mother, had loved both with a ferocity that she thought could never dim. But as the months passed, her feelings for the Texan began to fade. She might have hoped that their eventual parting would let her close the door on that part of her life, if not that of their daughter's. To her cost, she would find it was but the beginning.

Marcus Chapman insisted that he knew his rights. And those included first access to and then custody of little Jasmine. Ordered to fight the case in America, Morag had arrived in Austin with the youngster, filled with hope. But as the weeks dragged into months, her confidence, like her savings, began to wane.

From birth, mother and daughter had been inseparable. Now they were allowed only a few hours together once in a while after Jasmine was placed in the temporary care of the Chapman family. Battered by mounting legal bills, Morag acted like any loving mother. Throwing together her belongings and taking her daughter by the hand, she fled, and in doing so crossed from one state into another: from Texas, land of gunfighters and oilmen, to California and its gold prospectors and movie stars.

As a result, a warrant was issued for her immediate arrest, and the forces of law and order were called in to track down and seize her. It was alleged that she had abducted her own child, whom she had given birth to just two and a half years before. She would surely go to prison and possibly to death row, because abducting a minor could lead to the electric chair. And so she sought sanctuary at the British Consulate-General in Los Angeles.

A taxi would have taken them there from the bus station in moments. But Morag had no money, just a pair of stolen passports, a handful of cents, the return half of a long-distance bus ticket and the dread of what lay behind and ahead. There was just enough money in her purse to buy her daughter a hamburger and a drink of water, but not enough for food for herself. Sympathetic fellow travellers at the bus depot reassured her when she asked for directions. 'Don't worry,' they said. 'You'll be there soon.'

It was a walk of less than half an hour, no more than the distance that she and the little girl were used to walking each day to visit friends and not even long enough to tire the child so that she would stop and hold out her arms in the universal unspoken gesture that said that she wanted to be carried. Now it seemed so far as to be never-ending, an eternal and frightening journey

13

through strange, unfamiliar streets. And doubt ravaged Morag's mind. What would happen at the British Consulate-General? Would she be given help? Would it even be open?

Her worry caused her physical pain, and she twice had to stop and be violently sick. Even Jasmine was not untouched by concerns. Seeing so many Santas in the giant store windows, she had questions of her own, the most important of which was how Santa would be able to find her.

'Don't worry, sweetheart. Santa knows where every little girl and boy is.' But Jasmine remained unconvinced and wanted more reassurance. 'He'll probably sneak in the back door, sweetheart,' Morag replied, but it only led to many more questions. Who will leave the door open? How will Santa know where to get in? What if he doesn't find the door? These were important matters to a little girl and brought on an even more worried look.

'Mummy, can we go home? Please can we go home? Please, Mummy, take me home,' begged the little angel who was Morag's life. But home was in the north of Scotland, 5,000 miles away in a house overlooking fields where horses gambolled and dogs lapped and licked. Home was warmth and food. Home was where friends were decorating trees with gay lights, sending cards wishing happiness and good luck, wrapping gifts. Home was safety and comfort. Home was a lovely town called Forres, where Morag Dodds had lived with her little daughter until the child's father had started legal proceedings to take her into his custody and make her home with him in the Texan city of Austin.

'Sweetheart, not long now,' she promised.

Morag longed to stop, to rest and to cry – how she wanted to cry – but if she did, she knew the child would blame herself for her mother's sorrow. And so she struggled on, oblivious to the inquisitive stares of strangers who brushed past. Her mind was a turmoil of loneliness and despair. Slowly, she put down her cases, hugged her bewildered infant and wondered, 'What has brought us to this?'

1

Spreading Wings

There is a world of difference between the extravagant metropolis of Los Angeles, California, to which Morag and little Jasmine made their weary way, and the tiny village of West Allotment in Northumberland. One is a booming, flourishing giant, home to droves of celebrities who flaunt their way around Hollywood, Beverly Hills and Sunset Strip, the other a remnant of a once-thriving coal-mining area.

Morag was born in a little cottage hospital at Rothbury in the west of Northumberland in January 1964. Her dad Tony had fallen in love with her mother Flora after a chance meeting at a dance. Flora worked in the stables at Callaly Castle in Northumberland. After leaving school in Scotland, Flora's first job had been caring for polo ponies on an estate in Gloucestershire, but when the chance came to move back north she gladly took it because it brought her nearer to her family. On Tyneside, Tony was gaining practical experience on a nearby farm as part of his studies at an agricultural college. Like most young people, their Fridays and Saturdays were spent at dances in local village halls, when the highlight of the evening was normally a punch-up over a young woman. Happily, after meeting Flora, Tony was allowed to pursue his courtship relatively unchallenged. They married in Aberdeen and settled on a farm at Longframlington, again in Northumberland.

When Flora fell pregnant, the young couple were naturally overjoyed. There were no clouds on the horizon, until one day, with the baby not due for another five months, nature took a hand. Tony returned home as normal and told his wife that he had delivered a calf that day. Flora's mother and stepfather were visiting from their home in Scotland, and she left them with her husband to go to a weekly sewing class. When she returned, she could tell by the expression on her mother's face that something was wrong. 'It's Tony,' her mother said. 'He's had to take to his bed, and even getting there was a struggle because he's suddenly lost all feeling in his legs.'

Flora took one look at her husband then ran, her heart pounding, to a local public house, where she begged to use the telephone. She called the family GP, who initially assumed something was wrong with the pregnancy but quickly grasped what the actual source of Flora's distress was, and he wasted no time in dashing to her aid.

By the time the doctor arrived, Tony was in a bad way, paralysed from the neck down, unable to move a finger or foot. He was rushed by ambulance to hospital in Newcastle upon Tyne, where X-rays confirmed the experts' worst fears. Veins attached to the spinal column had burst, causing blood to leak into his spinal cord. It would require an immediate and risky operation, and there was no easy way for the surgeon to explain to the patient or his wife what the possible outcome of the procedure might be. 'You must prepare yourselves for the fact that Tony may never walk again,' he told them. 'Get set for the worst. Don't raise your hopes and expectations, and if we can do anything to improve his situation, then look upon that as a bonus.' It was a terrible blow for two young people who had been confident that they had everything to look forward to. Tony was 23 and Flora just 19.

Whether fate relented or the skill of the surgeon prevailed, no one can be sure, but the operation was successful. However, it would be many long months before Tony could walk unaided, and even before he had left hospital it was clear that he would never be able to return to the strenuous and often risky tasks involved in farming. This posed another problem: their house belonged to the farmer who employed Tony, and if there was no job, there was no home.

The farmer showed great kindness in allowing his erstwhile dairyman to remain in the house, but there came a time when he reluctantly had to tell the young couple that it was needed for Tony's replacement. By then, there was a growing hope that the patient might ultimately make a near full recovery, because he could stand and move about, admittedly with the aid of a walking frame.

Tony had the added incentive to recover when his and Flora's first child, a boy whom they named Stuart, was born in the cottage hospital in Rothbury. In fact, his recovery, while slow, was so sure that he began eyeing the possibility of driving once again.

Tony's family lived in the town of Tynemouth and were keen to have him, his wife and son living nearby. They announced that a terraced two-bedroomed house at West Allotment was on the market, and they were willing, and financially able, to donate sufficient cash for a deposit. It was good tidings indeed, but Tony and Flora soon had good news of their own. Flora was pregnant again. She had mixed feelings about giving birth a second time, because her labour with Stuart had lasted a full day, but the move to West Allotment, caring for her son and anxiously watching her husband hobbling about meant she had little time to worry. She had her pregnancy confirmed while living in Longframlington by the same doctor who had taken care of her while she was pregnant with Stuart, and he booked her into the Rothbury hospital once again, wisely believing that the familiar surroundings would give her comfort and reassurance.

On the day of the birth, she settled in between the hospital's crisp white sheets and prepared for a rerun of the first long haul. But it was not to be. She barely had time to take notice of her surroundings before she was wheeled to the delivery room. Within an hour, Morag had effortlessly and painlessly arrived, weighing in at 7 lb 13 oz.

Flora thought that her life was nearing fulfilment. Tony was improving – not at breakneck speed, certainly, but quicker and more completely than could have been hoped for at the time he fell ill. Indeed, he had been able to drive from West Allotment to visit Flora and his new daughter in hospital, although his movement was still severely restricted.

With just over a year between the children, Flora was continually on the move. She had never ceased to hanker for a return to her native Scotland, but she loved their little house in Lamb Terrace in West Allotment. Neighbours were forever popping in for a chat and to see the new baby. It was a good, friendly way of life, but it was incomplete. Tony, becoming ever more mobile, needed work and a long-term future. However, prospective employers were reluctant to take on a man whose fitness they judged to be in doubt, eager though he was to prove his capability and usefulness.

Despite the obvious hurdles, Flora and Tony thought that they still had sufficient drive and desire for a new challenge, and after talking to her family decided to move to a new environment. Before Morag was one, the Dodds family waved goodbye to their friends in West Allotment and set off on the long drive north to the village of Kingussie, almost at the midway point between the ancient and historic cities of Perth to the south and Inverness to the north.

Home was no longer a two-bedroomed terraced house in West Allotment but instead a magnificent stone-built edifice with nine bedrooms and three bathrooms. And as the weeks and months went by, it seemed that the move to Scotland was working out well. Tony found employment as a part-time delivery driver for one of the village shops, and for a time even had a second job serving behind the bar in one of the village hotels. When developers moved into Aviemore, 13 miles to the north, and began building a huge holiday centre, Tony also found work as a labourer. Meanwhile, he and Flora realised that their new home provided them with the means to cash in on the booming influx of tourists, and so they put up a bed-and-breakfast sign outside their front door. The idea was an instant success and business flooded in.

For the children, but especially Morag, those years in Kingussie were among their happiest. They had room to spread their growing wings, a myriad of things and places to discover, and the magic of the countryside to investigate. Although much of the house was made over to paying customers, they still had their own room above the kitchen from which they could smell the aroma of baking bread and hot breakfasts. Sometimes, Stuart would play tricks on his little sister, telling her that a ghost lurked in the house. Then, when she made her way downstairs to the toilet, he'd switch off the lights and leave her to scream in darkness.

The sheer volume of business meant that the children often had to make their own entertainment as their parents coped with the demands of their guests, and there were times when they landed themselves in trouble. One morning when Flora and Tony served breakfasts, Morag and Stuart filled up the petrol tanks of guests' cars with sand from their play area. One vehicle broke down later that morning in Aviemore, while another disgruntled motorist actually sent the Dodds a bill for the cleaning of his petrol tank and engine after his car had shuddered to a stop.

In the Highlands, there is a belief that nothing must be wasted, and Flora and Tony were adherents to this theory. Instead of dumping uneaten food from the breakfast tables into the refuse bin, they bought geese. However, the experiment did not last long, as the birds preferred pecking the children rather than slices of black pudding and rolls of bread. The geese had to go and were replaced by turkeys, which proved to be an ideal solution. The family had been promised that the birds were about to reproduce, and each day Flora and the children hunted about for signs of a newly laid egg. Day after day, they drew a blank until Flora discovered the reason. The nest was not in the gardens of the bed and breakfast but in the grounds of a nearby hotel, where staff had eagerly gathered their unexpected harvest.

It was a small deceit but one which upset the children, and Tony vowed to have his revenge. One night, he crept into the grounds of the hotel and removed two fresh eggs, replacing them with obviously rotten ones that Flora had discovered many weeks earlier, lying abandoned in her garden. The following morning, the hotel staff were said to be heard coughing and spluttering while they desperately opened the kitchen windows in an effort to clear away the all-pervading smell that had similar characteristics to mustard gas.

With each day, the bounty from their move to Kingussie paid the family with increasing happiness. They had an admirable way of life, a big house, a healthy income that left enough each year for the whole family to holiday abroad and money in the bank. It was hard work, but they felt they earned it fairly and honestly. However, there remained a feeling that they were not, and might never be, accepted by those born and raised in Kingussie.

'People who had spent their lives in Kingussie regarded the village almost as their own domain,' Flora remembers, 'and while they didn't mind strangers coming in to spend money before leaving, there was a certain resentment of anyone else moving there and making a good living. It was as if people like Tony and me were depriving the locals of something that they should have had. We had a sense that some people, particularly the older folk, were looking down their noses at us. It didn't bother us, as we were running an honest business that was successful because we put a lot of hard effort into it. However, one day we were told by a friend that a lady villager had been overheard saying we were lowering the tone of Kingussie because of our sign, which offered bed and breakfast for 15 shillings.

'Maybe we ought to have let it pass, but Tony was so angry that he telephoned the guilty gossip to say we had as much right to be in business as anyone else and that many other people with stores and pubs in Kingussie benefited from our guests. In short, he left her in no doubt what he thought of her and those like her. I agreed with him but believe he hadn't stopped to think that what he said might spread around the village and lose us friends.'

2

Breaking Up

M orag remembers growing up in Kingussie as the happiest period of her life, and her memories and experiences from that time were ones she always knew she would want children of her own to share. However, there is often a price to be paid for happiness. Morag discovered that the joy, warmth, safety and love that parents provide can quickly fade and disappear. Her sad lesson was one that would also be learned by Jasmine.

For approximately four years in Kingussie, Morag lived a carefree existence, basking in the freedom and innocence of childhood. She still remembers now the great fondness she had for her father in those days. And there is no doubt that her parents showered her with love. When her mother allowed her to help with even the simplest of household chores, it made her feel important. 'I loved those days when everybody seemed to be laughing all the time,' Morag says, 'and there was never any thought that I would grow up and it would come to an end. The primary-school teacher lived just around the corner and was a wonderful lady who was so kind to me, teaching me to read and write before I even began school. She gave me my very first book to read and my very first word to write on my first day at school. It was "cat" – I can still remember it clearly.

'I had so looked forward to that first day, meeting all my new friends, so proud in our uniforms with our hair neatly tied up.

Of course, it was sad for my mum. Having watched Stuart begin school, she now saw me follow, leaving the house empty of our shouts and laughter during the day.'

Tony, having scouted around for long-term employment, was made aware that the local hairdresser was contemplating retirement, so he set about seeking to retrain in this field. His disablement made him eligible for government funding, but the snag was that the course was in Glasgow, meaning that he would be away from home during the week, staying in lodgings. He caught a train south on a Sunday night, leaving Flora and the children on their own. For this reason, the family decided that it made sense to move to Aviemore to be near Flora's mum, who would provide company and help care for the children.

These were difficult times for Tony. The regular travelling and absence from home were taking their toll on a man who had fought back from total paralysis. The situation was not helped by an incident in Glasgow in which he was involved in an altercation with a thug who knocked him to the ground and kicked him in the head. He arrived home that weekend sporting a black eye and determined in future to travel from his lodgings to the college by car. This too caused problems.

Tony bought a car at auction without telling Flora. Tony's knowledge of motor vehicles was negligible and Flora knew it. If she found out what he had done, she'd give him a tongue lashing and point out that he should have consulted her or taken advantage of one of her close relatives who was a mechanic, so he remained silent.

One morning, he left his digs to find the car missing. That weekend, he returned home to Aviemore by train and said nothing to his wife about either the purchase or theft of the car. Flora was therefore surprised when a week later the police called to say that the family's stolen vehicle had been recovered, although it was damaged.

Most weekends, Tony would earn a few extra pounds by cutting the hair of neighbours and friends. Sometimes, customers would come to the Aviemore house, where Tony would snip away. From time to time, Morag would slip into the room and watch in fascination as strands of hair tumbled to the floor, listening to the click of her father's scissors. To a little girl, it was an impossible action to ignore. She only needed a customer, and her best friend Katrina was the guinea pig. Calmly, she proceeded not just to cut her pal's long and flowing locks, but left her all but bald – to the horror of both sets of parents. Katrina's father was especially enraged at this despoliation of his daughter's crowning glory. Undeterred, Morag next selected as her target the family three-piece suite, which was covered in a fur-like fabric. Huge chunks of fur soon lay scattered on the floor, and the suite took on a mottled appearance.

Eventually, Tony completed the course successfully, but while he waited for a full-time hairdressing opportunity to turn up, he worked in the trade part time and supplemented the family income by acting as a delivery driver.

The Kingussie house went on the market and was soon snapped up, giving Tony and Flora a healthy profit on their original investment. However, although the move had seemed like a sound idea, Flora found that she now had time on her hands – she was used to having her family constantly about her and a house filled with guests who needed clean rooms, freshly laundered beds and hearty breakfasts.

While in Kingussie, Flora had become friends – and at that stage no more than friends – with a local businessman by the name of Donald 'Donnie' Dempster, who owned a garage near the bed and breakfast. He knew Tony and the family, and would keep a kindly eye out for the children as they crossed the road each morning on the short walk to school. If the time for assembly grew near and they had not been seen, he would telephone Flora, who admits that when there were no guests she was notoriously unreliable at getting out of bed to remind the children that they should be up and on their way.

It was a friendship built on innocence, but not according to the village gossips, who missed nothing and were eager to pounce once they scented a whiff of scandal. The friendship might have dwindled because of the distance between them when the Dodds moved to Aviemore, but, as in so many rural communities where the population is sparse and entertainments few, it is difficult for paths not to cross socially. So, the Dodds and Dempsters regularly found themselves in the company of each other – too often for the liking of those who enjoyed maliciously spreading innuendo. And Flora and Donnie felt drawn to one another. Sometimes, if business took him near Aviemore, Donnie would call on Flora for a coffee and a chat, and he would ask about Tony and the children.

Inevitably, word reached Tony during one of his weekends at home. The children, used to hearing their parents chat and laugh pleasantly in the company of one another, now had to listen to shouts and screams that bewildered and frightened them. Flora insisted to her husband that she and the garage owner were simply good friends. The truth was that she and Donnie had become lovers.

A widening gap developed between Tony and Flora. What had seemed like a new beginning in Aviemore was in reality only a continuation of the decline in their marriage, and soon they were sleeping in separate beds. For the children, there ought to have been excitement at the move. Certainly, Stuart revelled in his new surroundings, and the new house meant that he and Morag had a bedroom of their own for the first time. Morag was even presented with twin beds so that friends could stay overnight and a vanity basin specially chosen for her by Flora. But the little girl had those feline instincts which despair of change. Instead of the move thrilling her, it was one that traumatised five-year-old Morag. She suddenly realised that when she began at her new school, she would no longer have the familiar faces of friends about her. At Kingussie, she had seen new starters reduced to tears as a result of being teased and mocked, especially by older children. And now she was convinced that she would face the same ordeal.

She spent her first days screaming and in tantrums. 'When my parents moved to Aviemore,' she remembers, 'I had to change to the primary school there. It was like being dragged away from everything and everyone I loved. The very first morning in class, I became hysterical. I immediately went nuts when I entered the classroom and tried to tear the place down, telling anyone who was prepared to listen that I refused to stay there. It was terrible not knowing anyone, and I could not see why my teacher from Kingussie, who had been so kind and whom I loved so much, could not have come with me. I did not want change. The teachers sat me down and tried to persuade me not to scream and shout and to be more sensible, but when I tried running out of the classroom they had to telephone my mother and ask her to come and sit with me.

'That worked for a while, but then I realised I could see our new house through the school windows, and I ran away to get to my room there. I was caught, of course, and brought back. Everyone was so patient and nice, but I just did not want to be there. I was crying because I missed my teacher in Kingussie so much – she had been like a kind granny to me and my best friend. Now she was no longer there. I was so miserable my mother even asked if she could drive me back and forward to Kingussie every day, but the school authorities would not allow her to do so.

'This was a time when I hated everything, including my school and my new classmates, whom I began pinching because I blamed them as much as anyone for my misery. At home, my mum and dad would yell and shout at one another, and I would be awoken at night to the sound of them arguing and screaming. I never knew what the rows were about, of course, but even then I told myself that when I grew up and had a little girl I would never make her so unhappy and force her to be frightened by the sounds of adults fighting.

'Sometimes my mother would sleep with Stuart, and that just seemed to make the turmoil worse. My parents' arguments disturbed me a lot, and Stuart was also upset. He was kind to me then. On my seventh birthday, he came into my bedroom. Mum

27

had given him a packet of felt-tipped pens, and he knew I was very keen on drawing, so he gave them to me. We had a lovely chat about painting and drawing, and I felt so close to him that day. But my happiness was not to last.'

One day not long after her birthday, Flora suddenly told the children to pack up. To Morag, it was a trauma equal to that of her school move. 'Mum didn't tell me or my brother where we were going,' she says. 'She just kept telling us to "Hurry up and get your favourite toys". She had a Mini at the time. It was parked outside the front of our house, and we were told to get in. Mum said, "If your father asks where you are going to be, tell him the doctor will know." We both asked where we were going, but she did not tell us. Neither of us could work out what was happening.

'That day, my dad came home earlier than expected. He parked in the driveway and saw Stuart sitting in the front of the Mini with me in the back. My dad went over to my mum, and they spoke, although we couldn't hear the words. Then Mum came to the car and told me to get out and speak to my dad. He picked me up in his arms and gave me a cuddle. Then he asked, "Where are you going, sweetheart?" I had to tell him, "I don't know, Daddy. My mummy says if you want to know where I'm going, you have to ask the doctor." My dad was holding me and tears were streaming down his face. He was desperately upset, and so was I. When he put me down, I got back into the car and we drove off. I remember turning around and watching him wiping away his tears as he waved.'

Flora drove the children to her mother's home, where the three would stay for some months, although Tony was a frequent visitor, often turning up just for a chat over a dram with his mother-in-law. Flora encouraged him to call often to see the children, not that he needed to be asked.

Before long, brother and sister were parted for the first time. Morag could have remained with her brother and mother but felt sorry for her father. 'You all have somebody, but my dad has nobody,' she told the adults. 'He's all alone, and I don't want him to be sad and unhappy. I want to stay with him.' She would eventually get her wish, but first she lived at her grandmother's in Aviemore and then moved to Inverness with her mother.

Stuart and Flora then went to live, temporarily, in a caravan in Kingussie with Donald Dempster before they transferred to a neat cottage in the village. But because it only had two bedrooms, pleas from Morag, backed by her father, for short stays with her mother and brother had to be turned down on the grounds that there was insufficient room and the children were too advanced in years to share a room.

Flora and Tony divorced, and Flora and Donnie became man and wife in a quiet register-office ceremony in Fort William. They then moved north to the town of Forres, east of Inverness, where they began building a beautiful bungalow in 16 acres of land with a stunning view over the Moray Firth. Tony remained in Aviemore and eventually engaged a housekeeper called Sue, who went on to become his wife.

Once in Aviemore, Morag would often regret the decision to move. Her grandmother had been the source of unlimited generosity, feeding her with tasty home-baked cakes and frequently putting a sweetie on her plate. The result was that she gained weight and took on a tubby appearance. 'Dad felt I was too fat,' she says, 'and Sue wouldn't let me have biscuits or bacon sandwiches, which I loved.'

Tony and Sue would ultimately move south to settle on Tyneside, where they still live. However, before the move, while living with her father in Aviemore, Morag looked forward to seeing her mother and Donald on a weekly basis on a Saturday, and luxuriated in being, as she puts it, 'spoiled rotten' by Donald Dempster. She would often go swimming and would be fed bacon rolls and coffee afterwards. These were happy occasions for her: 'I used to look forward to these visits. It was lovely to sit down in a café with mum for half an hour and be loved, and lovely to have something that I was not normally allowed.'

Her many changes of scenery and being in adult company as

a child left Morag with an ability to be independent, a trait not always found or encouraged in children today. Occasionally, this manifested itself as loneliness and insecurity, but Morag always felt her parents, even when parted, continued to love her.

However, Morag's independence and sense of being loved led her to believe that those close to her were to be trusted. Sadly, such blind devotion is frequently abused. As she entered her teenage years, Morag moved to Forres to live with her mother and Donald Dempster, but she took with her a memory and shame that can never be eradicated. And in order to understand the ferocity with which she would seek to protect little Jasmine in the ordeals that lay ahead and to better sympathise with her motives, it is essential to mention an especially distasteful series of incidents that were handled with crass stupidity and clumsiness.

During this particularly formative period, Morag was the victim of sexual abuse. It is not necessary to go into detail, other than to say that her experience was relatively minor, although still extremely traumatic. It happened on several occasions, and when she complained to an adult who ought to have acted with alacrity she was not believed.

Morag was 'counselled' by a GP who took her to one side and checked for evidence of the abuse. Her mother was not informed. The issue went no further, and the matter ended as far as the authorities were concerned. However, it was resurrected two decades later in a Texas courtroom, by which time Morag had suffered an even greater and more devastating abuse. That of being punished for loving her own child.

3

All at Sea

Morag looked forward to living with her mother, brother and Donnie in Forres. All four briefly lived in rented accommodation in the town until the newly built house was ready to open its doors to them. It was much admired, and Morag could sometimes see as far as the distant coastline of Caithness, where giant oil platforms were towed into the Moray Firth for repairs before heading back to stand far out into the North Sea as if on sentry duty.

Flora kept horses, and the house was a regular meeting point for the equestrian fraternity. She herself was training to be a driving instructor. It was a wonderful environment in which to bring up a child, and Flora hoped that some day Morag would have a daughter of her own to romp and run about the fields and surrounding woodlands. Like Tony, Donnie was devoted to Morag.

Morag found it easier to accept her mother being with another man than her father being with another woman. Like many girls, she was of the opinion that if her mother could or would not care for her father, then that task should fall to her and not a stranger. Morag's dislike of Sue had contributed to her ambition to be reunited with her mother, but when she moved to Forres to be with Flora she soon discovered that all was not as she'd hoped.

Morag followed Stuart to the local Forres Academy to complete her education but was in for an early shock. A girlfriend whom she had not seen for some years approached her on the first morning, a smile of greeting lighting her face. 'Morag, great, welcome back,' she said. 'How was boarding school?'

'Boarding school? I haven't been to boarding school.'

'Yes, you have. Stuart said you had.'

The idea of telling his school friends that Morag had been to boarding school was probably Stuart's way of avoiding prying questions that he did not wish to answer about where his sister had been and why she had not lived with him and his mother.

Another surprise followed that same day when a boy asked Morag, 'Dodds? There's a guy here of that name. Do you know him?'

'That's Stuart Dodds, my brother.'

'Brother! He never mentioned to anyone that he had a sister.'

To discover that her own flesh and blood had not acknowledged her existence was bad enough, but further disappointment was brewing at home when it quickly became apparent that things were not as they had once been between Flora and Donald. Cracks were appearing in the relationship, and they frequently argued.

As the time to leave Forres Academy drew near, it was obvious that Morag was a beauty in the making and was much admired not just by her fellow students but by others in the town. However, she seemed content with the friendship of a young man she had met during classes, and the pair frequently paid calls on one another. She became a keen partygoer, occasionally breaking house rules to join in the fun. One winter night when snow had fallen, Morag begged permission to join her friends in town but was refused on the grounds that it was too cold. The next morning, after she appeared for breakfast before heading to school, Donald took her outside and stood with her below her bedroom window.

'You go out last night, Morag?' he asked.

'No,' she replied, all innocence and sincerity.

'Well, you must have had a visitor.'

'A visitor? I wasn't aware of that. I was fast asleep.'

'Well,' said Donald, pointing to a series of marks in the snow leading to and away from her window, 'how do you reckon those footprints got there?'

'Must have been an animal,' she replied.

'An animal, wearing size-four pointed shoes?'

Morag had hoped that by once more linking up with Flora there would be a greater understanding of her emotional and social needs. Flora had been no shrinking violet herself, and her love of dancing and partying had clearly been passed on to her daughter. She sensed the need to rein in Morag from time to time, but putting limits into practice was no easy task as the jaunt out of her window into the snow demonstrated. Such surreptitious forays did not prove a setback to her education, but, like many who reach school-leaving age, Morag was eager to see more of the outside world and to have her own money in her purse.

Talking over sly cigarettes with her contemporaries at school, she would quiz her friends about how they saw their futures. Most were intent on simply leaving school, feeling that they had suffered enough learning, but Morag had developed a desire to look after others. Maybe it was the result of her own tangled development, of being a part of so much bitterness and disappointment, but she determined that she would become a nurse. Leaving the Academy, she applied for a place at Robert Gordon University in Aberdeen but was told that she was short on qualifications and was advised to continue her education for another year. That entailed going to college in Elgin, just a few miles east of Forres, to complete a health-studies course. Flora, sensing that the decline of her marriage to Donald could only adversely affect her daughter's ability to study, found Morag a flat in Elgin, which she shared with three other girls.

Morag was persuaded that by joining the Army she could pursue a nursing career, and after sitting an entrance examination she was accepted. But she turned the offer down, telling her friends, 'I don't think I could handle the discipline. I'll comply with discipline, but I don't like it, and in the long run I'd allow it to upset me.' So, instead, she worked hard in order to win the place she sought at university in Aberdeen, by now determined that she would become a nursery-school teacher. Her efforts paid off when she was accepted.

Despite her course at Elgin being partially funded by a local-authority grant, money, or the lack of it, was always a problem, and during summer and other holidays she took on a variety of jobs, including a stint as a waitress at a hotel in Ullapool to the far west of Scotland. She remembers the experience with fondness: 'It was good fun, and I was able to enjoy it more than the others because I knew I wouldn't be doing it for the rest of my life. I could afford to be flippant. If I got the sack, then so what? I didn't need a reference as a waitress when I was aiming to become a nurse. All the same, I did my best, although things went wrong from time to time.

'One of the guests, an absolute boor of a guy, was constantly rotten to his wife, pulling her up for everything: her dress, her make-up, the things she said. He was one of those people you can never satisfy, always condemning his food and drinks. One evening, he called for the dessert trolley, and I was right at his side when I spun it around too quickly and a big dollop of cream flew off the top of a cake and landed in his face. I apologised, because you had to be polite to customers, no matter how rude they were, and wheeled the trolley off before he could say anything. When I turned around, his wife was roaring with laughter, as were many of the other guests. It was the first and only time she had laughed during the entire holiday. It had not been deliberate, but I wished it had. Then, on the day the couple left, the man very generously handed me a £10 tip. For once, I was lost for words.

'Our head chef used to like a tipple. He wasn't a massively heavy drinker, not during the day, at any rate, but he would smoke a few joints and have a few cans of an evening. One night, he offered me a joint. The effect was horrendous. I felt dizzy and ill, and went outside for a walk to try to clear my head, but I ended up toppling into a ditch.

'He was supposed to get up in the morning to prepare breakfasts for the guests but never managed to make it, so the waitresses would do the job for him, because he was such a lovely guy. It was a fine arrangement until one morning the manager unexpectedly turned up and discovered the chef still sound asleep. The chef and I left the hotel at the same time: he for another job, me to study in Aberdeen.'

In Aberdeen, Morag threw herself into becoming a nursery teacher with gusto. Once again, money was a problem, but she showed considerable enterprise by leasing a flat and then subletting part of it to a fellow student whose monthly rent was enough to cover the lease. She also took on part-time weekend and holiday work as a cleaner in an ASDA supermarket. While completing her course, she worked for a time in a hospital in Aberdeen that specialised in the care of children with profound learning difficulties. It was more of a vocation than a task, and she thrilled at seeing the rare smiles that would creep over the faces of her patients when she appeared. But happy though she was, she wanted to see more of the world before she settled down to have the children with whom she was certain she was destined to share the remainder of her life.

Morag was aware that a sense of competition existed between her and her brother, and she told friends that Stuart was envious of her when she was accepted for Robert Gordon University. Stuart, though, proved he was just as capable of achieving success. He became a steward on the great Scottish-built passenger liner the QE2, visiting countries and ports Morag had only read about in books. He lived in Australia for a year and then in the late 1980s, with the help of shipmates, moved to the United States, finally settling in San Diego, California. Their paths were destined to cross there in the years ahead.

Meanwhile, Morag, who was bright and independent and had successfully completed her nursery-teaching course, became excited by a new career opportunity that promised adventure and comparative wealth. However, securing the job was a major challenge. Far out in the North Sea, men were earning big money from the oil industry. Drilling for and pumping oil was risky work, and there were strict safety rules, the three main ones being no alcohol, no drugs and no women. Females, it was argued, were not tough enough.

It was an argument with which Morag disagreed, and a refusal by one of the drilling companies to provide her with an application form was the equivalent of the proverbial red rag to a bull. As she saw it, the elements did not discriminate between the sexes. A man was just as much at risk as a woman, and, determined to have what she saw as her right to a job, she persuaded a boyfriend to telephone and ask for an application form. When they received her completed form, the oilfield employers, realising that they were in danger of being seen as chauvinistic, were forced to capitulate. As a result, Morag became one of the first four women to work offshore.

It meant a huge lifestyle change. Suddenly, she found herself working as a cleaner and stewardess, first in the Ninian and later Alpha fields, with a salary of around £18,000. The money gave her a freedom she had not known before. Now she could afford fine clothes, and instead of saving for a night out could enjoy herself whenever the fancy took her. Offshore, she worked in an accommodation module – in effect, a floating hotel for oilmen – making beds, serving food and cleaning. At night, Morag and her colleagues would sit around listening to music and chatting. Anyone found using drink or drugs was instantly dismissed. There were random checks, and Morag never tested positive for either. Indeed, her employers appointed her as a health-and-safety representative.

It is true to say that most people working on the rigs at that time treated drugs with suspicion and fear. Not so alcohol, which was looked upon with a certain degree of fondness. Booze was often smuggled on board. A favourite means was to buy bottles of mouthwash, pour out the contents and replace them with spirits. However, if she was offered drink, Morag refused. She had worked hard to get the job she loved and was not going to jeopardise her new career.

It was during a night out when she was back on shore that she fell in love for the first time. Donald Ross had the dark curly-haired looks that might have seen a movie producer snap him up for the role of a gypsy. Morag was captivated by his long eyelashes and serious, almost menacing, looks. Donald was from the east-coast town of Arbroath, and Morag was instantly attracted to him. She excitedly telephoned Flora the next day to tell her mother the news: 'I've met the man I want to marry, because I just know our babies will have beautiful long dark eyelashes like his.' The magnetism was mutual, and it was not long before Donald had moved into her flat in Aberdeen.

Approaching her mid-20s, Morag felt that she was nearly ready to settle down, and she missed Donald during her stints offshore. Their courtship was intense, but her frequent absences meant that they did not have the time or opportunity normally given to young people seeking to get to know one another. It was a deficiency that would later prove emotionally costly. They were married at a register office in Inverness in October 1990, with one of Morag's fellow oil-rig colleagues acting as her female witness. Afterwards, they set about buying a house in Marywell, not far from Donald's family in Arbroath.

'For the first time in her life, Morag felt settled and saw her marriage as the start of something wonderful,' Flora remembers. 'She had marvellous plans and was so looking forward to starting a family. She and Donald talked about building an extension to the Marywell house and using it to open a nursery school, because she loved working with children. Everything seemed to be right, but, sadly, the marriage was not a success, which was a terrible knock to all her hopes.'

Indeed, Morag's friends described the marriage as a disaster. Shift patterns meant that she could only see her husband every two weeks, and when she was ashore he was often away working, meaning that they had little opportunity to produce babies with long dark eyelashes. And her desire for those children was short-lived.

Just as she had watched the marriages of her mother and father, and of her mother and Donald Dempster, decay into bitterness and breakdown, her own crumbled before her very eyes, leaving so many dreams shattered. Realising that their relationship was doomed, Morag and Donald Ross went their separate ways. The marriage had lasted just three months. However, they did not divorce immediately, a fact that was to cause her problems later on.

Morag was heartbroken by the premature breakdown of her marriage, and it quickly became apparent that someone wished to add to her misery by making an innocent pet suffer. Like her mother, Morag loved all animals. After she split up from Donald, Morag bought a black Labrador pup to console herself. When she returned home on leave from her work on the rigs, the presence of the dog would mean that it would not be to an empty house. Morag's friends would look after the pet, whom Morag named Becky, during her absences.

One evening, she went out to meet with friends in Marywell, but when she returned there was no sign of Becky. The disappearance was puzzling, because Morag was certain that the doors of the outhouse, where Becky slept in a basket, had been locked when she'd left. When the animal failed to reappear, Morag contacted the police, but they were uninterested. What, after all, was a missing dog to them? Hundreds disappeared every day and most simply wandered home when they were hungry. But Becky did not return. Friendly neighbours and children mounted a full-scale search of the surrounding streets, gardens, wasteland and even garden sheds but drew a blank. Morag feared Becky had been kidnapped, and her persistence resulted in the police finally coming to see her to take a statement and a description of the animal.

'My dog has been stolen,' Morag insisted. 'She was locked in and had just been fed, so she wouldn't go wandering off, looking for food. Someone took her from the outhouse.' A week later, the dog was discovered lying dead beneath bushes in a nearby garden by tearful children. Flora, suspicious and upset, took the body to a laboratory in Inverness, where she paid for an autopsy. The results showed that there were traces of blue pellets used to kill off slugs in Becky's stomach. Laboratory staff theorised that Becky had been taken from the outhouse, dumped and had then tried to find her way home but had become so hungry that she had eaten the pellets. 'Whoever did it as good as poisoned her,' Flora told them, and no one disagreed.

The old proverb maintains that every cloud has a silver lining, and so it was for Morag. She still had her job offshore, although she returned to it thinking herself a failure because she had so desperately wanted to succeed at her marriage. However, the experience with Donald had not turned her against the opposite sex, as so often happens after a relationship has soured. Morag vowed that she would show greater circumspection where men were concerned in future, but her desire to find a loving partner had not diminished.

Back out in the cold North Sea, many of her colleagues went out of their way to be pleasant to her, despite initial reluctance because of embarrassment at not knowing how to sympathise or fear that they might upset or offend her. They must have been taken aback by her apparent indifference to her recent personal disaster but did not realise the hurt that she was inwardly experiencing at Donald's inability to appreciate his good fortune in having her. She had given herself to him freely, wholly, joyously, with hope and love, looking forward to their reaching old age together surrounded by children and grandchildren. That none of this would become a reality was a bitter pill. Those closest to her were shocked that such a beautiful and desirable young woman had to suffer the humiliation of a marriage dissolving so quickly. Morag did not seek consolation. But before long it would come from an unexpected source.

4

The Texan

Slim, elegant and blonde, Morag could turn the heads of most men. Oil rigs could be lonely places, and most workers, separated from their loved ones, suffered occasional spells of boredom. Rig operators had originally been worried about the possible effect the presence of an attractive woman might have on a male starved of female companionship or one emotionally vulnerable because of a failed relationship on land. Experiences of fights and jealousies among mixed crews in other parts of the world had made the bosses reluctant to integrate women into the offshore workforce in the North Sea. The job required men to concentrate solely on what they were paid to do, not on private passions. A slip could be expensive or even cost a life. When women were finally allowed on board, strict rules were introduced, and their quarters were off limits to men and vice versa. The result was that if there was fraternisation between the sexes it was done discreetly. No one wanted to lose a prized job. There may well have been sexual liaisons, but they were enjoyed behind locked doors and in strict silence. From the outset, Morag made it clear that while she was happy to make friends, she would allow it to go no further than that. Her feelings and desires remained locked inside.

Jack Reeves first met Morag when he worked as a cleaner in the Ninian South field. On the verge of being transferred to a rig in the

Beryl field, Jack, from the north-east fishing port of Fraserburgh, was asked to show his successor the ropes. His first impression of her was unforgettable: 'She was beautiful, a stunner, a cracker. When I saw this gorgeous young woman walking towards me, I assumed she was a visitor, perhaps someone from a television channel, a presenter researching a forthcoming programme. It was impossible to believe that someone with such looks could be working out at sea. Her place seemed to be on a catwalk or in a magazine. Morag wasn't just pretty, she was friendly and polite, thanking me for showing her around. I knew if I wanted to forget her, I never could.'

Soon after the meeting, he flew to his new posting but shortly afterwards learned that he would need to return to the mainland for a minor operation. Morag and Jack would lose contact for a considerable time, but the friendship that sprang up after their initial meeting remained. He would play an integral part in her story.

While her feelings for Jack were based around friendship, those for Marcus Chapman were vastly different. The Texan, who was two years her senior, arrived in the Beryl field armed with a bachelor of science degree in electrical engineering and a wealth of experience in the oil industry behind him. They met one day by chance in an accommodation rig, and Morag was instantly taken by his pleasant chatter and untidy brown hair. He found her almost too good-looking to be true, and they took every opportunity to engineer further meetings. When the time came for her to return to shore for her routine two weeks' rest, he followed. They met regularly, talked incessantly and fell head over heels in love. Morag felt no guilt at still being a married woman when they shared a bed, reminding herself that the marriage to Donald had lasted just three months and she had pleaded with him for a divorce.

'I met Marcus Chapman once or twice,' remembers Jack Reeves, 'and Morag told me she wanted to make her relationship with him last. She adored him and would have lived in a tent with him. She loved him to bits, but I thought he was a total prick.'

Morag was desperate to know more about the man who seemed to have appeared from nowhere and taken over her life. She was fascinated by what he had to tell her. Marcus came from a wealthy background. Born in Alabama in September 1962, his family moved to Germany before the time came for him to begin school, his father Jimmy Ross Chapman having been a lieutenant-colonel in the United States Army who had served two tours in Vietnam, in 1965 and 1969. When Jimmy suffered a heart attack in 1977, he quit the military, and after gaining a masters degree in computer science became a high-school teacher. Teaching ran in the family. Marcus's mother Lawilda had two masters degrees in remedial education and counselling and was the principal of an elementary school.

When he was 13, the family, courtesy of the US Army, moved to Hawaii, where Marcus was sent to private school. He would admit to Morag that he had run into problems with the teaching staff as a result of trying to show off to other pupils by answering back in class and, less publicly, by smoking marijuana. His parents, who were strict disciplinarians, became worried by his behaviour and arranged for him to be interviewed by a child psychologist, who described the teenager as bright and probably bored by school.

The family eventually ended up in the little town of Woodville (population 2,400) in Tyler County, Texas, deep in the American Bible Belt, where religious fundamentalism is rife. In Woodville, Marcus graduated from high school and then went on to achieve his engineering degree at university. The qualification meant that he had no difficulty in getting a job, and he secured his first post, with Western Atlas International, in 1985, continuing with the company for eight years. After training in Texas, he worked for the company for five years in Saudi Arabia and then six months in Malaysia before being transferred to Scotland, where he met Morag in 1991.

Morag wanted to know if Marcus had been married before. He said that he had been but was reluctant to tell her more. However, Morag was insistent on knowing all that there was to know about the woman who had once held his heart. When he was twenty-two, he told her, he had married a hair stylist who was eight years his elder and who already had a daughter from another relationship. Within a year, they had separated and divorced. 'She was interested only in socialising and going out every night, while I was coming home from work tired and only wanted to stay indoors and relax,' he told Morag. Neither Marcus nor Morag knew it then, but another meeting with his ex-wife lay ahead.

Like any dutiful daughter, Morag wanted Flora to meet the new man in her life. Flora remembers the introduction well: 'Morag telephoned to tell me she had met this quiet American who had arrived on the rig where she was working. She sounded so excited and wanted to bring him to meet me. I had arranged to attend a car auction near Inverness and was there when they arrived. They joined me and stayed until the end. We then went back to the house, which Marcus much admired.

'He was polite and interesting and told me about his business interests in Texas. At one point, he used my telephone to call Lawilda and discuss a property deal. He and Morag walked down to a whisky distillery near my home, and he came back clutching a bottle of malt, which he clearly liked to drink.

'They appeared to spend most of their time in bed, but then isn't that what most young people do when they first meet and are attracted to one another? It was obvious that they were very taken with one another, and Marcus managed to get his shift pattern changed so that his followed Morag's.'

Before the year was over, Morag had to tell her employers that she was pregnant. The baby was due in May 1992, and she knew that she would have to quit work as soon as she delivered the news. There was a total ban on pregnant women working in the oilfields. If anything were to go wrong, there was no gynaecologist on the workforce, and in the event of bad weather no way of getting the patient to land.

Having to leave her job did not dampen her enthusiasm for Marcus, but her mother felt that the interest Marcus had shown in Morag before she fell pregnant had waned after he had received the news that he was to become a father. 'Morag telephoned me with the news that a baby was on the way,' Flora remembers. 'She was clearly delighted, and so was I, although I wondered if it was slightly early in the relationship and thought that perhaps she hadn't given herself sufficient time to get to know him. Had Marcus been a Scot, then it would have been easier for us to acquaint ourselves with him and his family. We would naturally have visited one another, meeting his parents and extended family to get a fuller picture of the sort of person he was. But because his folks lived thousands of miles away, you could not really judge what he or they were like. Meeting him only every couple of weeks because of his work patterns made it difficult for me to gauge much about him. I told myself at the time, "This is all happening too quickly."

'Morag's excitement was infectious. She was dead thrilled. For a long time before she met Marcus, she had talked about having children. Now her wish was coming true. Her whole life seemed to revolve around having children, and it was impossible not to feel happy for her. But the joy didn't spread to Marcus.

'He seemed to change and didn't treat her with the respect that I would have wanted. They were living in Aberdeen, because Marcus, maybe not unnaturally, did not want to stay in the house she had once shared with Donald Ross. A friend with whom Marcus had worked in Malaysia moved in with them. While they were living together, I called in one day to see how Morag was. She told me that she was expected to cook for both men, which I thought was wrong. Under the circumstances, I'd have expected the other chap to have found his own accommodation, leaving Morag and Marcus, who were more or less newly weds, to have some peace and privacy.

'While Morag was making our tea, Marcus came into the room carrying a pan of red cabbage. He laughed and said, "This is what you are expected to eat for your tea." That upset Morag, and she complained that Marcus had refused to go with her to antenatal classes, even though he was off work all day and it would only have taken an hour of his time. However, he preferred to watch television.

'Later on, I found out that when Marcus was working offshore, his pal expected his tea to be prepared on time at five in the afternoon. It meant that Morag, who had joined a computer course at a local college, had to rush home to heat up a pizza or a burger, food he could easily have prepared himself.

'One morning, his friend insisted on having a cooked meal that evening, even though Morag was especially busy. She suggested a liver and bacon casserole, and he agreed, so she called in at a pet shop on the way home and asked for liver for a dog. She served it up piping hot, and he ate the lot, even complimenting her on the standard of her food.'

During the pregnancy, Marcus attended a short work-related course in Dundee and returned home clutching flowers. Morag had no way of knowing what had happened while he was away, but the gesture seemed unusual. It was so out of character that she telephoned her mother and said, 'I have a funny feeling that he's had a fling with someone he met on the course, and this is his way of easing his guilt.' It bothered her, but she was too concerned with the unborn baby to make a fuss.

The flowers were a rare act of romance. Morag later confided to her mother that on one occasion shortly before Marcus left home to return offshore, she had suggested that they make love, but he had declined, telling her that he had a headache. It was another example of Marcus's growing indifference and demonstrated that his heart wasn't in the relationship.

Marcus decided that Morag should meet his parents, so he arranged a trip to Texas for her and her mother. Flora vividly recalls what a bizarre visit it was: 'In the run-up to Christmas

1991, Marcus announced that he was taking Morag to Texas to meet his family. She really looked forward to the trip, having never been to America, and he asked me if I would like to come along, too. I decided to kill two birds with one stone by first going out to meet up with Stuart, who had by now settled in San Diego. I would then take him with me to Texas. At that time, I visited Stuart in America every year. He had done well for himself and was moving into business as an outside caterer, supplying food and meals for dinner parties and functions, using some of the knowledge that he had picked up on a hotel management course in Scotland. He was also buying up older cars and hiring them out to Brits, mainly Scots, who were looking for inexpensive car hire.

'Before leaving for Texas, Morag came to Forres, full of hope for the future. It was a hope I shared, and I told her, "Just think, after the baby is born, I'll have two homes to visit – one in Texas and one in California. Imagine all those rodeos I'll be able to watch." While she was with me, she made Christmas cakes from an old family recipe – one for her and Marcus, another for his parents and the third for his grandparents.

'So, late in December, I set off to San Diego, the arrangement being that Stuart and I would then be met at Houston airport in Texas and be taken to the Chapmans'. But, instead of Marcus being there to meet us, we were met by Lawilda and Morag and given the excuse that Marcus had been spending most of his time visiting relatives and had a prior arrangement to see a family member.

'Lawilda seemed more interested in playing up to the attentions of Stuart than talking to me, and so Morag and I left them together and set off to do some Christmas shopping. Stuart appeared glad when he spotted us returning, because he'd evidently found it hard going entertaining Lawilda. It was a long drive to the Chapman home in Woodville, and on the way I realised why Stuart had looked so relieved when he had seen Morag and me. It was difficult to find any common ground with Lawilda, and when

Stuart, Morag and I chatted amongst ourselves she seemed to be analysing our every word.

'We assumed that Marcus had told his parents that Morag was four months pregnant. It would, after all, be only natural for him to want to break the news to his family. What proud father-to-be would not want to tell his parents? But we found out after we arrived that he hadn't said a word, and it had been left to Morag to make the announcement while Lawilda was showing her into the spare room, where she was to sleep.

'At Woodville, we met Jimmy Ross Chapman, who was a nice man but rarely smiled. And we also met Marcus's grandmother, who was an astonishing woman. She was aged about 80 and had a boyfriend. They would go off together line dancing for the weekend.

'One day, we went to the shops to get some things for the baby. When it came to actually making the purchases, it wasn't Marcus who gave Morag money but Lawilda. She held the purse strings, and when a cheque needed to be written she signed it.

'I recall that at one point I said there seemed to be nothing but churches between Woodville and Houston. Afterwards Lawilda said to Marcus that I had been rude by asking about Catholic churches. Well, I'm not worried about one church or the other, and I don't think I mentioned Catholic churches, but my impression of Lawilda was of someone who liked to stir things up.

'Just before Christmas, Jimmy Ross hooked up a boat to the back of his car, and we all went down to Lake Austin. There was quite a crowd of us in the little boat, and I told Marcus that I wasn't too keen on water and asked him to take things slowly. Instead, he opened up the throttle and went flat out. He seemed to think it was funny that I was frightened.

'Marcus and his dad had brought a shotgun with them. They threw some tins into the lake and began shooting at them. At one stage, while the boat was rocking with the recoil from the gun, Marcus looked around and said to me, "Watch out, there are crocodiles in the lake." I thought, "You are simply being nasty.

You're not really as nice a guy as I once thought you were." He seemed to take pleasure in intimidating me. If he said something that he realised had caused upset, he would carry on talking in the same vein.

'The Chapmans had fostered a teenage boy who was introduced to us only as "Sam". It appeared to be an unusual arrangement, as it wasn't organised by a social-work department but instead agreed privately with Sam's parents, who could not afford to put him through school. Sam was a normal kid, who was due to stay at Woodville over Christmas. But the arrangement did not last long. He was late coming back home for a meal, and as a punishment was ordered by Jimmy Ross to dig a hole five-feet wide and five-feet deep. Morag went out to ask Sam what he was doing, and when he told her she asked what the point of it all was. According to Sam, Jimmy Ross had told him that just as being late was pointless, so was digging a useless hole, and that was the lesson he had to learn.

'Sam wanted to visit his parents on Christmas Day, but the Chapmans refused, as they did not think it was convenient. They had bought Sam lots of presents, which seemed to be their way of showing him how much they loved him. But they also acted quite strangely in some ways. For example, they caught Sam smoking at one point, something to which they vigorously objected. They realised that he was partial to a cigarette, so they bought a whole carton and left them in the house where he could see them and ordered him not to touch them. If he did and was caught, he would be asked to leave. It seemed to us that this was some sort of test, even a torture, and Sam, by that point, had clearly had enough. Some time later, he opened the carton and was told to leave.

'At seven o'clock on the morning of Boxing Day, Marcus left with Stuart, telling Morag that he needed her brother to help him deliver a refrigerator to one of his properties, an apartment he rented to two girls. He said that they would be back that evening. It seemed strange, in that case, that Marcus took a suit with him, and it was obvious he had no intention of returning that day. In fact, it was the following night before they reappeared, and this set off a shouting match between Marcus and Morag, who was rightly angry at having been left behind, pointing out that she and I were as much guests as Stuart. Morag was then taken to a motel after she suggested that they had spent the night at one of Marcus's properties in Austin with some women.

'I felt sorry for her being abandoned in that way, because there were only other houses and a lake in Woodville, and it was winter, so we couldn't even go out for a walk. Morag spent so much of that holiday in tears. She was pregnant with her first baby and staying with people she did not know in a strange country, but the father of her child had gone off and left her.

'While Marcus was away, Morag mentioned to Lawilda that he made her sleep on the floor in Aberdeen, that she was expected to cook for him and his pal and that he was forever being rude about her food. Lawilda listened but commented only that Morag was lucky to be with Marcus. Then she pulled out one of the family photograph albums to show Morag pictures of Marcus's ex-girlfriends. It was very belittling and unnecessary.

'I later learned that Marcus had taken Morag to the motel and left her there without food or drink. When he came back to Woodville to face the music like some naughty schoolboy, he was ordered into his mother's bedroom and the door was shut. He was in there for about an hour while Lawilda went through all of the things that Morag had complained about. The next morning, it was time for me to leave. I did not see Lawilda, who had not reappeared from her room, or Marcus, and I didn't know where Morag was. Jimmy Ross drove Stuart and me to the airport and just kept apologising, saying, "I'm sorry about this." I'm sure he meant it, but then he was used to Lawilda's ways.

'Because I was flying back to Scotland via San Diego, Morag was due to arrive home first, and we arranged for her to collect me at Glasgow airport and drive me to Forres. But Marcus banned her from picking me up, telling her that he didn't want her talking to me again, because he thought I was a bad influence. That showed how little he knew her. She set off to meet me in her old Lada, but the police pulled her over on the way, pointed out that she had a bulb missing from one of the headlights and told her not to drive the vehicle until it was fixed. It was early morning, which meant she had to wait until daylight before trying to find an open garage. There was no way that she could make it, so she left a message saying that I would have to make my own way home. Because it was still the holiday season, no trains were running, so I had to take a series of coaches. I eventually arrived home tired and angry, and although Marcus later lifted the ban on Morag seeing me, I thought that his attitude was silly and pathetic. It did not bode well for the future.'

5

Jasmine

Morag and Flora had returned from their brief visit to the Chapmans sad and worried. It was clear to Flora that the relationship between Marcus and her daughter was already in danger of falling apart at the seams. Had this simply been a case of a young couple mistaking lust for love, realising that there was insufficient mortar to hold together the bricks of their future relationship and agreeing to go their separate ways with no hard feelings, then no real harm would have been done. But this was different: a baby was on the way, a child who would need the energy of both parents to be channelled into his or her growth and not into maintaining a struggle against one another for supremacy. She had gone through all that and survived. But she did not want her daughter to suffer in the same way.

Having broken up with Donald Dempster, she had a new partner with whom she was determined to spend the remainder of her life. Don Evans was a social worker who also ran an antiques business near her Forres home. Many families, particularly those forced to manage amidst the detritus of violence, drugs, alcohol, fear, hunger and poverty, find themselves being visited by social workers whose limited experience of life and middle-class backgrounds makes them unsuited to doling out advice. Don, on the other hand, was an ideal candidate. Glasgow born and streetwise, he had battled against alcoholism and depression, and during a horrendous journey to victory over his problems had been dismayed by what he saw as the frequent inadequacies of those in the social-work field. His solution was to become a social worker himself, giving up a possible career in medicine and emerging from the University of Glasgow with a degree in pure science and a post-graduate diploma in social work. In the field, he reasoned that his role was to act as a friend and not a lecturer to his clients, although at times he found that tough love was more effective than quoting from regulations.

Don met Flora when she enquired about becoming a foster mother. He was of the opinion that Flora's bungalow and fields were an ideal setting in which to soothe the suffering of children, but she would ultimately decide not to proceed, realising that her own daughter needed the help and succour that she had thought to give to others. However, from their first meeting, Flora was taken with this straight talker from the Moray Council Social Work Department. They began dating, and Don eventually moved in with her.

Flora told her friends that Don was her partner for life, but when it came to marriage for a third time, she baulked. Don asked her but she felt that it was wiser to wait and see. 'Third time lucky,' friends assured her.

'I've never been lucky,' she responded. 'That's why I'm letting time make the decision.' She also wondered whether Don's professional expertise might be needed to advise her own family out of the mess that it seemed to be heading towards.

Meanwhile, Morag had more than just the concerns of imminent motherhood on her mind. She had kept silent about what had really happened when Marcus and Stuart had returned from their shindig in Austin. After pushing her into the family pickup and driving angrily to the motel, he had checked into a room, where he had made fierce love to her before hurriedly dressing and leaving, simply telling her, 'I'll be back.' She had then been left alone to wait and wonder what was going on, without money or food, uncertain as to what was happening to her mother or brother. It was after lunch the following day before Marcus had returned. 'I'm starving,' she had protested. 'You forget I have two mouths to feed, and this cannot be doing the baby any good.' He drove her back to Woodville to collect her belongings before the time came for them to return to Scotland and prepare in earnest for the arrival of the baby.

It had not been a happy Christmas as far as Morag was concerned. There had been too many rows and, as she saw it, too much rudeness shown towards her and her mother. These were, she knew, relatively small matters in the overall scheme of things. It is inevitable that there are uncertainties and suspicions when two families meet for the first time. But something that Lawilda had said to Morag niggled away at her and would not vanish from her memory. Marcus's mother had told the warring pair, 'If you two continue to argue, I will take this child from you.' They were words that would haunt the pretty young mother-to-be.

The time for the birth grew near, and having been paid off by her employer as a result of the pregnancy she began buying voraciously, emerging from shops with her arms weighed down with every conceivable item that could be remotely useful in a baby's upbringing. And everything had to be duplicated: one set in pink, the other in blue.

She had once set her heart on caring for the children of others; now she was about to have a baby of her own. She did not care whether the child came with long dark eyelashes any more; all she hoped and prayed for was the same as all expectant mothers: a healthy child. When she was a youngster, she had once been asked by Flora as they drove along in her Mini, 'When you grow up, Morag, what kind of motor do you want? A nice wee Mini like this?'

'No, Mummy, I want a bus.'

'Why a bus? Isn't it too big?'

'No, I want a bus because it is big, because I'm going to have so many babies it will need a bus to carry them all.'

The baby was due towards the end of May 1992, but it was only when the time for giving birth drew near that it became physically

55

obvious that Morag was pregnant. 'When I was expecting, they asked at hospital check-ups if I wanted to know if it was a boy or a girl, but I didn't want to be told,' Morag remembers. 'I was sure that it was a boy, because I didn't have a bump – not until the very last month. As a result, nobody knew I was having a baby.'

As the final month of pregnancy dragged on, Morag became increasingly anxious that Marcus would be on hand to drive her to the hospital in Aberdeen for the birth. They had moved out of the city to Drumoak, a quiet village a dozen miles to the south-west of Aberdeen. A close friend who had given birth herself told Morag, in answer to her question, that when her waters broke it would be 'like filling a bucket of water', and that is what she expected. Her friend also told her that the signal that nature was on the move would be back pains and contractions. Morag began to feel these and was constantly running to the toilet only for nothing to happen. She got out her ironing board and ironed everything she could find to see if that eased the pain. It did not. When she rang the hospital for advice, she was told to take a bath, but that did not seem to help either. The pain remained, and so early one morning, at around six, she woke up Marcus and ordered him to drive her to Aberdeen. 'You're going to have to take me,' she said, 'because something is kicking so hard inside me that it seems as though it is going to pop out at any minute. Oh, gosh, it's got to be a boy, and he's going to be a footballer.'

Morag was extremely relieved that Marcus had been at home with her, but on the short journey a thousand thoughts ran through her mind. She had pestered her mother and friends with questions about what it was like to give birth and always the first thing she asked was, 'Will it hurt?' Every answer was different but all had a common theme: 'You'll be all right, and so will the baby. Don't worry.' She tried running through what she had been advised at antenatal classes, and once again wished Marcus had gone along with her. She had rehearsed over and over what the nurses had told her would happen and what she must do, but her mind was a blank, everything was forgotten and it was no use asking Marcus.

She willed herself to stay calm. She told herself that it was maybe not that she couldn't remember, but just that she could not concentrate, and this brought her some relief.

The journey was no more than half an hour, but the car seemed to hit every bump. 'Slow down, slow down,' she urged Marcus, at the same time wanting the journey to end. It seemed to take an eternity. Every set of traffic lights seemed to be stuck at red. Road junctions were busy. She silently pleaded for the lights to turn green and the junctions to clear. And then, suddenly, they were there, and Marcus was helping her through the hospital doors.

A gynaecologist looked her over and said, 'You're a bit early, but you live in the country, so we're not sending you back.' This comforted her, because she dreaded having to return home and endure the awful stress of another trip to hospital. The doctor then said, 'I think that your baby is due at around five this afternoon. You can have a painkilling tablet in the meantime.' At antenatal sessions, she had been advised that she would be allowed two painkillers and then an epidural to ease the discomfort to her back, but she had suffered back problems in the past and had made it plain that she did not want an epidural. She decided to hang on and not take anything until the pain became unbearable.

While she was waiting, she realised that she knew one of the midwives – they had trained together as nursery nurses. It was clear from the woman's surprised expression that she also recognised Morag. 'Are you sure that it's OK for me to deliver your baby, because you know me?' she asked.

'Sure,' replied Morag. 'No bother. There's no problem.' So they chatted about this and that, and it took her mind from the situation. They gossiped about people they knew, what they had done with their lives, who had married who, who had children and so on. Eventually, pain took over, and Morag asked for a painkiller, only to be told that it was too late. The gynaecologist smiled and said to her, 'The baby's head is here.'

Morag had persuaded Marcus to stay with her in the delivery room, wanting him to hold her hand and reassure her that all was going well during the birth. Earlier, a kindly nurse had shown her a tube and face mask. 'If you feel overanxious or breathless, just place the mask to your mouth and breathe in,' said the nurse. 'It's a mixture of gas and oxygen, and it will quickly settle you down and relax you.' Morag was grateful for knowing it was there, and as the baby slowly emerged and the pain continued she reached for the mask. It was only then that she realised Marcus was holding it to his face and was telling her in between huge gulps, 'It's working, honey, it's working. This is great.' She screamed at him through lips drawn tight in pain, 'Well, fucking give it to me then.' But he was too engrossed in what was happening around him and overcome by the feeling of goodwill and well-being that the gas had given him to listen to her. Then, almost more to his relief than Morag's, the baby arrived. 'You have a girl,' the mother and father were told.

Without the aid of painkillers, injections or gas, Morag had experienced a totally natural birth. The baby had not arrived exactly on time – three quarters of an hour after the gynaecologist's estimate, in fact – but she had arrived and that was all that mattered. In a moment of relief that all had gone well, Morag told herself, 'My baby could have nine arms and ten legs and she would still be the most beautiful baby ever born.'

Tiny and with a mop of black hair, the little bloodstained bundle immediately began making sounds that heralded a determined fight for life. A nurse was on the verge of taking the newborn off for a wash, but Morag insisted that they put the baby on her breast straightaway, and so they did. Later, she told her mother, and anyone else willing to listen, 'When she was just out of the womb and still covered in blood, I breastfed her straightaway and only then had a shower and let them clean her up. I wanted our bonding to begin the very second that she appeared in the world.' It was 25 May 1992, and the first shot had been fired in a transatlantic war.

Morag is still critical of Marcus's behaviour both in the labour room and outside, complaining, 'Marcus wouldn't give me a card, he didn't give me flowers, and he didn't even take a photograph of me and my child together. I took one of him and her when she was newly born, but he didn't do that for me. It's one of my big regrets, not having a photograph of me and my baby just after she was born.'

The infant weighed in at just over five pounds. Hundreds of miles to the south, Flora and Don Evans were holidaying in Turkey. They had telephoned every day for news, but Flora was not unduly worried about her daughter. She was healthy, young, strong and, perhaps most importantly, desperate to care for her baby.

'What are you calling her?' asked Flora when Morag told her that she now had a granddaughter.

'Jasmine Jamee Chapman,' replied Morag.

'Why Jasmine?'

'When I was a little girl of 11, I remember experiencing this wonderful scent and an uncle telling me that it was jasmine. It was so special, and even though I was young I thought, "When I have babies, I'm going to call my first girl Jasmine, because I love jasmine so much." I never thought about a name for a boy. When I told Marcus I was naming her Jasmine, he said, "You can't do that." But I told him, "She's my daughter, and I can give her whatever name I want." He said, "You can't call her Jasmine unless I can give her a middle name." "What middle name is that?" I asked. "James," he replied, after his dad. I thought, "Well, it's double-barrelled, but it's not too bad. Jasmine James." Then Marcus decided that it had to be the name his dad used – Jimmy. I asked if he wanted to settle for Jamee, which sounded the same but was a girl's name and probably more appropriate. He thought about it for a while, then came back and said, "You can call her Jasmine, but you have to have Jamee first." However, I put my foot down, and she will be christened Jasmine Jamee.'

When Flora and Don returned from Turkey, they made a beeline to see the new arrival. Flora was enchanted by the tiny face topped with black hair and was thrilled to see her daughter looking so well. 'I thought you told me having a baby wasn't painful,' Morag said. 'Well, it's not true.'

Flora offered to stay with Morag to help care for the infant, but after looking through the mountain of pink and blue clothing she realised that her daughter was well prepared and would probably not need her assistance. And she noticed a strange expression of almost menace on her daughter's face when she offered to babysit. But Flora did not know that the words Morag recalled from an exchange many thousands of miles away were running through her mind: 'I will take this child from you.'

6

Flight

Morag loved her little daughter from the moment that she first set adoring eyes upon her. 'You are beautiful, so beautiful,' she would tell her baby as she hugged her to her breast, convincing herself that Jasmine was listening and understanding her every word. She tried to refrain from thinking about anything going wrong and prayed that her precious daughter had not been born carrying a defective gene that had so far gone undetected. She was also terrified to let Jasmine out of her sight for fear that by some awful freak the child would vanish or be snatched from under her watchful eyes by a jealous woman

Every hour on the hour she would slip out a breast and offer it to Jasmine. She had bought a tiny listening device that would lie beside the baby's cot and shriek out a warning signal if it failed to detect movement, an indication that the infant had ceased breathing. But no sooner had she left the room after laying Jasmine down to sleep, than she would return to check that she had missed nothing on her previous visit. Her every waking minute was taken over by thoughts of her daughter. She was possessed by a great desire to enfold her in a love so strong that it would destroy any invading malady or harm seeking to attack this precious mite who had caused a change in the lives of so many.

Some months passed before she gave in to pleas from her mother and friends to treat herself to a night out. It was the first time mother and daughter had been parted. Flora drove to Drumoak, collected Jasmine and a bottle of breast milk, then returned to Forres. Within two hours, she was joined by Morag, who had set off to join her friends but had realised that she could not bear to be apart from Jasmine. She spent the evening at the bungalow doing what she had done since the moment the child was born: watching over her.

The satisfaction she gained from watching the baby slowly grow made up, in some measure, for the lack of a physical relationship between her and Marcus. Their affair had been consummated almost from the moment it began, and she had found their intimacy fulfilling and enjoyable. So she became disappointed and frustrated when Marcus began to lose interest in sex, at least with her, after the birth.

Because of Marcus's work patterns and shift arrangements, Morag and Jasmine were often left alone for days and even weeks. She sometimes visited her mother in Forres, but it was as much to assuage her loneliness as to carry out any filial duty. During the few occasions when Marcus was at home with her and Jasmine, Morag was thrilled to feel that the family unit was complete. But these were mere dots in the ocean of their existence. What she lacked was stability and having a partner who would be there for her when she needed help and reassurance. At other times, she would be in Forres when Marcus returned for shore leave, but he made little or no effort to visit his daughter, evidently preferring to remain in Aberdeen.

Morag had been conscious of his indifference during her pregnancy, but such was her pleasure at the prospect of having a baby that she did not allow it to overshadow her joy. If the worst came to the worst and they parted, she would have been content to continue on her own. But having seen her own parents divorce, she determined that her child would grow up with both a mother and a father to give their love and support. But another cloud appeared on the horizon. 'Not long after Jasmine was born,' Flora recalls, 'Marcus announced that his employers were sending him to work in Syria. "Sending or have you asked to go there?" Morag asked him. He protested that he had no alternative but to move, so she pleaded, "Please, Marcus, can't you see that Jasmine needs a dad at home, not thousands of miles away?" But off he went. What was most humiliating was that he would not telephone for weeks at a time, and when he did and was asked why there had been a delay he would claim that it was difficult to get to a working telephone. But when she challenged him and said, "Yes, maybe so, but I bet you can always find one when you need to call your mother," there was no dispute.'

Morag had always remained in contact with Tony, who was now living on Tyneside with Sue. He told Morag that her grandmother had gone into a retirement home, leaving her house empty. If she wished, she could have the use of it. It was an attractive offer, and there were other advantages to moving. Tony had made a success of hairdressing and now ran a thriving business. He was comfortably off, and Morag knew that she could turn to him for financial help should she need it. Additionally, he could offer her practical training as a hairdresser. Morag discussed the various options with Flora, and after talking things over asked her father if she and the baby could stay with him and Sue. The answer was an immediate affirmative, and she moved to the north-east of England with Jasmine.

It was a development with which Marcus was clearly unhappy, sensing that there was a real danger of a complete breakdown in the relationship. Suddenly, there were telephone lines everywhere, and he made frantic calls to Morag, begging her to move back to Scotland. 'There's absolutely no point in my doing that when I'll simply be on my own,' she said. 'It is no basis for a relationship between you and Jasmine if you continue working away from home for months at a time. What happens is up to you, but you have to see that unless you can arrange for us to be together as a family unit then it would be best for all, especially Jasmine, if you simply did not come into her life.'

She was giving him a stark choice between doing nothing or

changing his career. He opted for the latter but pointed out that it would mean a change for her, too: 'If I stay in Scotland, the only work I'm going to get is in the oilfields, and that means being offshore much of the time. If you want me around, we have no option but to move to Texas, where I reckon I can get work that will let me live at home.' It meant uprooting from family and friends, but now that he had effectively called her bluff, she had no option but to go. She talked over the idea of settling in America with Tony and Flora, who both pointed out that if there were problems she could simply come back to Scotland. 'And never forget, we're only a few hours away – just a plane ride or two,' they told her. Others in her close circle were less reassuring. One of her closest friends warned Morag, 'You are making a big mistake. If he really cared, he would settle here.'

Marcus, Morag and Jasmine flew to Texas in February 1993. With them went her furniture and a superb chocolate-coloured Labrador Morag had named Dillon. She had bought the dog from a local vet and had him hip scored to assess his breeding value. He scored a better than perfect zero-zero. Dillon was thought of as being part of the family.

The family settled in Austin. Marcus's years of travelling in the oil industry had made him a wealthy man, and he decided to concentrate on managing his and his family's property investments there, thus ensuring that he could be a full-time father to Jasmine. However, according to Morag, it was clear, almost from the moment that she carried Jasmine across the airport tarmac, that what had started out as a fine passion had become a sad and futile excuse for a relationship. It had been such a hot-and-cold affair – admittedly, mainly cold – but there had been moments of apparent tenderness.

In April, the couple made a declaration before officials of Travis County to the effect that they wanted to publicly acknowledge that they were common-law man and wife. It was an official statement, and the nearest thing to actually getting married, but romance had nothing to do with the development. Marcus would later confess that his motive was to ensure that Jasmine had joint citizenship of the UK and USA by formally becoming her father. And that could have a crucial bearing should there be any dispute between mother and father as to who was to have custody of the child in the future. However, his plan hit a snag: Morag was still married to Donald Ross at that time, but she kept silent about this. When it transpired some time later that she had come close to committing a technical form of bigamy, the declaration was declared invalid and the common-law marriage annulled.

The declaration was, however, but a single star shining in a black sky, because if Morag had hoped that Marcus would honour his public commitment to her by an equal show of devotion in private, she would soon be disappointed. Morag and Marcus continued to share the same bed, but she says that they did not make love: 'He just didn't seem interested any longer. I tried coaxing him, but it made no difference. It was so humiliating lying next to a man and trying to entice him into having sex and being rejected.' There were constant fights and bickering, and almost every dispute was about Lawilda's interfering or, at least, her dominance over her son. 'Why must you consult her on every decision you make?' she would demand to know. 'Stand up for yourself. If there are things to be discussed that involve Jasmine, then it's me you should come to, not your mother.'

The bitterness increased with claims and counterclaims of violence. At one stage, Morag rang a child-abuse line after accusing Marcus of striking Jasmine with a telephone receiver as she toddled about their luxury house. There were other allegations, all of which Marcus would go on to deny.

Throughout the rows and insults, Morag would close her eyes and see only the sandy beaches of Northumberland and majestic heather-coated hills of Scotland, imagining her daughter paddling in the sea and chasing ponies at Flora's. She longed to be away from the shouting, swearing and threats. Back in Scotland, Flora realised all was not well when she received a postcard from Austin. It was signed simply from Morag and

Jasmine. Flora wondered why Marcus was not mentioned. 'What has happened here?' she thought to herself. 'Something is wrong.'

She was disappointed that there were problems and believed that if Marcus split from his parents to live with his wife and daughter, it would make him more appreciative of his good fortune. But the simple truth was that things were not going well. Morag would allege to various family members that he had threatened her with a gun.

She told the story to Tony when he and Sue visited in May 1993. Tony's response was to gather up any weaponry he could find, hire a boat and sail it into the middle of Lake Austin, where he threw the hardware overboard.

There was now no doubting that the relationship was beyond repair. Morag felt that she had given it her best, joining in community activities, trying to get to know Marcus's friends and becoming acquainted with what appeared to be a sizeable number of Scots who had settled in Austin. But she was convinced that Lawilda held too great an influence over her son and thus over her and Jasmine. That alone made her unhappy and afraid that Marcus and his family would seek to drive a wedge between her and her baby daughter. For the moment, Jasmine was too young to even be aware that things were not as they should be between her mother and father. But Morag wondered how this coldness, this estrangement, would affect her relationship with Jasmine as time went by. Would the child not be more susceptible to influences from the Chapmans? She was, after all, in their country, hearing their language and growing up following their customs.

The more she thought about the future, the lonelier and more depressed she became, but there was no husband to put a loving, reassuring arm around her. She was on her own, and she was convinced that moving to Texas had been a mistake. The only solution was to go home to Scotland.

When Tony and Sue visited in May 1993, Tony could see

Morag's sadness and worried about the safety of his daughter and granddaughter, so he determined to take them back to the United Kingdom with him when he returned. The house where Morag and Jasmine had lived before moving to Austin with Marcus was still empty, but Tony said that he would understand if she opted to go back to Scotland to stay with Flora. His first consideration was the happiness and well-being of Morag and her baby.

By taking Jasmine out of the country, Morag was legally doing nothing wrong. The baby had been born in Scotland, and in order to prevent Morag from taking Jasmine away Marcus would have needed a court order giving him some form of custodial rights in Texas. No order existed. He could not claim Jasmine was an American citizen and subject to Texas law because she had not lived in the country for the necessary six-month qualifying period. It was true that he and Morag had gone through a form of civil-marriage ceremony in Texas, but that declaration was effectively invalid. At the time that it was made, Morag no longer thought of herself as being the wife of Donald Ross, but until the marriage was formally ended the law saw it differently. So, there was legally nothing to prevent Morag from leaving with Jasmine, and Tony was in no doubt that she wanted to return to the UK. He agreed that when he and Sue flew home, mother and daughter would go with them.

The plan was straightforward. When Tony and Sue set off for the airport, Morag and Jasmine would accompany them. But did Marcus somehow get wind of their scheme? Was word of what was in the air passed to him? If so, by whom? Whatever the answers, and whether his move was purely coincidental or deliberate, Marcus vanished with the baby, now just over 12 months old, on the eve of Morag's intended departure. Tony waited as long as he dared, but in the end he had to leave.

Although she couldn't be certain, Morag was convinced that Marcus had made for his mother's home in Woodville. Everything Marcus did seemed to be controlled by Lawilda. Morag wondered whether he had suspected that she was on the verge of doing a runner with Jasmine and had sought advice from his mother, who had suggested that he bring the baby to her home until Tony and Sue were safely gone.

When she telephoned Woodville and asked to speak with Marcus, Lawilda was adamant that he was not there. 'Why are you asking?' she said. 'He's with you. Why would he come here?'

'Because you want my baby,' Morag replied and hung up.

There was only one way to find out the truth and that was to go there herself. But that meant a journey of just over 200 miles, and Marcus had taken their only vehicle. She had never before been parted from Jasmine, apart from the brief interlude when Flora had volunteered to babysit, and the worry of not knowing her daughter's whereabouts was breaking her heart. In desperation, she got on a long-distance coach for the journey to the Chapmans'.

Morag later told her mother, 'When I arrived, Lawilda didn't seem unduly surprised to see me. I told her that Marcus had absconded with Jasmine, and I believed he was there, but she denied all knowledge of him having been anywhere near. I didn't believe her, but what else could I do? Call out the police? There was no alternative but to go back to Austin and wait.'

Back at an empty home, Morag decided to seek official advice. She called the offices of the British Consulate-General in Houston and explained what had happened. They were sympathetic but officially unable to act. However, that did not prevent a kindly lady worker passing on a helpful tip or two: 'Go out and buy enough food for you and the baby to last until you can get back home. Think of yourself as being under siege, and if necessary, once your daughter is back with you, barricade yourselves into your home until someone tells you that tickets are waiting at the airport. Whatever you do, once she is back with you – and he'll have to return her or else you can formally call in the police and tell them she has been abducted – do not let her out of your sight.'

It was advice that she took immediately, writing a cheque for around $200 to pay for her purchases at an Austin supermarket. What she did not know was that earlier in the day Marcus had cleared out their joint bank account. When the store presented the cheque to the bank, it bounced and an official complaint was made to the local police. Officers began making inquiries about Morag, but it was too late. By the time a warrant for her arrest was issued, she was back with her father in England.

How that came about is one of the more remarkable episodes in a quite astonishing story. On the day that she wrote the cheque, Marcus returned to the house with Jasmine, who appeared to be well and happy. There was nothing to suggest any harm had come to her, but he refused to tell Morag where he had been or why he had disappeared with the baby. 'I've been worried sick,' sobbed Morag. 'You know I went to your mother's home looking for you. She said you weren't there, but I know that's not true. How could you do this to me?'

Before leaving the country, and before the police were aware of the bouncing cheque, she made a formal complaint in Austin that she had been assaulted. The police the world over are consistently reluctant to investigate allegations of domestic abuse, and the officers in Austin were no different. By the time they decided to look into Morag's complaint, she was already back in the UK, so no charges were laid against Marcus, the police taking the view that there was no point in trying to take a man to court when the only witness was thousands of miles away.

Marcus's unpredictable behaviour made Morag even more determined to flee Texas and make her way home to the UK. That evening, she busied herself in the kitchen and changed Jasmine before putting her down for the night while Marcus watched television and then went to bed. Morag continually asked herself if what she was planning to do was fair but then rebuked herself for having doubts. There was no way she could continue to live in Austin with Marcus. The dawn of each new day simply heralded more misery, and the prospect of her sorrow rubbing off on Jasmine terrified her. All she longed for was for her child to be happy, which did not seem possible without a major change in their surroundings.

At one stage, Marcus called down to ask Morag what she was doing, and she replied that she was having a fresh coffee before turning off the lights and joining him. It was essential that the baby was asleep, because she could not afford her coming to life and screaming to be fed or changed and, in the process, rousing Marcus. At what seemed minute intervals, she checked on the barely moving babe, then quietly opened the door and took her outside, hiding her under a bush outside the front door in her cot. It was a warm, balmy evening, and she knew Jasmine would only be there for a couple of minutes. If she awoke and called out, Morag would hear but Marcus would not. Then she waited until she was certain that Marcus was asleep, at one point even creeping into the bedroom to check that her suspicions were correct.

There was no time to lose. She pulled a bag packed with some personal belongings and baby clothes and nappies from a hiding place in a cupboard and sneaked out of the front door. She silently closed it behind her and picked up Jasmine, making off on tiptoe. She knew where she was going. A month after arriving in Austin, Marcus had introduced her to a near neighbour named Roberta Reid, a fellow Scot who had lived in Texas for some years. The two women had become good friends, and Roberta, who lived with an American boyfriend, was fond of Jasmine. She had been enchanted by the child and angered by the apparent indifference of Marcus to the unhappiness of Morag. Nevertheless, she was taken aback when she heard a knock at her door in the early hours and discovered Morag standing there clutching her daughter. 'I can't stand his threats any longer,' whispered Morag. 'I just have to get away. My dad was buying us a ticket home, but Marcus ran off with Jasmine, and he had to fly back without us.'

Roberta ushered them into her home but knew that it was vital to get Morag and Jasmine out of the neighbourhood. Should Marcus wake up and discover them gone, he could easily call the police, who would surely blanket the entire area, making escape difficult. Marcus knew about the friendship between the two women, and Roberta realised that in the event of a hue and cry Marcus was certain to direct the police to her door. 'We have got to get you out of this street right away,' she urged and picked up the telephone, asking the operator to connect her to the battered-women's refuge in Austin. She explained the young Scot's predicament, and the refuge promised that within minutes a female worker would be sitting outside Roberta's door in an American Cab Company taxi to take them to safety.

While it was on the way, Morag rang her dad to tell him what had happened. 'Try not to worry, and I'll arrange to get money wired out to you tomorrow,' he promised. By the time she had replaced the receiver, a cab was sitting outside Roberta's, and it was not long before mother and daughter were in the refuge.

Morag knew that she would only be safe and remain undiscovered there for a limited time. Her major problem was the prospect of Marcus seeking an injunction to prevent her from taking Jasmine out of Travis County. He just had to state that his daughter had lived in Texas for six months. It was admittedly untrue, but while the claim was being investigated Morag would be forced to remain in the country. Alone, broke and a stranger to the American legal system, she would be vulnerable to having Jasmine taken from her and put into state custody. That would inevitably mean a long fight to regain control of her daughter, one that she feared she had little chance of winning. So, the quicker she disappeared, the better.

Staff and other women at the refuge were immensely protective. One mother, her arm in a sling and bandages swathed about her legs from a beating, said, 'Honey, try not to worry. If anyone comes here and insists on poking about, we'll just shout rape, and they'll soon go away. But you have to get away from here soon. The social-work people regularly come around checking, and if they find you they'll begin asking all sorts of questions

71

and want to know why you've run away. These people just love taking children from their mothers.' If a spur was needed, that was it.

Morag found it difficult to sleep that night. The next morning, she rang Western Union, and they confirmed that the money from Tony had arrived – enough to cover the cost of a flight back to Britain. Morag again rang her father, who told her, 'Make sure you don't take a direct flight. If Marcus has started a hunt for you, they'll be checking all the expected routes. Come home via Florida. No one will expect you to turn up there.'

In the afternoon, Roberta drove Morag and Jasmine to Austin airport. 'Morag was basically a nervous wreck,' Roberta would later say in an affidavit. 'She was extremely anxious and frightened of what Mr Chapman might do to her, and so she wished to go back to the UK as quickly as possible.'

It was 2 June 1993. At four in the afternoon, their jet soared high into the sky, and Morag and Jasmine looked down over the city that had brought them so much misery. They had left virtually all of their belongings, clothing, furnishings and toys behind them, as well as Dillon the dog.

A few days later, Roberta had a caller: Marcus Chapman. 'He asked me to ask Morag to get in touch with him,' she continued in her affidavit. 'He obviously presumed that she was still in the country, but that was not so. I did not tell him that she had gone back to England with Jasmine, because I did not want him to know. I was aware of how he had been treating both Morag and Jasmine, because she had told me about the many incidents that had taken place. I can recall that on one occasion Morag told me that Mr Chapman had hit Jasmine on the hand with the telephone receiver, and as a result Morag had telephoned the Texas Department of Human Services child-abuse line in order to obtain advice.'

Roberta sent Marcus packing and then remembered her parting from Morag and Jasmine at the airport. Morag had given Roberta a hug of thanks, and the women had wondered what Marcus's reaction had been when he'd woken up to an empty house. 'He'll ring his mother,' Morag had said, and they'd laughed. 'I don't expect I'll see you again, Roberta. Maybe you've saved my life.' Then, with a slight skip, she was gone.

Six thousand miles to the east, Morag arrived in Newcastle to be met by her dad. 'Let's go home,' he said.

7

Sprouting Menace

Morag had chosen to return to her dad, rather than Flora, because her grandmother was still in the retirement home, leaving her house vacant. It was there that Morag and the baby settled. She knew that it wasn't a permanent arrangement, because the house would be sold at some stage. But her first thoughts, shared by the entire family, were of relief that the Texas trauma was over. At the same time, they were under no illusions that the matter had ended. Lawilda, in particular, said Morag, would not allow her son to give up. 'They'll be back,' she warned. 'Mark my words, they'll be back.'

Deciding the best form of defence was attack, Morag wrote to Marcus giving him her telephone number, telling him where she was and even enclosing a handful of snapshots of Jasmine so that he could see for himself that she was well and happy. She then applied for a council house. It was explained that she might have to wait a while, but if she was prepared to take pot luck and accept the first suitable house that became available, no matter where it was in the local-authority area, it would speed up her chances. 'After what we've been through, we'll live anywhere,' she told startled housing officers. 'So long as it's not in Texas.'

Before the council found permanent accommodation for Morag, she had to move out of her grandmother's house, so the council offered to put her up in a local hotel that was used to house homeless families. She was promised that it was a short-term arrangement. 'I can't afford that,' she protested.

'Don't worry,' she was told. 'We'll take care of the bill.'

Morag didn't think that it was fair to live at the expense of her father, and so she went to the local offices of the then Department of Health and Social Security (DHSS) and applied for help. For all of her adult life, she had earned her own keep, becoming used to a healthy income and a good standard of living. Many people in her position might have felt shame at now expecting others to provide for them, but Morag knew only happiness and relief that months of fury, violence, threats and madness were over. And thanks to the handsome financial rewards of working offshore, she had invested well in her various properties, buying the former council house in Elgin and selling it at a profit before taking on the home in Marywell, which she knew would now have to be sold to help support her and Jasmine.

While she waited for good news to drop through the letterbox about a house becoming available, she made friends with another young woman who had a baby the same age as Jasmine. Most days, the two women would take the children to a nursery, but her friend noticed that Morag always appeared vigilant, nervous almost, especially when strangers approached.

Morag waited to hear from Marcus – waited for the father who so professed his love for his daughter to tell her that he would be sending regular cash to help her support the child. Morag was not concerned about herself, knowing that either her family or the social would provide enough money for her to live on. But Marcus had made such a fuss of wanting Jasmine that she was sure that he would naturally want to help her through life in some tangible way. Nothing came.

Two months after returning to the UK, Morag was allocated a two-bedroomed home in the new town of Killingworth, a short bus journey from Newcastle upon Tyne. Her rent would be paid by the DHSS, and she began gathering together furniture

– some old, some new, some borrowed. When she had upped sticks and moved to Texas with Marcus, she'd left her furniture behind but had taken her family heirlooms, such as treasured medals and photographs. Now they were on the other side of the Atlantic.

Her new address at Garth in Killingworth was a far cry from the house overlooking Lake Austin, but instead of the screams that had echoed through the walls of that home, here there was only laughter and childish giggles. Conscious of the danger, however unlikely, that Jasmine could be snatched away from her, Morag was pleased to see that the back garden was enclosed by a fence and padlocked gate, which always remained locked.

What remained of the summer was a happy time. Morag placed a paddling pool in the garden and playfully taught her daughter to pretend to cook and bake. And she joined Jasmine in a nearby nursery, allowing her and her daughter to broaden their circle of friends.

From time to time, Flora would visit. And her old colleague Jack Reeves, who Morag thought of as a godfather to her child, regularly called from the rigs, wanting to know every detail of what Jasmine had been up to.

That summer, Morag also took Jasmine to nearby baths to teach her to swim. She knew that Marcus would make contact at some stage and bid to take his daughter back to Austin and his house by the lakeside, even for a brief spell. If and when he did seek to have his daughter return to Texas – and Morag was convinced Lawilda would not cease to urge her son to do so – she wanted the reassurance, with the lake such an attraction, of knowing that Jasmine was able to swim. In this way, Morag wished to demonstrate that she had prepared her child to face whatever the future held.

At that time, Jack was working as a steward on one of the supply ships that bustled between accommodation rigs in the North Sea, picking up cargoes in ports such as North and South Shields on the River Tyne and ferrying them to their destinations. Whenever

77

he docked, Morag would make an effort to call on him, and she frequently came away with gifts and food.

As a result of her training with children, Morag was of the opinion that Jasmine needed a father figure in her life, but Marcus made no effort to weld the family together, and so she came to rely on Jack to play the role of what was effectively a surrogate dad to Jasmine. It was one he accepted happily.

A divorcee with no children of his own, Jack was generous to both mother and daughter, realising how difficult it was for Morag to survive on what was a meagre income compared with what she was used to. He saw that behind her mask of pleasure there lay occasional spells of great melancholy and loneliness.

To Jasmine, Uncle Jack was the bee's knees. He was kind to her, and even at the age of 18 months the infant would have been sufficiently perceptive to tell that he was kind to her mother.

At Christmas 1993, Jasmine received many gifts, but none from her father, not even a card, even though he and his parents had been sent further photographs of the youngster so that they could remain acquainted with her development.

Flora's visits were sporadic at that time, as she was working to build up a horse school at the bungalow in between offering driving lessons. From time to time, she would detour to Killingworth on her way to or from horse sales in England. She knew that her daughter missed the physical presence of a man. The danger, as she saw it, was her defences being dropped for the wrong one.

Flora had never been a fan of Jack and didn't think that he was the man for her daughter. She readily acknowledged his generosity and thought that it shamed the parsimony of Marcus to an even greater degree, but there would never come a time when she would welcome Jack as a candidate to be Morag's permanent partner and protector. And her outright dislike of him was entirely mutual. But at least they shared a disgust of the way in which Marcus had treated Morag and Jasmine.

In Killingworth, Morag and Jasmine were visited by

Lawilda and Jimmy Ross Chapman. Morag had no problem with their decision to see the child. Indeed, she was delighted, wanting them to play a full part in the development of their granddaughter. She shared a similar hope for Marcus but was disappointed by what she saw as his indifference to Jasmine. Her nursery training had instilled in her a belief that Jasmine needed to develop within a settled environment surrounded by the love of parents and grandparents alike, even if some lived many thousands of miles away.

Although their meeting at Woodville had been brief, Morag liked Jimmy Ross. She thought that he was a gentleman of the old school and admired the disciplined way in which he conducted himself, no doubt a result of his having spent years in the military.

The sight of the new town with its packed rows of brick houses must have taken the Chapmans by surprise after the wide-open spaces – too wide open for Morag's liking – of Texas. Eager to demonstrate her enthusiasm for their retaining contact with Jasmine, Morag invited the couple to stay in her home, even though it meant her giving up her own bed to the Americans. She placed no restrictions on their movements with her daughter but would, in time, wonder if this had rebounded on her. She told Flora, 'One day, Lawilda and Jimmy Ross took Jasmine out to a park where there were lots of children of her own age playing, their mothers watching and chatting. When they came back, they asked if it was appropriate for Jasmine to be mixing with kids from council estates. Once they had left to go back to Texas, I asked Jasmine what had happened. She said that she had wanted to join in a ball game with the other children but Lawilda and Jimmy Ross had prevented her from doing so. The impression I had was that they thought that youngsters from council estates were not good enough to mingle with Jasmine, yet they were just little boys and girls of her own age with whom she loved to have fun.'

Flora is in no doubt about the motive behind the Chapmans'

visit: 'It was a spying mission. They came over to check up on Morag, to see what she was up to and who she was seeing, whether she had a lover or boyfriend staying in the house with her and Jasmine, if the home was clean and well kept, and if Jasmine was being properly cared for. You can bet your bottom dollar that they took a good look around the place and searched for anything that might have shown Morag in a bad light so that they could report back to Marcus what they'd found. But if he was so interested and concerned, why did he not come over himself?'

Marcus had an explanation for his inability to travel to Killingworth. He had quit his work in the oil industry to bed down – unsuccessfully as it turned out – in Austin with Morag and their daughter. In July 1993, a month after they had fled back to the north-east of England, he started work for another engineering company, Thermal Wave International, based in Austin. He surmised that it would be unreasonable to ask new employers for time off almost as soon as he had begun working for them, and so he and his parents agreed that it made sense for them to go in his place. On the other hand, is it unreasonable to ask why, when he would later show such concern for the well-being of Jasmine, he did not explain his worries to his new bosses, who would have been heartless to refuse to allow him time off? As it was, his parents could only have told him that his daughter was safe, happy and growing up in a clearly loving environment.

Because of the continual worry about Jasmine's future, Morag contacted lawyers with a view to gaining some form of legal right to take care of her daughter. On Christmas Eve 1993, her representatives wrote a letter to Neal Pfeiffer, Marcus's lawyer in Texas, that would have far-reaching consequences. It explained that they had already written to Marcus to tell him that they had applied to the local court in North Tyneside for Morag to be given a residence order so that she would have the 'care and control' of Jasmine. A residence order simply lays down formally where and with whom a child is to live. The letter went on to say that Morag was not intending to put any obstacles in the way of Marcus keeping in contact with Jasmine, but if he wanted to see her it would have to be arranged in advance. It concluded by asking whether he would object to the proposal in court.

So, the first shot had been fired. Morag's letter was the first of scores of documents from both sides of the Atlantic, all of which were packed with legal jargon, but in reality said, 'Jasmine should be with me.' No one could have foretold the far-reaching effect her letter would have, but was it a sensible move to make at that stage? What if she had simply let matters remain as they were for the foreseeable future? What if she had waited longer before seeking to make her custody of Jasmine official? Marcus had not seen or contacted his daughter in the six months since she and Morag had fled from America. How would it have looked had she waited several months more and been able to tell the authorities that the man who was insisting he should take his little girl to Texas had still shown no interest? More significantly, perhaps, should she have been advised to move back to Scotland, the country where Jasmine had been born, and to seek to gain custody there? Would, at that time, a judge have taken custody of a child from a mother with a spotless record of care and given it to a man who had seemingly made no effort to see his daughter for months on end?

There were even those among her friends who believed that following the response to her initial letter – a response in which the Chapman representatives expressed an interest on Marcus's behalf in taking control of Jasmine – she should simply have left Killingworth, moved to Scotland and effectively gone into hiding. Then she could have sat back and defied attempts to be found. The thinking was that Marcus would have eventually given up searching. It was true that there were plenty of potential bolt holes and enough supporters who would have been glad to give shelter to Morag and Jasmine. But this was almost certainly not a viable or sensible idea. It would have been relatively easy for lawyers to have the jurisdiction of the English courts extended to their Scottish counterparts, who would then have had to enforce orders for her to produce Jasmine. But to this day there are many people close to Morag who believe that she ought, at the outset, to have waged her legal fight in her homeland and not England.

In the New Year, there was a communication from Texas, but it was not a belated greetings card. It was a development Morag had dreaded from the moment she'd fled from Austin. But the die had been cast, and she had begun a skirmish that was heading towards all out war. The response, dated 10 January 1994, from Neal Pfeiffer made it plain that Marcus was prepared for a stout defence. It was polite and clearly meant to be as helpful as possible. It indicated that Marcus was not in Austin and attempts to contact him had been unsuccessful. But Pfeiffer confirmed that he represented Jasmine's father and that there had been attempts by the Texan, when Morag and Jasmine were living in Austin in June 1993, to have his marriage to Morag legally ended. That did not necessarily worry Morag; the relationship had long been over as far as she was concerned. But what she saw when she read on caused her to fret. Pfeiffer left no doubt that while Marcus wanted either an annulment or divorce, he was so worried about Jasmine that he wanted as much access as he could legally obtain.

Within days of this correspondence being received and discussed with Morag, a response was on its way to Texas. It stated that the magistrate at the court hearing in Tyneside had requested that both parents write out statements giving details of what each thought should be the arrangement for looking after Jasmine and for their having contact with her. The letter also asked if Marcus objected to Morag being given a residence order and what his intentions were: 'Is he asking that the child be returned to America to live with him or is he merely requesting regular contact?' Significantly, it went on to warn that if Marcus tried to secure a residence order allowing him to take his daughter to Texas, it would be 'strongly contested'.

When Neal Pfeiffer replied on 25 January 1994, there was no longer any doubt that the bell had been sounded for a bloody head-to-head encounter. His letter made it clear that the Americans intended to step up the pressure in regard to the future of Jasmine. Morag rang her mother and said, 'Marcus says it would be better for Jasmine if she lived with him. I just can't believe he'd say that. His lawyer says if they can't get that, then they'll settle for a court over here ordering Jasmine to live with me provided it's in England and they know where we are. They are going to ask the courts here to rule that Jasmine should spend most of her school summer holidays in Austin with the Chapmans and stay over there every other Christmas.' The letter added that Marcus was willing to come to England to either confirm to magistrates that he and Morag had agreed to Jasmine's future or, if that had not happened, to argue his own case.

The tone of letter was polite and reasonably friendly, but behind the words lurked menace. Marcus wanted Jasmine to go back to Texas to live with him, and the extent of his fury with Morag was demonstrated by the fact that within two days of her leaving Austin he had started action to have the common-law marriage wiped from the slate. It was also evident that he believed she had somehow remained in the USA for several days or even weeks before heading home.

Morag thought it was unbelievable that a man who had ignored his little girl for so long should now, out of the blue, dispute her right to care for her daughter and state that he would prefer to take her away from her mother completely. The best Marcus was prepared to offer was Jasmine staying in Killingworth but spending weeks of the year with him during those holidays when Morag would have expected to be able to spend quality time with her daughter: to take her visiting in Scotland, to ride ponies, and to call on Uncle Jack in Fraserburgh and their many friends in

Aberdeen and elsewhere. Jasmine had never been out of her sight, apart from the brief disappearance in Austin, and the thought of losing her for weeks at a time appalled and frightened her. Morag was confident that no court would consider sending the toddler to live with a stranger, which is what Marcus would be to her, in a far-off land. But what scared her was the idea of a compromise in which the suggestion that Jasmine stay with him during holidays was accepted.

What would happen, she asked herself, if Jasmine was put on a plane to Texas and did not return? Who was to say that courts over there wouldn't take the view that the youngster was better off staying with a wealthy father and rich, intelligent, influential grandparents? How would she go about getting her back? Marcus had enough money to be able to start an expensive legal fight in England, but she depended on social-security handouts. Would she be given legal aid to take a fight into America if he decided to hold on to Jasmine? These questions and more raced through her mind.

Morag had known that Marcus would make a move at some stage but after his lack of contact she had dropped her guard, believing that he might have given up on Jasmine. Morag suspected that Marcus was offering a compromise so that he could later take Jasmine away from her, but there was no way that she would allow that to happen. Morag thought that Marcus was playing mind games and deliberately setting out to wound her by applying pressure to her weakest spot: her devotion to her daughter.

And so the airmail letters flowed back and forth. She had been happy for Marcus to visit them at Killingworth whenever he wished. But she told her lawyers that there was no way that he was going to be allowed to take Jasmine for holidays in America, no matter how many promises were made that she would be sent home on time. 'I don't trust him,' she told them. 'He's run away with her once. He's unpredictable, and who is to guarantee he won't do it again? He's just not having her.'

As the weeks passed, it was evident that the matter was becoming more serious. So serious, in fact, that it was not long before the case progressed to the courts in London and became a morass of mind-boggling complexity.

8

Summoned

As the lawyers rattled out letters and ran up fees, Morag spent the winter trying to shelter her daughter, now heading towards her second birthday, from the legal battle waging over her. There were still those among her friends who continued to urge her to move back to Scotland and seek shelter from the courts there. They warned her that a day would come when it would be too late to turn back. Some even suggested that she shouldn't trust the English legal system, arguing that it would let her down if she wasn't careful. But Morag continued to be guided by her Tyneside lawyers.

When snow fell, the two threw snowballs, squelched their way along slushy streets, Morag merrily pulling her red-cheeked child on a sledge, and watched robins scampering through their garden, pecking up breadcrumbs thrown by Jasmine. They were happy days, but Morag knew they might not last. Jack Reeves visited with words of reassurance, but a letter that she had been dreading arrived from her lawyers in March – the one that locked her into a legal merry-go-round from which there was no escape. It was now that she had second thoughts about her decision to fight on English soil, but the time for self-recrimination was past.

Ripping open the letter, she read the words inside with dread. She called her own lawyer asking for a brief interpretation, then, her eyes filling with tears, called Flora. 'Mum, I've had another letter.

Marcus has hired some solicitors in London, and they are insisting we give them my address. My lawyer says that this is so I can be served with legal papers about Marcus wanting to see Jasmine. They say that they've been to court and now, legally, Jasmine has to stay here. I've also got to hand over my passport.' It effectively made her a prisoner – but an angry prisoner, determined to fight to retain her flesh and blood.

In the spring, Morag was called to a hearing in London at which the future of Jasmine was to be decided. She found it remarkable that despite the wealth of Marcus and his family, he had been granted legal aid and told that his bills for attempting to take a Scottish child away from her mother to live in Texas would be picked up and paid by British taxpayers. She was loath to take Jasmine, fearing that if the decision went against her she would be made to hand over her child there and then. And so Uncle Jack agreed to babysit at Killingworth in her absence, taking time off from his work on the rig supply vessel. She trusted Jack with her daughter, and the youngster enjoyed being around him.

Jasmine wanted to know why Morag was leaving. Morag was unable to stem her tears. 'Sweetheart, I have to go a long way away to tell important people that I love you and want you to live here with me,' she replied.

Morag then asked Jasmine if she would like a present to be brought back for her. 'Geese, Mummy.'

Her daughter's request led Morag to remember her days as a child in Kingussie when she had been chased around the big stone house by geese. 'Wouldn't a dog be nice, sweetheart?'

'Oh yes, Mummy.'

'Why don't you think of a name and tell me what it is when I get back?'

'Yes, Mummy.'

'Then if I win what I have to do, I'll buy you a real dog, sweetheart.'

In the High Court, a judge ruled that Jasmine should stay with her mother but Marcus ought to be allowed reasonable access. It was all that she could have hoped for, and she headed back to the North East filled with joy and laughter. 'It's finally over,' she told herself. 'It must be. Surely this is the end of the road, and we can get on with our lives.'

Once home, Morag kept her promise to Jasmine. A neighbour's bitch had pupped, and they needed to relieve themselves of her litter, so a little black-and-white puppy soon began snuggling up to Jasmine. He was a mixture of countless breeds but was the most beautiful animal she had ever seen, and she called him Frostie, because he had been born during the winter.

Frostie became Jasmine's friend and playmate. One day, Morag heard squeals and barks from the kitchen. She ran in to find Jasmine with her sleeves rolled up to her elbows, standing on a stool over a sink filled with soapy water. Frostie was being held on his back by Jasmine, and his face could just be seen peering through the foam. Water and suds were splashing everywhere.

'What the hell are you doing?' asked her bewildered mother.

'Mummy, Frostie dirty,' Jasmine replied. She then continued to vigorously apply soap to the protesting pup and then dunk him up and down in the water.

'Look, sweetheart, that's not how you wash a dog. I'll show you,' said Morag, rescuing the grateful animal and enfolding him in a towel.

Although he escaped from drowning on that occasion, Frostie was later to have an even closer shave with death. Standing at the foot of the staircase one day, Morag spotted her daughter and the dog above her. 'Get Frostie down here, sweetheart,' she called and waited for the pup to scuttle down. Instead, Jasmine picked him up and threw him over the banister. He landed shaken but safe, and headed for comfort and security beneath his favourite chair. 'Jasmine, you cannot do that to Frostie,' Morag said. 'I meant you to carry him down or give him a gentle push to let him know where you wanted him to go.'

The paddling pool that Morag had bought the previous summer was still in the back garden, and she would regularly fill it with clean water. She also bought Jasmine a small chute so that she could slide down into the water. It was the source of immense fun. Jasmine loved the thrill of hitting the water and watching it splash over her and anyone standing nearby. It was an experience that needed to be shared, and one day she discovered the ideal companion: Frostie. Morag, hearing a commotion, emerged from the house to see the pup being urged to climb the little steps and then given a helping push down the slide. But the dog was no water baby and obviously did not share Jasmine's enthusiasm for the game. Frostie had to be once again rescued by Morag.

It was during just such an afternoon of high jinks that the telephone rang. Jack Reeves was visiting his goddaughter and watched her splash in the pool as Morag hurried indoors. She emerged minutes later, pale and shocked. 'Go inside and pick up the phone,' Morag said. 'Don't say anything – just listen.' He did as he was ordered. Before he even reached the phone, he was able to make out the ravings and rantings of a male voice with an American accent. Threats and obscenities thundered across the Atlantic, and it was evident that Marcus had not abandoned the fight for his daughter.

'I'd heard some fairly choice language on the rigs and supply ships in my time, but this was pure vitriol,' Jack recalls. 'I gathered that Marcus was livid that Morag had defied him and that he would have to come to England if he wanted to see Jasmine. What was astonishing was that this was a guy who was claiming he had the sort of nature that made him an ideal candidate to take care of a small girl. I was furious that he would talk to Morag in this way without realising that Jasmine might have been standing beside her mother listening in, and I eventually got her to end the call. When she did, I asked, "Why put up with that? Why not just tell your lawyer and change your number?" But Morag thought it would be wrong to deprive Marcus of the chance to maintain contact with the child. I told her, "You're crazy. No one else would stand for being yelled at like that." But she simply shrugged and asked what else could be expected from a guy who had dumped her on her own in a motel at Christmas.'

As the summer of 1994 approached, Morag would have loved to have been able to take her daughter for a holiday abroad. Although her parents were long divorced, they would have happily chipped in to send her off for a break, as they both felt that she had earned one after the struggles and heartbreak of the previous 12 months. Almost every day, she listened to other young mothers as they happily gossiped about their own holiday plans, showed photographs of themselves and their husbands or partners romping on foreign beaches with kiddies of Jasmine's age, or demonstrated the nut-brown effect on their complexions of two weeks under a cloudless Continental sky. But she was not jealous of them. Her pleasure came from having Jasmine close by.

Morag's passport had been returned, but her lawyers had warned her not to stray far from her home. Marcus had announced that he intended to appeal against the decision to let his daughter stay with her mother. He was set on having the case heard in Texas, where he was confident he could rely on a home-town decision in his favour. Far from allowing the door to close on the matter, Marcus had wrenched it wide open again.

'Does this mean we have to go back to court to fight the whole thing all over again?' a distraught Morag asked her lawyer.

'I'm afraid it does,' he replied.

'But he can't win, surely. Why doesn't he just let things stay as they are? He knows he can come and see her regularly.'

'It's not as simple as that, Morag. Now he's arguing that the case ought to have been heard in Texas in the first place, on the grounds that Jasmine is an American citizen.'

'But she's not. She was born in Aberdeen. She's Scottish.'

'His lawyers are going to argue that she's American because of the time you spent living in Austin.'

'Four months?'

'He will argue that it was six.'

'That's not true. We were only there for four months.'

'You'll have to be prepared to go to London at short notice again, I'm afraid. There is nothing we can do.'

As she waited for the summons, she increasingly regretted her decision to live in England after her flight from Austin. Night after night, she lay awake, tasting her own salty tears on her lips, fearful of what was happening around her. She dreaded the arrival of the postman each day, expecting only bad news and blaming herself for the uncertainty about Jasmine's future. The child had been conceived and born in Scotland. Flora and Morag's friends had insisted that she should have moved back to Scotland as soon as Marcus had indicated that he wanted Jasmine to live in Texas. In her own country, the sympathy of the courts and community would have been with her. The Chapman lawyers would have had to track her down, and if they'd succeeded in taking the matter to a custody or access hearing, then that hearing would have been in a Scottish courtroom. That would have been where a decision was made. A Texan would have had to ask a Scots judge to take a Scots child from her Scots mother and hand her over to a father who lived thousands of miles away and who had not made personal contact for many months. They might have granted Marcus visiting rights and possibly have ordered Morag to take Jasmine to Texas to see her father and grandparents from time to time, but the odds against his winning custody would have been astronomical. English judges had come down on her side once before, but a different panel was now going to hear Marcus's appeal. They would effectively have two aliens before them, one claiming that the child had American citizenship.

'Why did nobody tell me when all this started that all I needed to do was go back to Scotland and let them come for us there?' Morag asked. The truth was that her friends and family had, but her lawyers had not. It was now too late for regrets. The great steamroller that is the judicial system was in motion. With the summer at its height, she was told that an appeal hearing was to be held in London.

Morag believed she had right on her side, but often what is right is not reflected in legal rulings. Courts are notoriously fallible to the mercy of clever words as opposed to facts. Marcus insisted that it was only right that the question of custody of his daughter should be heard in Texas, claiming she was an American citizen, having lived there for six months. It was a claim Morag disputed, pointing out their sojourn had lasted just four months. Jasmine, Morag's lawyers argued, was Scottish and did not come under Texan jurisdiction. Two of the three appeal court judges were sympathetic to her, but, at the end of the day, they ruled against her and she lost.

Shocked and in tears, Morag sat outside the courtroom and asked her lawyer what it all meant. 'Jasmine must be sent to Texas for the courts there to decide who shall have custody,' her lawyer explained.

'On her own?'

'You don't have to go.'

'Let me get this right. The court says a two-year-old girl who has never been parted from her mother should be put on a plane to Texas for people over there she does not know to decide whether she will come back home to me?'

'You can travel over if you wish.'

'I'm not letting my daughter out of my sight. It's unbelievable. This is a human being, a wee girl, we're talking about here.'

'If you make it clear you are going with her, then we'll make sure Marcus is told by the court to pay your costs and to look after you while the case goes on in Texas.'

'Ordering him to do that is one thing, getting him to cough up is another. We should never have fought this case in English courts. A Scottish judge would have looked after us.'

Morag's lawyers asked the judges to ensure that Marcus was formally ordered to provide for her in the States. The court concurred and laid down a series of conditions: that he would pay the cost of flights for Morag and Jasmine from Newcastle upon Tyne to Austin via Gatwick in economy class plus £75 to cover travelling expenses; that he would pay $6,000 into an account administered by lawyers in America; that he would pay dental fees in America for Morag; that he would not try and take Jasmine from Morag's care and control; that he would find Morag a two-bedroomed apartment in a 'reasonable' area of Austin at a cost of between $750 and $850 a month and would pay any advance rent; that he would hand over $1,200 a month maintenance for Morag and their daughter; that he would not 'assault, molest or otherwise interfere with the mother or Jasmine'; and that he would not 'seek to have access to Jasmine save in accordance with the agreement of the mother'. But the crunch of the ruling was this: 'The child Jasmine Jamee Chapman be returned forthwith to the state of Texas, United States of America, namely on 10 August 1994.' And that judgment was given in the late afternoon of 29 July 1994. Morag had less than ten days to prepare before she had to uproot her life once again.

By 8 August 1994, two days before she was due to arrive in Austin, Marcus's lawyers promised that $6,800 dollars had been paid into a fund from which she would receive $800 when she set foot in Texas and another $1,200 a month from that point onwards. His attorney, Neal Pfeiffer, offered to let Morag and Jasmine stay in a two-bedroomed property that he maintained in Austin until they could find somewhere else. Pfeiffer's letter said, 'I would prefer for Ms Chapman to select her own apartment upon her arrival when time permits, for which Mr Chapman will make payment.' This was in direct conflict to the ruling by the London judges, and Morag thought that it was an omen for what lay ahead. She turned down the invitation to use Pfeiffer's apartment. As she and all those around her saw it, why should she stay in the lion's den when Marcus had agreed to provide an apartment for her? Once in Pfeiffer's flat, Marcus's lawyers would have complete access to her and be able to monitor her every movement and visitor. Her every action would be scrutinised, to the potential

94

detriment of her case. She demanded the privacy Marcus had agreed to provide.

Morag was shattered by the developments, unable to grasp that her pleadings for justice and help appeared to have been trampled over and ignored. It was as though Marcus was hell-bent on grinding down her resistance, knowing that he had the strength and financial backing to continue the fight for Jasmine indefinitely. She was confident that she would defeat him, even in his own backyard, but wondered whether it would end there. Just months earlier, she had celebrated, thinking that it was all over. Now she had to start all over again. Was it, she asked herself, his aim to battle on and on until she crumbled beneath the joint pressures of trying to raise her daughter while attempting to fend off subtle and cruel attempts to part her from the child.

Morag had been warned that the case in America might drag on for several months and had no option but to inform the local housing department that she would need to vacate her Killingworth home. They were sympathetic but had a long waiting list to satisfy. 'Tell us when you come back, and we'll make sure you get priority,' they promised.

'Oh, I'll be back, but not to England,' she told them. 'I have made that mistake once, and it will not happen again. I want to be among my own.'

9

Silver Lining

The ruling by the appeal court was based on human-rights legislation, which determined that child-custody cases should be fought in the country of which the child was a resident, and Marcus had somehow successfully argued that Jasmine was American. It was a flawed decision, but there was no going back, and it meant that Morag had to dismantle her home and life for a second time. To see the furniture she had scrimped and saved to buy being carried outside was heartbreaking, and at times she had to sit alone in her empty bedroom with the door closed, sobbing silently for fear of her own distress causing similar misery to her daughter.

The belongings would be put into storage and then sold to raise cash for the legal fight that lay ahead. Jack Reeves had arrived from Fraserburgh to help, and Flora had hired a horse trailer, hitched it to her car and driven south from Forres during the early hours. When she reached Killingworth, she could see that Morag had been crying, but there was little time to sympathise. The next morning, a plane would fly them from the airport on the outskirts of Newcastle upon Tyne to Austin. Tony also turned up, worried by Marcus's record of breaking promises. He was terrified that his daughter would touch down in Austin only to discover that none of the promised funds were available, so he handed her an envelope packed with £1,500 worth of US dollars.

When Flora left for the long drive back to Scotland, knowing that she would need to immediately return to collect the rest of Morag's belongings, Frostie lay beside her in the car, miserable at being parted from his little bubbly chum. Flora's ears rang with the promise forced from her by Jasmine that he would be well looked after. But it was difficult to concentrate on what to do with Frostie when the bigger picture involved her own daughter and granddaughter: 'I felt terrible about the whole affair, knowing that it would have been avoided if Morag had lived in Scotland, and was worried in case something went wrong and we would not see Jasmine again. The sight of Morag's eyes, red and hurting from crying, made it seem worse. It was just awful having to help rip her home apart. She had only just installed a new fitted kitchen, most of which would have to be abandoned.

'Jasmine carried Frostie around as if he was her favourite toy, desperate not to be separated from him, and at one stage she clutched the little dog so tightly that he bit her.

'About an hour out of Killingworth, I felt my own sadness welling up and broke down crying. The tears came like a torrent, and I couldn't see to drive, so I pulled into the entrance to a disused farm, switched off the engine and let them flow. I was asking myself, "Why has my life gone so wrong? What did I do to deserve this?" I felt bitter towards Tony, who had done really well for himself financially. With his wealth, he could have done so much for Morag. With different legal representation, the whole Texas trip could perhaps have been avoided and the matter resolved in England.

'My sobs must have woken up the sleeping Frostie, who was whimpering. Frostie, I knew, would be a problem. I had to find a place for him to stay and a new owner, someone who would be kind to him, for the simple reason that he seemed to be a part of Jasmine and to have been the cause of the puppy suffering would have meant that I had abused the trust that Jasmine had put in me.'

Eventually, Flora reached Forres and unloaded the furniture with the help of a friend and Don Evans. Before setting off back to Killingworth, she found a good home for Frostie.

When Flora returned to what had been her daughter's home, she discovered Jack Reeves standing guard as crowds of youngsters used the offer of helping as an excuse to steal. Adults arrived seeking bargains, and Flora was forced to sell belongings that would not fit into her trailer. Among the last possessions to leave were the beds in which the travellers had slept, and by the time the house was empty and locked up for the last time Morag and Jasmine were in the air.

For Morag, it had been a harrowing experience: 'I had to explain to Jasmine that we were going back to America. With the curiosity that all children have, she wanted to know why. I could not bring myself to tell her that it was because her daddy wanted to split us up, so I simply said that we were going on holiday. I thought that would have excited her, but it did not. Instead, she looked sad and thoughtful, and I'm sure she suspected that there was more to it. I tried to make everything happy for her and didn't really tell her what the hell was going on, which was a heck of a lot. There were days before we left when I was sure I was going to break down in tears in front of her.

'We had had such lovely times together, but now I was scared that our happiness together might come to an end. So many things were racing through my mind. I remembered, for instance, the time earlier that year when I'd decided to give her a treat, and we'd gone to Edinburgh and stayed in a cheap hotel for a couple of days. Jasmine loved wildlife, and I took her to Edinburgh Zoo. She was so excited, because she had seen photographs of the penguins doing their walk and wanted to watch them. How she loved that.

'Then, just before we were leaving, we discovered that it was feeding time for the seals. We stopped to watch as the keeper threw them fish for which they would leap and splash. Jasmine was enthralled, squealing in delight, and the keeper asked her if she would like to help. He gave her a fish and told her to throw it to the waiting seals. She took careful aim and threw, but as she did so it slipped from her hand, went in the wrong direction and hit a chap smack in the face. It was a pretty smelly fish, and everyone thought it was very funny. Some of the spectators were just about in stitches. Of course, the victim wasn't too pleased. He turned beetroot red and was obviously furious but too embarrassed to say or do anything. Jasmine and I laughed about that all the way back to the hotel and again the next day when we returned to Killingworth. But as the time drew nearer to go to the airport, it didn't seem so funny any more.

'At the airport, I was determined that I would not cry in front of her, but as we were strapped into our seats and the plane was heading down the runway to take off she suddenly looked up at me and asked me who was looking after Frostie.

'I said to myself, "I'm going to die here. How do I handle this?" I then told her, "Don't worry, sweetheart. Don Evans will look after Frostie. Frostie is going to be OK, because Don likes dogs, and he loves you, too." But the truth was that I didn't know where my mum was going to find a home for Frostie. All I wanted was to be nice and act like a normal mum, although I kept telling myself that no normal mum would ever find herself in the position in which we now were.

'I thought the kindest thing was not to tell Jasmine the real reason for us being on that aircraft and hoped that she had accepted what I'd said about her dog. But about halfway through the trip, she woke up from a nap crying. She again wanted to know what was going to happen to her dog. "I've told you. He's going to be OK with Don." It was a terrible thing to look at her little face, wipe away the tears and not know what lay in store for either of us or for Frostie.'

Because Morag had been warned that the proceedings would almost certainly drag on for months, her immediate priority was to find an apartment. She eventually settled for rooms in the Georgian Apartments, a huge complex of rented properties in

Georgian Drive, Austin. It was hardly the Ritz and very basic, but she had limited funds and was soon to run into difficulties receiving the money promised by Marcus.

First, however, the legal process got under way, and it was during a visit to her lawyer in Austin that Morag met Randy Berry for the first time. Tall, gangling, not unlike the comedy actor John Cleese and a veteran of the Vietnam War, Randy took an immediate liking to the slim blonde who looked so lost and defeated. Richard Jones, one of Randy's colleagues, was Morag's lawyer, and Randy would become Flora's legal representative after she was advised that it was in her interests, as Jasmine's grandparent, to have a lawyer of her own. Unlike the United Kingdom, American courts could award custody to a grandparent, so Flora asked Randy to represent her and keep a watching brief. Being in the same practice as Morag's lawyer was clearly a huge advantage.

Randy did not look like an affluent, successful member of the legal profession. Often untidy and occasionally known to appear in court with a stitch or two missing from his clothing, he cut an unkempt figure. But what he lacked on the sartorial front, he more than compensated for with a heartfelt eloquence. He made clients feel confident in his ability. From the very first time they met, Morag thought that she had at last found someone she could trust. There was an instant rapport between them on a personal and professional level, even though he was 20 years Morag's senior. Trapped in an ailing marriage, Randy was flattered by the interest and attention Morag showed in him. As time went on, they became increasingly close. They soon fell in love, became lovers and saw a future together.

Randy regularly telephoned Flora to bring her up to date with progress in the case. She liked his no-nonsense attitude and the fact that he approached the legal dispute with the same care and determination as he would have prepared for a full-scale conflict in Vietnam. And because of the simple fact that the majority of their conversations were taken up talking about Morag, she suspected that Randy had a keen personal interest in her daughter. But she said nothing.

Randy announced that he would fight the case on the basis that if Morag and Flora won, the Chapman family would be ordered by the trial judge to pay his fees. 'What if we lose?' asked Flora.

'Well, then, so do I,' he replied. In fact, he did receive a fee of sorts when Flora agreed to pay a parking fine of $30, which he had incurred after giving her a lift to court one day.

Shortly after Morag's arrival, the case was formally begun at a preliminary hearing before a judge in Austin, who was astonished to learn that the matter had been sent from the London courts. 'I really don't know why you are here, Miss Dodds,' the judge said. 'We do not have jurisdiction in custody matters over a citizen of another country, and your daughter is clearly a citizen of the United Kingdom. But if they don't want it, then we'll have to take it. If your country won't take responsibility, then I guess we'll have to.'

As is the custom, the case began to drag once the initial legal formalities were over. Morag and Jasmine had a single room in the furnished Georgian Apartments and were expected to share a solitary bed. Morag had not brought her daughter up to be cosseted, but the spare furnishings and sleeping arrangements meant that there was no alternative to their sleeping together, something she'd always resisted in the past. Finance was an ever-present problem. From time to time, the funds Marcus had deposited for Morag, and on which she relied, would go astray in the mail. It meant trooping to the offices of her lawyer to begin the wearying process of making contact with Marcus's solicitor in order to have the cash redirected. As the days became weeks, boredom set in. When it rained, there was nothing to do but sit in the dreary apartment, playing games or flicking through bland American television shows.

'Jasmine wasn't so conscious of the feeling of being prisoners, because I tried to keep her occupied,' Morag remembers. 'But I knew she needed the companionship of children her own age. Right across from our building was a nursery school, and she used to gaze out of the window at the kids having fun. Sometimes, when we went out for a walk, we would pass right by them, and we could see them splashing about in a play pool like the one Jasmine had loved when we lived in Killingworth. I could tell she just longed to be there among them, and one day she asked, "Mummy, can I go and play, please?" I went to the people running the nursery school, explained who we were and asked if my daughter could take part. I said that I was happy to pay and was desperate for Jasmine to find other children to be with, because at home she had always been surrounded by friends. I told them that she loved to watch the others in the pool or on the swings, and her reaction at being left out was so sad. But they told me, "This is for American citizens only. Your daughter is not eligible."

'I said, "Come on. She's only a child of two. She's stuck on her own, and I promise she'll behave and not cause any problems." But they were adamant. I tried again, pointing out that I was a trained nursery-school teacher and offering to help, but it made no difference. They really were not interested. OK, maybe there were rules and regulations, but it seemed too cruel to force my little girl to be an outsider. I said, "If this was my country, we would always let your children join in. We'd never allow them to be unhappy." If I thought that it might have worked, I would literally have gone down on my hands and knees and begged, but they would have been unmoved. They could see Jasmine staring at the other children, and it was obvious that all she wanted was to play with them. It was disgusting that people with the job of looking after nursery-school kids had given her the cold shoulder.

'On the way home, Jasmine asked me, "Mummy, can I go tomorrow?" I had to tell her, "No, sweetheart. The adults say there is no room for you." It was a lame excuse, but what else could I say. She burst out crying, and I wanted to join in with her, but I stopped myself, thinking, "She's suffering enough. Don't add to it."

So, day after day, she would watch the others, and I'd sit with her and be mum, dad, playmate and friend. It was very hard going and horrendous when it rained, as there was nowhere to go.'

However, it turned out that there was some consolation from the nursery-school ban for Morag and Jasmine. One of Morag's near neighbours in the apartment complex was Jake Harris, a divorcee who although parted from his wife Caroline had remained friends with her. She was more than happy to let Jake take care of their children Olivia and Helen while she worked and for him to see them whenever he wanted. Morag bumped into her new neighbour one day and they began chatting. She told him that Jasmine had been refused a nursery-school place. 'Don't worry,' he told her. 'Jasmine can play with my kids. They'd love to meet her.' And so Anglo-American relations were somewhat repaired thanks to Jake and his daughters' kindness.

Jake and Morag became good friends. Sometimes he would drive her to the supermarket, and when she was sent bundles of the inevitable forms, which seem to be the bane of every American's life, and needed help to understand and complete them, he would pore over them with her until they were filled in. During her telephone calls home to her mother, she was able to tell Flora, 'Things are really beginning to drag here, but at least I've found friends for Jasmine.'

Elsewhere in Austin, a judge was examining the files on the custody case and concluding that it was time to make progress. In the city police headquarters, a clerk was updating records on outstanding crimes, including one from the previous year in which a store had alleged that a young woman from the United Kingdom had paid for a giant pile of groceries with a bad cheque. 'I wonder where she is now?' he mused.

10

Bringing Trouble

Courts everywhere are accused of being slow, cumbersome and often difficult to understand. Those in the USA are no different, and the argument over who should have custody of Jasmine would drag on well into 1995. In an attempt to speed matters up and save both parties considerable expense, Judge Jeanne Meurer decided to offer them a solution. It was a simple one: get together and come up with a compromise. But it was soon apparent that meetings at which Morag and Marcus would jointly hammer out their various demands were simply not going to take place.

Morag would blame her one-time lover for the failure of the judge's proposal, claiming that he never showed up or always had an excuse for not attending. It was frustrating for her having to hang about in the hope that something would happen, and some of Morag's friends in Austin wondered if there was another, hidden, agenda at work. Was the delay being engineered by the Chapmans in the hope of driving Morag into some indiscretion, such as having a drink?

It was a miserable time, filled with fear and uncertainty. Night after night, she sat in the miserable, dull apartment, desperate to hide her tears from her sleeping daughter, and unable to step outside, because there was no one she could trust to look after Jasmine. Her friends felt justified in asking whether the delay was deliberate but knew they would never get an answer, cruel though her predicament was. And downright dirty tricks were soon to be employed against Morag. At the same time, a development that played into the hands of the Chapman cause, and which could have spelled disaster, was in the process of formation. It was as an act of pure kindness but had the same effect as an earthquake on a house of cards.

Since the day when he had helped Flora clear the last of Morag's belongings from the house at Killingworth, Jack Reeves had been in constant touch with Jasmine's mum. He took seriously his responsibilities as godparent and had told Morag before she left to keep him up to date with developments by telephoning him whenever he was at home in Fraserburgh. He fumed when she told him that Marcus was using what seemed to be delaying tactics.

'In Scotland, Marcus was far from the day-to-day influence of his mother, but once he went to America there was no doubt that she ruled the roost,' Jack says. 'You need only to think of the Christmas at Woodville to appreciate just how much she dominated her son, even though he was a grown man. Morag told me that when she broke the news about the pregnancy to Lawilda, Marcus's mother had replied, "I hope it's a daughter. I've always wanted a daughter, and now, maybe, I'll get one."

'The impression I've always had is that if Lawilda had stayed out of it and not pushed her son into demanding custody of his daughter, none of the bitterness and destruction that followed would have happened. Morag was absolutely under Marcus's spell. She would have done anything for him, and he appears to have been genuinely fond of her, so you must ask why everything went wrong. Was it Marcus and his odd behaviour or his mother, pulling strings and making her son jump, who pushed Morag into a corner from which her only escape was to return to Scotland, thus breaking up the relationship? Who really wanted Jasmine? Marcus didn't come over to visit her, but his parents did.

'After she went to Austin with Jasmine, Morag would often

telephone me, reversing the charges. As you can imagine, my phone bills were astronomical. During one of the calls, I realised that she sounded depressed, frightened and worried. This was no surprise, because she was in a strange country, and while there were expats over there who would later step in to help, it wasn't the same as being at home. It was obvious she just wanted the whole thing over and done with. When she arrived in America, she was angry to be told by a judge, "You don't have to be here. There's no need for you to be here." But by then it was too late to turn about and come home. Her attitude was, "Well, I'm here now, so let's get this over with." I had urged her to let the battlefield be a courtroom in Scotland, where she was sure to win, although I doubt whether the Chapmans would have pursued it had she done that, because they had no mud to sling at her at that time.

'Morag was a good mum. She would give up anything so that Jasmine could have the best. I know that's true of most mothers who love their children, but Morag happily made many, many sacrifices for Jasmine, who was always an exceptionally happy, well-brought-up child. Now Morag sounded emotional and distressed when I talked to her on the phone. I could almost see her tears and felt helpless. Jasmine was obviously too young to understand what was going on around her and unable to appreciate what her mother was going through. Morag's distress got to me. She was alone in a strange country fighting for her own daughter, and I did not like what was happening to her. It felt as if the Texans were ganging up against her, so, when a six-week leave came along, I decided to go over to the States to give her moral support. In any case, I hadn't seen Morag or Jasmine for several weeks.'

Jack arrived in Austin and was appalled to find that Morag had to share a bed with Jasmine: 'I could not believe that a court in London had ordered her over there, away from her lovely home in Killingworth, without having first ensured that she would have a standard of living at least equal to that which she and Jasmine had been made to leave. It was dreadful that Marcus who was professing such love for his daughter was prepared to let her live in conditions that I felt were bordering on squalor.

'When I arrived, I was met by Morag, Jasmine and Jake Harris, who had driven them out to the airport. Jake was a good guy: very kind and helpful, and a great ambassador for his country. I admit that I was tired when I got to Texas, having worked hard offshore. I'd come straight off the supply ship, immediately packed a bag and left for the airport to catch my very long flight. In fact, I hadn't slept for something like three days, apart from the occasional doze on the way over.

'I was excited to see Jasmine and Morag, but I hadn't eaten much and had had a couple of drinks. From the airport, Jake drove us back to the apartment block. We put Jasmine to bed, and then Morag and I had a good talk. I could tell how desperately worried she was about what might happen to Jasmine when her future was eventually decided by the courts. She broke down several times when it was mentioned that there was a possibility Jasmine would be taken from her and placed with the Chapmans. It was awful listening to her pouring out her heart about trying to get through the long nights on her own. I had a few drinks, and at times I too was in tears. But I certainly wasn't drunk. And because it was a warm night, I only had on a pair of jeans.

'At some stage, it must have been around three in the morning, Morag went out to call on Jake Harris and ask if I could sleep in his apartment. No sooner was she out of the door than people began rushing into the apartment. My immediate thought was, "Marcus and his pals are here, and they want to take Jasmine away," so I rushed into the bedroom and bent over the bed to protect her. It was then that I realised the intruders were, in fact, policemen. I was standing there clenching and unclenching my fists when they waded in and arrested me for being drunk and disorderly. But I did not realise this at the time and could not understand why they were there. I had done nothing wrong, and Morag was blameless. Had she been present, she might have been able to explain what was going on, but all the policemen seemed to be shouting at me at the same time, and I could not make out what they were saying. Evidently, they were unable to understand me either. At one point, I said, "If you're ever in the UK, I'll come and find you and kill you." Perhaps it was not the wisest thing to say, but I had done nothing wrong, and none of the neighbours had complained that we were making a racket or disturbing anyone.

'It appears that the police turned up because someone contacted them to say that there was a warrant out for the arrest of Morag for the bounced cheque and to tell them where she was living. They also said that people in the complex were angry at the noise coming from a loud party in her apartment and that someone was screaming and arguing. All of that was simply not true. There was hardly any noise – no shouting, screaming or music playing – and certainly not enough to wake up Jasmine, who was asleep in the next room.

'While the identity of the informant was never revealed, very few people knew about the warrant, and Morag suspected that the person who directed the police to her apartment that night was Marcus.'

Jack had only added to the confusion and suspicion by instinctively rushing to protect Jasmine when the apparent intruders entered the apartment. Police pouring in, not knowing what to expect, saw, through the glare of their torches, a semi-naked man leaning over a bed in which lay a little girl, still sleeping and naked having earlier refused to wear her customary pyjamas because of the heat. It was a wholly innocent act, but the police were not to know that. They automatically assumed the worst and pounced on Jack, dragging him away, oblivious to his protests and cries of concern for the little girl. What happened next between Jack and the police is a mystery. But he is in no doubt that he was given a savage beating by men who were angered by his pledges to kill them and assumed the worst after spotting him next to Jasmine's bed. Such was the ferocity of the beating that he passed out, and it was only later that he was able to piece the likely events together.

'The police station was only a ten-minute drive from the Georgian Apartments, and I was arrested just after three, yet I was told it was seven o'clock before I reached the station. What happened during those four hours? I don't know, but things that happened later gave me a pretty good clue as to what had gone on.

'I woke up that morning in a cell not knowing where I was. I found myself sharing a cell with a boy who had been arrested because of some unpaid parking tickets. He told me that he had come into town to watch an American football game but a policeman had recognised and nabbed him. As the day progressed, I was becoming anxious about when I would get out, but my cellmate tried to reassure me by saying that there would be a court session later in the day. "Don't worry," he said. "You're sure to get out. By the way, what are you in for?" I didn't know, so I questioned one of the police officers. "Excuse me," I said. "What am I in for?" He asked me my name, and when I told him who I was he said that it was for being drunk and disorderly. "Oh, you'll be out in two hours," my cellmate said. But by three in the afternoon, nothing had happened, and I was really anxious, thinking I would be spending the night behind bars. Then, a couple of officers came and took me to be fingerprinted. I was shackled in a chain gang made up of other prisoners.

'When the cell door opened, Morag was standing there. "What are you doing here?" she asked. "What the hell are you doing here?" I replied. We weren't supposed to talk, but the cop said, "As you come from Scotland, you can speak." She told me that she had been lifted as she came from Jake Harris's apartment, about 20 minutes after leaving me. There were police cars waiting for her. When she gave the police her name, she was asked to wait, before being told that she was being arrested because of a problem with a cheque.

'We chatted for a while before we were separated once again. Morag told me that she would deny everything, no matter what was put to her. "I have a good lawyer who will sort this for me,"

110

she said. "It's Marcus who ought to be facing the music for this, not me. He was the one who took all the money."

'At seven that night, I went in front of a judge. I really didn't take in much that was going on. I was in a foreign country, before a foreign court and faced more time in a foreign jail, so when I was asked how I was going to plead I told them that I was guilty, because I just wanted out. I was fined $110, but because I'd been in jail overnight they deducted $50. All I had on was a pair of jeans, and I was wondering where I could get the rest of the money when a sergeant called me over and ordered me to pick up a bag of rubbish and carry it a short distance from one side of the room to the other. Once I had done so, he said, "I'll give you $30 for that. That leaves $30 to pay, so we'll just forget about that, shall we?"

'At the time, I didn't think anything about the remark, because I was simply glad to be getting out. Morag had been released earlier, so I telephoned the apartment, and she said she would come to collect me with Jake Harris.

'Back at the apartment, we started cleaning up. I was worried, because I seemed to have lost my wallet, which had been in the pocket of my jeans. We found it in Morag's bag the following night when we went out to a restaurant for dinner. When I'd arrived from the airport, I had between $200 and $300 in my wallet, plus English money. Now, when we checked it over, the dollars were missing, and that set me to wondering about the generosity of the police in letting me off with the fine. Had I paid it in advance, I thought.

'We talked over what had taken place and came to the conclusion that the police had been sitting outside watching the apartment, because they barged in within a minute of Morag leaving to go to Jake's. The only solution was that someone had tipped them off that Morag, wanted in connection with the bounced cheque, was living at the apartment. We reasoned that Marcus knew about that cheque, because after it was refused by the bank and a complaint made, the police, wanting to talk to Morag, would have made their first point of call the address where she had lived in Austin. And that was the home she and Marcus had shared. So, Marcus knew about the cheque, and because he was paying for the rent of the apartment knew where she was staying. We were in no doubt that it was Marcus who rang the police, making out that he was a resident in the apartments who could not sleep because of the noise coming from Morag's apartment.

'It was a rotten thing to do to a young woman already suffering because of the prospect of losing her daughter, and, of course, being arrested and accused of theft was certain to portray her in a bad light.

'I continually pondered what could have happened to me in between my passing out and arriving at the police station. It was something like four hours, and I knew that for part of that time I'd been beaten up by the police. Just how savage that beating had been and how long it must have lasted emerged two days later when huge bruises came out on my back, knuckles and shins. The police had been careful about how they beat me up, hitting me nowhere that would show up unless I took off my clothes. So, OK, I'd had a few drinks, but I wasn't causing any trouble and yet the police broke in.'

After arresting Morag, the police realised that they had a problem on their hands: what to do about the sleeping Jasmine. She could hardly be dragged along with her mother or arrested for sleeping in the altogether. And it wasn't feasible to leave a police officer to guard her until her mother was released. In the end, they begged help from Morag, asking her if she knew of a friend who would look after Jasmine until her business at the police station was completed.

Following her return to Austin, Morag had rekindled her contact with Roberta Reid, now no longer a neighbour but living in another part of the city. Roberta was in a relationship with an American by the name of Warren Peters, but the couple had been experiencing difficulties, so Morag had largely left them alone, not wishing to intrude. Now she needed Roberta's help and gave her friend's address to the police, who arranged for Roberta to collect and care for Jasmine. Later in the day, Jasmine was returned to Morag, but the story would take a new twist at that point.

Jack stayed on for a further trouble-free two weeks. But the damage had been done. The Chapman camp could now bombard her with questions about the presence in the apartment of a drunken semi-naked man being alone with her daughter. They would even use the event to assert, wrongly and unfairly, that if Jack had been drinking then it stood to reason that Morag had been too. There was no evidence to support the allegation, because Morag had behaved impeccably, and she could argue, rightly, that her appearance in court because of the problem with the cheque had been Marcus's fault. Nevertheless, the events that had led to the joint arrests would constantly be thrown at her from then on. Increasingly, her depression grew and mood darkened. She felt the light she had once seen at the end of the tunnel was fading.

11

Ordeal

G uardian *ad litem* is the official term for a professional appointed by a court to represent someone who is unable to make decisions for themselves, usually because of their mental inability or their youth. It is a responsible post, because whoever holds it must be able to work out what the individual they are representing would want to do. Almost as soon as Jasmine reached Austin with her mother, a guardian *ad litem* was appointed for her by the offices of the Juvenile Court of Travis County. It is no exaggeration to say that Morag did not like or respect the guardian *ad litem*, believing that he showed bias towards Marcus Chapman from the beginning. That was a view which would come to be shared by others and led him into public humiliation and shame.

Richard Jones, Morag's lawyer, was duty bound to tell the guardian *ad litem* about his client's arrest and that Roberta had agreed to look after Jasmine until her mother was released from the police station. That night, Roberta returned Jasmine to Morag, but within a couple of days the guardian *ad litem* had intervened to insist that the child could not stay with her mother. It was a standard ruling in circumstances in which a child or children lived in a home where there had been any sort of domestic dispute. Until the problem was resolved, the warring adults made peace and the threat of violence or abuse had abated, the guardian *ad litem* would normally arrange for the children to be taken to relatives or foster parents. In this case, the guardian *ad litem*, with the approval of Morag, asked Roberta to again look after Jasmine while he investigated whether or not the young girl was in any danger from Jack or her mother. After talking to the police, neighbours and Richard Jones, he quickly concluded Jasmine was not at risk and even raised no objections to Jack Reeves staying on in the apartment after being given assurances that he would be sleeping on a settee. Had the guardian *ad litem* disapproved of Jack remaining, Morag would have forced him to move to a hotel. And so Jasmine was quickly returned home, a move greeted with relief by her mother, and not just because it meant being reunited with her precious daughter.

According to Morag, Warren, Roberta's boyfriend, a man twice Morag's age, began taking an especially keen interest in her. What happened between them would be the subject of intense questioning when Morag had to make a formal deposition to lawyers involved in the custody case in late November. It was an interview session at which she was already under stress and deeply worried about the future of Jasmine. The idea of the interview was to allow the various sides to go over affidavits and statements already made by Morag so that they could prepare for the full custody hearing. A trial date had not yet been set, and it increasingly seemed to Morag that it never would be.

And so Morag, with her lawyer Richard Jones, went along to the offices of William Powers, the local Austin attorney hired by Lawilda and Jimmy Ross Chapman and a man regarded by his peers as a formidable opponent. It was a crucial session. Every one of Morag's replies would be carefully analysed to ascertain whether it could be exploited to the benefit of the Chapmans. It was a dreadful ordeal for a young mother to be put through. Strangers would prod and poke her life, friends and family. Her background would be torn apart. Her interrogators would try to turn innocent situations against her in order to build up a case that showed her to be an unfit mother. To them, it was just business.

There was nothing personal – it was just an everyday attempt to destroy an unwary victim.

Morag knew she had done nothing wrong. She only wanted to tell the truth, but she also knew that sometimes the truth could be made to sound sinister and imply guilt.

Within minutes of the questions starting, she felt like the accused in the dock, having to justify the actions of others, realising that the consequences of what they had done were being made to reflect not against them but against her. There would be times when she wanted to break down in tears, to run away, but bravely she stuck it out, and many of those present would afterwards concede that she emerged with considerable merit.

After examining her background and how she came to meet Marcus and be in America, Powers turned to her relationship with Roberta. His intention was to show that the decision by Morag to let her friend care for Jasmine was flawed and demonstrated poor judgement on her part. Morag wanted to scream that the guardian *ad litem* was also guilty if that was the case, but she was restricted to answering questions only and could not include her own comments, however valid they might be. The attorney, never one to miss an opportunity, pounced on what had been, for Morag, a no-win situation, and he cleverly introduced Jasmine to the equation.

Powers wanted to know why there had come a time when Roberta had said she would no longer watch over Jasmine. The reason, Morag told him, was that her friend had separated from her partner Warren. The matter might have ended there, but instead it was turned against Morag. The young Scot admitted that during her visits to Roberta's home, Warren had begun to take a keen interest in her. Too keen for her liking. She made it plain to Warren that her interests lay not in him but in fighting for custody of her daughter, and she also explained that Roberta was her friend. Warren clearly did not want to take no for an answer and began telephoning her late at night, asking her out for dates and wanting to chat. Eventually, Morag complained to Roberta, who lost her temper. 'She hit me twice,' Morag told the lawyer. 'Then, I said I would hit her back if she hit me again. And then she attacked Warren.' Morag suffered two broken front teeth in the attack. 'She was just hitting him and punching him,' Morag continued, 'and he fled into the living room.' Worse was to follow. After being dragged away by Morag, Roberta picked up an axe and smashed the windows of Warren's car. He fled.

'Have you filed charges against Roberta?' asked Powers.

'No.'

'Why not?'

'Well, I did file charges, but Roberta called me, and we had a chat. She wanted to know a bit more about everything, because she'd lost her temper. She had a nervous breakdown straight after, because she was under a lot of pressure leading up to that point. She didn't know about the charges, and I just offered to drop them. She didn't ask me, I just said I would. I felt she'd been through enough the past few months.'

Morag's last sentence might have prompted the comment that she too had been through a lot in the past months, but no one said it, and no one asked a question that gave her the chance to do so. She had been honest with her friend, helping her and saving her from possible arrest. These were kindly actions, but Powers only wanted to know if Morag had told the guardian *ad litem* 'that Roberta had a habit of assaulting people when you were recommending that she care for Jasmine'. Morag wanted to protest that Roberta had never struck a child, but she thought that no one would listen.

Inevitably, Powers wanted to make the most of the incident involving Jack Reeves, by now back in Scotland. Jack, Morag said, had really come to America to see Jasmine. 'Jasmine is very fond of him,' she said. She continued that Jack had brought his own drink and that after chatting for a couple of hours while Jasmine was asleep, she had also gone to bed.

'Then what happened?' asked Powers.

'He tried to go into my bed.'

'And what happened then?'

'I got out, went into the bathroom, got dressed and went and asked Jake Harris if he could stay at his house or if he'd come up and speak to him.'

'Was there any loud noise?'

'No, and none of the neighbours heard any when I asked them.'

'Did he make sexual advances to you?'

'No, he just tried to come into bed, and I just, you know, said, "No way."'

Morag then explained what had happened when she'd returned ten minutes later: 'There were police cars all over the place. They had arrested Jack for being inebriated, or something like that, and they then told me they were arresting me because of the cheque.'

Once again, an innocent situation had turned against her. She had chatted, soberly, with Jack Reeves, had gone to bed and when he tried to climb in with her she had gone for help. Powers was endeavouring to make out that, as with Roberta, she had unwisely chosen Jack as a friend.

'You indicated to us that you thought he was inebriated,' Powers said. 'Did you think that he could hurt Jasmine just by virtue of the fact that he was drunk?'

Morag's response was simple and adamant. 'No,' she said. Morag felt frustrated but kept her irritation and anger in check. She then went on to explain that Jack's reaction on hearing the door burst open after she had gone to see Jake Harris had instinctively been to protect Jasmine from what he had believed to be kidnappers. She wanted Powers and everyone else in the room to understand this. She was desperate to make them see that Jack Reeves was devoted to little Jasmine, and had been kind and caring towards the child; that Jasmine loved him as he loved her; that he had flown thousands of miles to be with them, knowing the strains Morag was under and realising that if he could lighten her burden by showing her some support then he was also helping Jasmine.

He had come in kindness, and Morag and Jasmine had welcomed him. Yet that generosity had rebounded on them.

Morag wondered whether it was a coincidence that the tip-off that led to her arrest was made on the same night that Jack Reeves, a surrogate father to Jasmine and a friend to Morag, had arrived in town, and she hoped that the question would be asked during the deposition. But, knowing the likely answer, the Chapmans' attorney did not ask it.

Powers did try to tar Morag with the same brush as Jack Reeves, a man whom he portrayed as liking a drink: 'Are you currently seeking any counselling for substance abuse or alcohol abuse?'

'No.'

'Do you feel like you have any problem with regard to the use of alcohol?'

'No.'

Even though she answered truthfully, the fact that the question had been asked insinuated that there was no smoke without fire. And yet Morag had voluntarily undertaken alcohol and drug testing as part of her own case, intending to show that she was completely clean. Her drug was her daughter. Her stimulant was seeing Jasmine laugh and her little eyes sparkle. But at least Morag was now coming to appreciate how dirty a war it was into which she was being dragged.

12

Raising Doubts

As the questions continued, Morag increasingly felt like the proverbial lamb being prepared for slaughter, surrounded by a pack of wolves intent on ripping her reputation to shreds and along with it her case for retaining custody of Jasmine. She took a break for lunch – a sandwich and bottle of water – but as the afternoon session got under way, her friendship with Roberta and Jack brought increasing and savage insinuations that she had an uncontrollable drinking problem, suggestions based on the fact that before her axe attack Roberta had been drinking wine. The women were friends, so it was inferred that if one had a problem, then the other must too. It was simply not true that Morag had been anything other than sober and alert, but she could tell from the persistence of questions along this line that false allegations of alcohol abuse would inevitably be the strongest possible challenge to her claims that she and not Marcus was the more suitable to be Jasmine's full-time carer.

When the deposition taking had begun, it had been a novel experience to Morag. Had she been versed in the ways of courtroom procedures then she would have known what to expect. Her initial excitement based on curiosity had not lasted. She had expected that an answer given honestly and truthfully would be accepted as such, and the questions would then move on to another subject. That this was not the case came as a surprise, even though her own lawyer had told her to expect the probing to be persistent and even unpleasant at times. She found it difficult to keep her concentration, her mind drifting to wondering what Jasmine was doing and to how things were at her mother's back in Scotland. She also realised that she could understand movie scenes in which prisoners confessed to crimes they had not committed, simply to stop incessant probing and accusations.

William Powers returned to the night that Roberta Reid had set about Warren Peters's car. Powers immediately wanted to know what alcohol had been consumed that night. 'Did you have anything to drink on that occasion?' he asked.

'I had a glass of wine after it was all over – only one glass, because Warren offered me vodka, and I said, "No, I don't drink spirits."' It was a simple answer, but it brought an admission that she had taken a drink. Only one, but it was what the lawyer wanted.

Before she could elaborate and justify her actions, Powers moved on to the night the police raided her apartment and discovered Jack Reeves. He said a police report into the incident stated that they had responded after someone called in to say that they could hear a woman screaming in the area. Was it Morag, he wanted to know. He gave no indication as to who the mystery informant was, and almost as soon as the question had left his lips Morag wanted to ask one of her own: who made the call? She was confident she knew, but her task was to answer questions, not ask them, and so her query went unspoken. Morag replied that two Mexicans had been having what she termed as a 'severe argument', but it had been some distance away from the apartment.

Powers then asked her how she felt about Jack Reeves' behaviour that night. Morag answered honestly: 'I was really annoyed. He didn't really understand what was going on. He didn't understand the American accent and what they were saying to him. I'm really annoyed with him.' The trap had been set, and in her candour and naivety she had taken the bait. It was obvious what would come next. 'And so you invite this man who you were really annoyed with back into your home for two weeks as soon as he gets out of jail. Why did you do that?'

Afterwards, Morag would never know why she did not tell the lawyer that the arrangement had only come into place after the guardian *ad litem* had satisfied himself that Reeves' presence would not pose any threat, particularly to Jasmine, or that Jack doted on the little girl. Instead, she blurted out, 'Because I've known him ten years, and it was just a case of he maybe had too much to drink and was exhausted.' It was neither an adequate explanation nor a good answer. She had been caught out by her loyalty and gratitude to Jack Reeves for his help and support.

Next, Powers turned to her feelings about his clients, Jimmy Ross and Lawilda Chapman. He wanted to know if Morag thought that they loved Jasmine and whether they ever mistreated her. 'I don't know,' she replied. 'I haven't seen them with her lately. I don't know them that well.' Once again, they were candid responses. It was correct that she did not know the Chapmans well, and it had been months since their visit to Killingworth. How could she interpret whether their feelings towards Jasmine had changed in the intervening months? But her responses perhaps gave the appearance that she was indifferent to them, or even disliked them, and Powers would use this as ammunition in the trial to show that Morag was biased towards the Chapmans and unfair in her assessment of them should they decide that they wanted to be the custodians of Jasmine. When she told the lawyer that she did not find their home to be a pleasant environment and that they had 'peculiar tendencies', he was getting the reaction for which he had hoped. 'What do you mean?' he asked, and Morag told him about Sam being forced to dig a hole because he had returned late one evening and about the carton of cigarettes being used to tempt him. She added, 'I find it peculiar that the older brother doesn't visit and he's – all his possessions aren't in his room any more, yet Marcus's are. His room has been left the same, which seems peculiar, because my mother keeps two rooms in her house for me and my brother, and they're the same as they were when we left. Not that they have to be, but she doesn't treat one of us different from the other.'

The attorney moved in for the kill and asked Morag to tell him what she thought should happen to Jasmine if the jury at the forthcoming custody trial decided that neither she nor Marcus should win custody. It was a full-blown hint that the grandparents would make a play to keep the child. Powers did not expect Morag to support such an idea but wanted to demonstrate that any assessment of them by her would not be reasoned and fair. By achieving that, he could ask a jury to discount her views.

Morag prevaricated. The obvious alternative to Jasmine staying with either parent would be for her to live with grandparents, but she instead said that the court would have to place her daughter in care. Powers asked if Morag would want that. 'I wouldn't want her to be in care at all,' she said. 'She's perfectly healthy and well balanced.'

But Powers persisted: 'Would you rather she was in foster care or placed with a relative?'

Still Morag refused to give him the answer he was looking for, which was that she would be content with Lawilda and Jimmy Ross caring for Jasmine. 'I have no relatives in this country,' she told him.

Finally, he himself suggested the response he wanted: 'So, your answer is what? You want her in foster care rather than staying with Mr Chapman's parents?'

Morag replied, 'I think it would be less damaging for her, considering the way they've brought up their children.' There were some present who detected a slight smile cross the lawyer's lips. He had demonstrated the extent of Morag's dislike for his clients, something upon which he could make hay in court. On the other hand, she had bravely stuck to her guns, maintaining that Jasmine was happy and healthy thanks to having lived with her. Why should there be any need for her daughter to be given to anyone else? It was the crux of the whole case. Could the attorneys representing Lawilda, Jimmy Ross and Marcus damage Morag's argument that she was a good mother sufficiently to create doubt in the minds of jurors that the youngster should remain with her mother? If they did that, then with whom should Jasmine live? Could they show her view of the grandparents to be unreasonable? Powers sensed that he could.

Next, the lawyer wanted to know how Morag would react to Marcus seeing his daughter if she won custody and took Jasmine back to England. This was tricky ground for the attorney. He was there to represent the interests of Marcus's parents, not Marcus, and if their son was painted as uncaring and unfeeling, then that would be in their interests. But he did not want to be seen to be openly criticising Marcus. Instead, he left that to Morag.

What kind of relationship should Jasmine have with her father if she returned to England, he wondered. 'I think he should be able to visit,' Morag replied.

'Tell me to what extent should he be allowed to visit.'

'Well, during the holidays, while she's not at school full time and other occasions when he can manage to get over.'

'And your position is that he should come to England to see her rather than she be allowed to come here. Is that what you're telling me?'

'I can come here during school holidays, there isn't a problem there, but during the school session it makes it very difficult for me to get here.'

'And should he be allowed unsupervised visits with her?'

'I'm still very scared about that, but I suppose there should come a time when he could.'

'If Jasmine is left with either Mr Chapman or with his parents, do you think you should pay child support?'

'No, because I'll be fighting to get her back. He has never paid for the child ever, apart from a short four-month period and a period of two to three months after she was first born.'

'And how did she survive after that?'

'I used my money to support her.'

'What was the source of your money?'

'Previous work. It was a very high wage.'

Powers knew he had done well. He had raised doubts about Marcus and Morag by using her own honesty to discredit her. Now it was the turn of Neal Pfeiffer, the attorney representing Marcus Chapman. Morag had already dismissed suggestions by Powers that she drank, but if she had hopes that the subject would be allowed to fade away these were soon dispelled. Pfeiffer persisted with questions about alcohol, and Morag continued to deny having any sort of problem. Having failed to gain ground on that subject, Pfeiffer tried the subject of drugs, but Morag was able, with some pride, to tell him that she had consistently passed random tests on the oil rigs.

Pfeiffer then changed the subject again. Was it true, he asked, that Marcus had physically abused her in the past? 'Yes,' she told him and went on to give answers to a long series of questions he posed on the subject. Morag also told Pfeiffer that in April 1993 she had made a formal complaint to the police in America that Marcus had struck her. 'He hit me quite severely,' she said. 'I had bruising and a cut lip, which the police included in their report.'

She continued that there had been other attacks but these had not been reported to the police: 'Probably about every other week, he'd either grab me or hit me in some way, or he'd really beat me up, and on three occasions he put a gun to my head.'

In further questions, Pfeiffer asked Morag about other allegations she had made of being attacked by Marcus. He questioned her about an affidavit she had signed, which alleged that Marcus tried to strangle her. 'He pinned me down with his elbow on my windpipe, putting his full weight upon me,' she explained. Pfeiffer also quizzed her about the times she said that Marcus had threatened her with guns. In the same affidavit, she had stated, 'I really believe he would use guns, especially when he's in an intoxicated state.' Pfeiffer wanted to know if she thought Marcus had a drinking problem, and she replied, 'Sometimes he drank far too much and would get really weird.'

In answer to a question by the lawyer, Morag then said that Marcus had disappeared with Jasmine on three occasions. And on one occasion, he had called her and threatened that she would never see her daughter again. The lawyer wondered why he would do this. Morag told him, 'I think he was generally being nasty, you know. Trying to scare me and being nasty.'

Pfeiffer then asked Morag, 'Do you have any reason to believe that Marcus was mistreating Jasmine when he had her in his sole possession?' To this she replied that there had been an occasion when Marcus had agreed to look after Jasmine to allow her to concentrate on cleaning their Austin home. She then said, 'But he hadn't fed her all day. He just turned up at five o'clock and said, "I don't know why she's screaming," and I said, "Haven't you fed her?" and he said, "Well, she was asleep when I stopped for lunch."'

She was also questioned about Jack Reeves. 'He drinks quite a bit, doesn't he?' asked Pfeiffer.

'Not really, no. He does have a drink every now and again, but he works away from home for six weeks at a time, and he's maybe only home for two or three weeks.' Once again, it was an attempt to show Morag in a poor light by suggesting that she allowed Jasmine to be close to a man who had a drink problem. Inevitably, this led to further questions about the night when Jack had been arrested. 'Who do you think it was that reported you to the police that night?'

She was in no doubt as to what the answer was: 'I personally think it could well have been Marcus.'

Flora holds baby
Morag after her birth
in Northumberland
in 1964.

Vivacious and smiling, Morag with her mum
Flora during a night out in October 1990.

Morag and wealthy Texan Marcus Chapman holiday together during happier times after meeting while working in the oil industry in 1991.

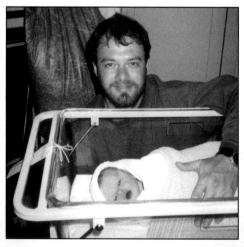

Marcus shows off his daughter Jasmine Jamee on the day of her birth in Aberdeen in May 1992.

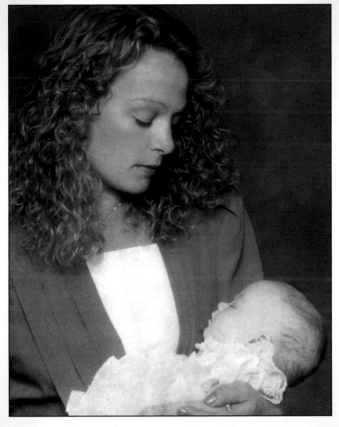

Attractive and overjoyed, Morag poses with newly born Jasmine during a visit to Texas to introduce the Chapmans to their newest family member.

TOP LEFT: Lawilda Chapman with baby Jasmine in 1992.

TOP RIGHT: Former army officer Jimmy Ross Chapman, Marcus's father, relaxes with granddaughter Jasmine.

LEFT: Morag celebrates with dad Tony after returning from Texas following a short but unhappy attempt to settle in Austin with Marcus. She fled back to England with Jasmine after just four months with air tickets paid for by her father.

Local playgroups refused to allow Jasmine to join while she and Morag waited for the beginning of the custody case, forcing the child to play alone.

Following Morag's arrest and imprisonment, she was eventually allowed bail on condition that she wore an electronic ankle tag. Two friends examine it during a visit as she awaits the start of the custody hearing.

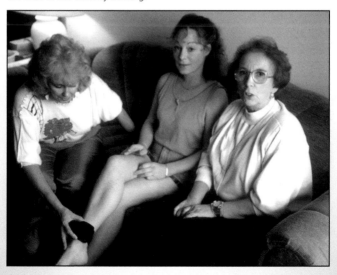

Morag was refused permission to see her daughter after her arrest. Flora was horrified at how distressed and unhappy Jasmine was when she met the child during an organised meeting in an Austin park.

The courthouse at Austin, Texas, scene of the custody hearing.

Former social worker Don Evans, who gave crucial evidence for Morag.

Jasmine's godfather Jack Reeves was a witness for Morag at the custody hearing, despite being arrested during his first visit to see mother and daughter.

Morag and Jasmine visited Judge John Dietz after the conclusion of the case. The judge presented Jasmine with a toy wand.

Jasmine (centre) shortly before she was taken into care.

LEFT: Jasmine, aged seven and a half, chose this Christmas gift when Flora visited Killeen in 1999 and met her granddaughter for the last time.

ABOVE: Morag is unable to hide the desolation of not having seen her daughter for more than ten years.

Flora on her property in Forres, where Morag and Jasmine stayed after returning from Austin in 1995.

13

Changing Strategy

As Morag made her deposition, she felt that her very soul was being ripped apart, but she knew there was worse to come. Marcus and his parents now had scandal on which to feed. She would never openly, or even privately, blame Jack for the criticisms made of her as a result of his visit, because the fact was that his behaviour, however reprehensible, was not the cause of the police raid. That, she would for ever be convinced, was the work either of Marcus or one of his cronies.

But Jack had been drinking. If he had arrived in Austin and gone straight to bed, the worst that could have happened as a result of an anonymous call to the police would have been Morag being picked up because of the dodgy cheque. But because of his antics, the door had been left open for the Chapmans to steam in and question whether it was appropriate for Morag to rely for help and friendship on the likes of Jack and Roberta when she had responsibility for Jasmine.

Morag now wondered what there was to look forward to: more reports, investigations, statements and questions all aimed at chipping away at her once confident hopes that she would return to Scotland with Jasmine safely hers. Jack had threatened to kill the police. He had been drinking and caught half-naked over Jasmine's bed. True he had given an honest explanation, but who would accept his behaviour was reasonable or acceptable?

The Chapmans? Not likely. A judge? Hardly. It was correct that his antics alone had not resulted in Jasmine being placed, albeit briefly, with Roberta, because Morag had also been arrested. But the whole episode had raised massive and potentially disastrous doubts as to her judgement where the care of Jasmine was concerned. Morag may have trusted Roberta, but the fact was that she knew her friend enjoyed a drink and could be violent. Morag herself had been on the receiving end of her frustration, and she had witnessed Roberta's bizarre attack on Warren's car. However much Morag herself was happy at Roberta looking after Jasmine, others were not so sure that she had been a wise choice.

The deposition had also hinted that the Chapmans might be changing their strategy. Questions had been asked that suggested Marcus might not be the ideal candidate to have custody of his daughter. And at least half of the time had been taken up by William Powers, the attorney who was looking after the interests of Lawilda and Jimmy Ross. Morag had been able to speak of Marcus as a man whose behaviour with his daughter bordered on the immature. Admittedly, forcing a young man to dig a hole in woods because he arrived home late was hardly rational behaviour, but of all the black marks against the interested parties it was probably the nearest to grey, the least dangerous if not the least bizarre.

Once again, Morag was frightened when she recalled Lawilda's words: 'I will take this child from you.' And there were genuine grounds for her fear. Morag and Marcus had initially appeared before Judge Meurer, who had told them that even if they could not settle their differences they should at least come to a sensible compromise. Some two weeks before the taking of the deposition, Morag and Marcus had been called back before the judge, who, irritated to learn they had made no progress, ruled that Jasmine would be placed in the custody of Lawilda and her husband for two weeks. Once the two weeks were up, Morag could see her daughter during the daytime for two days, but

Jasmine had to be returned to her grandparents each evening. If Marcus and Morag had still not shown any enthusiasm for arriving at a settlement by that point, the child would be placed in the temporary care of the Chapmans until the custody dispute came to trial. And that was weeks if not months into the future. It could hardly be called a fair judgment, and Morag protested that it was Marcus's failure to show up for meetings that had halted any progress. Further, the Chapmans had indicated, if only through the presence of their attorney at the taking of the depositions, that they intended to offer themselves as permanent custodians of Jasmine. Now they were being handed the child on a plate, giving them the ideal opportunity to bond with her and thus be able to return to court at some future time and show that Jasmine had become part of their family.

Flora was furious when she learned of the judge's decision: 'Jack being discovered by the police leaning over Jasmine's bed when he was drunk was exactly what the Chapmans wanted. It played into their back pocket. They were able to point out that there was something not right about the situation, when, in fact, up to that point everything had been fine. As a result, Jasmine was tested for signs of having been given alcohol and drugs. Needles were put into her arms and legs, and the marks were covered by plasters. It was a terrifying experience for a tiny child, especially when her mother wasn't there to give her reassurance.

'It was wrong of the judge to hand Jasmine to the Chapmans, because it was Marcus who was at fault for not sitting down with Morag and working out some sort of custody arrangement: who would pay maintenance, how much and how her schooling was to be funded.'

The ruling left Morag in tears. She was worried and, for the first time, genuinely alarmed about her long-term prospects with her daughter. When she left England in August, a development such as this had not been on her list of possible outcomes.

Morag had been forced to face the barrage of questions at the deposition with this sad prospect running through her mind and had consequently found it difficult to concentrate on what was being asked. Often, she was not even aware of the content of the questions, simply nodding or answering 'uh-huh', because by doing so she was giving the response the questioner sought and the interrogation would therefore be over all the more quickly.

Now she was totally alone. Jasmine was in Woodville with the Chapmans, just over 200 miles away, and when Morag had telephoned to ask for a brief word with her daughter she had been told not to call again but to speak to the judge if she wanted to make contact. Flora was in Scotland, as was Jack Reeves, while her father was still running his flourishing hairdressing business in England.

Morag often thought about her little house in Killingworth and how Frostie was doing. She also wondered how she was going to handle being separated from Jasmine at Christmas. Her daughter would be just over two and a half, and more than capable of appreciating a Christmas tree with lights and a fairy, of singing along to carols, and of asking about Santa Claus and desperately trying to remain awake in order to catch sight of him and his reindeer as they hurtled from chimney pot to chimney pot. But Morag would share none of these things. Instead, a judge was about to rule that Jasmine live for the duration of the custody trial in Woodville, which had such unhappy memories for Morag.

Sitting in the dark of the apartment watching the lights of Austin, hearing children in the streets laughing and shouting, Morag felt a madness gradually encroach. Not long after moving in, she had been forced to complain to her landlord that she was under surveillance. A stranger had been hanging about and following her wherever she went. The landlord saw the stranger and demanded to know who he was and what he wanted, only for the man to produce a private detective's licence. He refused, however, to name his employer but was warned not to hang around the Georgian Apartments any more. He was not seen again.

Now, in just four days' time, Morag would see Jasmine for

what might be the last time in many months. She had put up with the barrage of questions at the deposition and had sat alone each night wondering what her daughter was doing, but she could see no light at the end of the tunnel. All that lay ahead was a continuation of an ordeal that was sapping her sanity. She was depressed, and there was no one to comfort her; no one to put a kindly arm about her shoulder; no one who would hold her. She did not know how she would hold up when the Chapmans brought Jasmine to see her and realised that she would be counting the hours throughout each of the two days.

Even now, she finds it difficult to talk about that first morning: 'I was to have her from 8 a.m. to 4 p.m. on each of the two days – this child who had never been away from me in her life, other than when her father took her away. Now it seemed to me that his own parents were doing the same thing. The first morning, Jimmy Ross carried her in while Lawilda remained in the car. Jasmine was crying. She grabbed me, threw her arms around my neck and kept saying, "Mummy, Mummy, can I come home, Mummy? Take me home, Mummy."

'She had a little blanket with her, which she was using as some sort of comforter, holding it against her face and hanging on to it as she crawled around the floor. I was horrified. She had never needed anything like that in the past. If she wanted some love, she came to me and I would hug her. Now she was clingy and frightened, crawling around with her head down and coming up to me and saying, "Sorry, Mummy." It was just the worst experience of my life.'

Flora remembers a sickening telephone call from her daughter: 'Morag rang and was in such a distressed state that it was difficult to get her to calm down and explain what it was she was saying. But when she gained her composure and began talking, it was me that felt as though I would break down. "Mum, this is the first time I have had her from the Chapmans," she said, "and she is crawling around the floor, behaving like a baby all over again. She follows me everywhere, and even if I go to the toilet she's

133

banging on the door shouting, 'Mummy, Mummy, Mummy.' She keeps giving me things, as if she's a pet dog wanting affection – a pat on the head for doing well. She brings them to me and looks up for a friendly word or a hug. It is as though she is afraid she has done something wrong and the result has been that she's been sent away from me. She cannot understand why we have been separated, and it's just ripping me apart. I don't think I can put up with this any longer. I just don't know what to do. She has to be handed back at four, and I'm going to spend the entire night dreading what she'll be like when they bring her tomorrow. Why should I have to put up with seeing everything I've done for Jasmine being torn apart? She can't even walk. What should I do?'"

Her mother's reply took some seconds to sink in. 'Get the fuck out of there,' Flora told her.

14

On the Run

Ten minutes later, Morag called her mother again from Jake Harris's apartment, where Jasmine played happily on the floor, unaware of the unfolding drama. 'What do you mean, get out of here?' Morag asked.

'They're making a fucking mess of Jasmine's life, that's what. Get out.'

'I can't. They've taken away my passport.'

'Get some clothes together, and get Jasmine away.'

'Where?'

'Any fucking where. Just get away. I'll try and get you a passport.'

'But I've got nowhere to go.' Then she thought about her brother. 'Give me Stuart's address in San Diego.'

'I don't think he'll help, Morag. He's trying to stay in America and won't do anything that could mess up his chances.'

'Well, somebody has to help. I have to get out of this country, because they are destroying me and my child. I suppose all I can do is go on the run. What I really need is a passport. You can't go anywhere without one.'

'Both of us, Don and I, want the best for you and Jasmine. So I'll try everything I can to somehow get hold of a passport for you both, but it's not going to be easy. I can't, in fairness, ask Don to get involved. But I can't let you carry on like this. It's destroying you, and they will also destroy Jasmine's love for you. So get away. Stay in touch and all the best. Please let me know what you do, and make sure you get in touch when you reach San Diego.' The line went dead.

As she replaced the receiver, Morag turned to Jake Harris. 'Jake, you know I have to go away. I can't handle this any more. What they are doing to Jasmine is killing me.'

'OK,' he replied. 'Where are you going to go?'

'I have a brother in San Diego. My mum doubts if he'll help, but he'll surely not turn us away if we can get to him.'

'How will you get there?'

'Well, I expect when they come for Jasmine at four and she's not here, they'll go straight to the police. It won't take them long to work out that I need a passport to fly anywhere and don't have one, so they'll reckon I'm either still in Austin or I've gone off by bus somewhere. They're bound to call on Roberta, and when they realise I'm not there they'll start searching buses. I desperately need a passport. Mum's ringing around her friends to see if anyone can help, but even if someone can it means having to hide up until she can get it to me.'

At that moment, Flora was making telephone calls to all her horse-owning pals, asking them if they had a son or daughter the same age as Jasmine: 'I knew it was wrong, but I was sure my daughter's life was at stake. There was no way she could have coped with Jasmine being taken away to Woodville for weeks and more likely months. I rang dozens of people, but either the kids with their own passports had dark hair or they were on passports with their mothers and the mothers had dark hair or the mother had light hair but the kid had dark hair. And all of which was hopeless, because both Morag and Jasmine had fair hair. So, I told Morag to get hold of some black dye. Then, if we could persuade a family to part with a passport on which the mother or child had black hair, she should be prepared to change the appearance of herself or Jasmine. But by then, even had we been able to find a suitable one, time was running out.

'Morag was having no luck, either. She said that she didn't know where she could get a passport for a little girl with fair or black hair, and I said, "It doesn't matter about the sex of the child, because nobody looks that closely. Just get hold of a passport and you'll be fine."'

Jake Harris was hovering as Morag finished the call. 'Any luck?' he enquired.

'No, she says just to get any passport. It doesn't matter if the kid on it is a boy or girl so long as they have fair hair.'

'When do you need it?'

'Right now. They'll come for Jasmine at four. We need to give ourselves some breathing space.'

'OK, Morag, come on.'

'Where are we going?'

'Caroline's house. She's blonde and so is Olivia, and Jasmine looks pretty much like her. I'm sure she could pass as Olivia.'

'But what will Caroline say when she finds out the passports have gone?'

'I'll just tell her that she must have mislaid them. You might be able to send them back to me before she discovers that they're missing. She'll not mind. She likes you, and the kids love Jasmine. They'll be thrilled to know they're helping her.'

He drove her to the home of his ex-wife and within minutes was back in the car handing two passports to Morag. When she examined Caroline's photograph, she gasped. 'She doesn't look anything like me,' she said. 'They'll spot it right away.'

'No, they won't,' he assured her. 'Nobody looks that closely.' He went on, 'If I were you, I'd try getting a flight from San Antonio. 'I know Austin is much closer to us, but there's always the possibility somebody there might recognise you. Once they start checking up to see if you've caught a flight, then that's the first airport they'll look. We can be in San Antonio in an hour and a half.'

'Jake, I've got no money.'

'How much do you need?'

'I dunno. I think my mum said that when she and Stuart flew

from San Diego to Austin to meet the Chapmans the tickets were about $600.'

'How about if I loan it to you? Can you pay me back?'

'Sure. As soon as I'm home, I'll send the money. Once I'm in San Diego, I'll try for the British Consulate-General in Los Angeles, tell them our passports have been stolen and ask them to get us temporary replacements. I'm certain they'll help.'

As they headed to San Antonio airport, Morag began coaching her daughter in her new identity: 'Sweetheart, we're going to play a little game. I want you to call me Mummy, and I'm going to pretend you are Olivia, the little girl you sometimes play with.'

'Yes, Mummy.'

'If someone calls you Olivia, look at them, but whatever you do you must not say, "That's not my name. My name is Jasmine." Do you understand?'

'Yes, Mummy.'

At the airport, they went to buy tickets for San Diego. Jake handed over his bank card but was told after a slight delay, 'Sorry, sir, but the payment is being refused. Do you have enough funds to cover this?' Jake realised that his account needed to be topped up. 'Sorry, Morag,' he said. 'I can't do it. I'm short.'

'You fucking idiot. You bring us all the way out here then tell me you haven't enough money for the tickets. What the hell do we do now?' Instantly, she realised that she had been harsh on her friend, who was risking so much for them. She reached out a hand and grasped his in a gesture of apology and reassurance that he still had her confidence.

Jake sensed that her words were triggered by disappointment and worry, and turned towards her and smiled: 'There is only one thing we can do. Go back and try again tomorrow. I'll make sure the account is topped up.'

'What about Jasmine? I'll have to hand her back to the Chapmans. If she breathes a word of this, we're all in jail.'

'Talk to her. Just make sure she doesn't speak about having been to the airport.'

On the drive back to the Georgian Apartments, Morag explained the situation to her daughter: 'Sweetheart, I need you to keep a big secret.'

'Yes, Mummy.'

'You must not tell anybody you've been to see aeroplanes. They'll ask what you've been doing today and where you've been. Just say, "I was out visiting places and looking at things." Can you do that?'

'Right, Mummy.'

As they parked the car, with little time to spare before the Chapmans arrived, Morag said, 'Jake, please, you must get that money in the bank tomorrow, because I only get to see her for one more day. After that, I might not get to see her for months. Please don't let me down.'

There was a worrying incident for Morag when the Chapmans came to collect Jasmine. Her landlord, who had settled in Austin from China, began haranguing Lawilda and Jimmy Ross, telling them, 'You can see how you are distressing everybody by what you are doing. The child should be with her mother. Leave her alone and go home.' His words had no effect and Morag feared that the Chapmans might try to use the incident as an excuse for not bringing Jasmine back the next day.

She spent an anxious night wondering if Jasmine had kept the Chapmans in the dark over her secret trip and used the time to pack the clothing and toys she considered essential. Morag also decided to take along the child's pushchair, realising that it could be used to carry their heavy cases.

At one stage, she called her mother to tell her what had happened and to ask again for her brother's address in California. 'Don't count on Stuart,' Flora reminded her. 'When it comes to the crunch, the one person he'll think about will be himself. Remember when he and Marcus went off while we were in Woodville? Stuart is desperate to get a green card, allowing him to live and work in America. He doesn't want anything to stand in the way of that, even if it means refusing to help his own sister.

He will not risk being told that by helping you and Jasmine he has broken any laws and is going to be deported back to Scotland. You can try throwing yourselves on his mercy. He might feel sorry for Jasmine and decide to help, but don't be disappointed if he refuses.'

Morag was even more worried in the morning as she waited to see whether the Chapmans would return with her daughter. Sure enough, they did – bang on time. 'See you at four,' they called to Jasmine as they left.

Morag answered for her, but under her breath: 'Like fuck you will.'

Morag waited for a quarter of an hour in case the Chapmans returned and then banged on Jake Harris's apartment door, praying that nothing had happened that might bring about a change of plan, such as a problem with getting the funds into his bank account. Her concern on that score was instantly forgotten. 'Money's in. I've already checked,' he said.

They carried the suitcases and pushchair to the car and set off for San Antonio. 'Remember, Jasmine, just call me Mummy and don't say your real name. You still have to pretend to be Olivia.'

'Yes, Mummy. Right, Mummy.'

When it came to pay for the tickets for the 1,100-mile trip to San Diego, Jake's card was instantly accepted. Clutching the tickets and the stolen passports, Morag made her way to the departure area. She wanted to tell Jake that she knew how much he had risked for them, but the words would not come, and instead she brushed his cheek with her lips. Then she turned and was gone.

As they boarded the aircraft under the names of Caroline and Olivia Harris, Morag was unable to stop her entire body from trembling. She thought that her legs would give way, and her hands quivered so violently that a stewardess, thinking she had a highly nervy passenger on her hands, fastened her seat belt and tried to reassure her that everything would go smoothly.

Later on, Caroline would be called into court at the custody hearing to give evidence as to what she knew of Morag. 'She is a very good person, a nice mother, dependable and wonderful both to her own daughter and my children,' she said.

'And did you realise that Miss Dodds used your passport and your daughter's passport in an attempt to get out of America?' The question dumbfounded Caroline, because up to that point she had no clue that either her or her daughter's passports had been taken.

'Caroline nearly fell out of the witness box with shock,' an onlooker told Flora.

On the flight, Morag sang songs and told her daughter stories, hoping that this would take her mind from telling anyone about the little game they were playing. When they landed at around lunchtime, Morag telephoned Stuart but got no reply, so she called a gay friend of her brother's who Flora believed had a key to his apartment. She explained who she was and said, 'We've come as a surprise and don't want Stuart to know, so if you see him don't mention that I called. But how about if we come over from the airport and you let us into his flat?'

'Stuart has already telephoned to say that you might be in touch and has told me not to help. He's already been warned that you are on the run and that there's a federal warrant out for your arrest.' Morag was convinced that her brother's informant had been Marcus. The friend added, 'But if you get to the flat and explain to the woman who looks after the apartments who you are, I'm sure she'll let you in. Good luck.'

Morag was still on tenterhooks as they collected their luggage and headed out of the terminal in search of a taxi. 'Look, Mummy, there's Granny,' shouted Jasmine. 'There's her car.' Morag thought she was about to die from heart failure; she had palpitations and could feel erratic pounding in her chest. She had the terrifying thought that Lawinda had somehow driven to San Diego and arrived there in time to take Jasmine back. But when she looked, she saw only a Lincoln the same style and colour as that driven by Jimmy Ross Chapman.

Stuart's friend turned out to be correct. When Morag explained to the owner of the flats who she was, the woman produced a master key and let mother and daughter inside. 'What a wonderful surprise Stuart is going to get,' she said. She had no idea that they were on the run. 'You need anything?'

'No, thanks. We'll be fine. What time does Stuart normally get home?' The landlady said that she thought he would be home at around teatime, and they settled down to wait. Morag picked up her brother's telephone and called Flora to reassure her that they had arrived safely: 'Mum, call Randy and tell him what's happened. He'll worry when he finds out we've gone, and I don't want to phone him myself in case the call gets put through to Richard by mistake. If anyone thought Randy might have been in on this, he would be in big trouble, and I don't want that happening to him. Tell him I'll try to call him when I can.' Flora thought that her daughter's concerns about a man who was not even her own lawyer went much farther than she was letting on, but she was glad to think that Morag was prepared to entrust her greatest secret with him: that of her whereabouts.

As they waited for Stuart to return home, Morag discovered a bottle filled with dimes, tipped it onto the solitary bed in the apartment and began counting. 'I sat down on the bed with Jasmine and asked myself, "What the hell am I going to do now?"' says Morag. 'Obviously, I wanted to cry, but I couldn't in front of Jasmine. I didn't want to hurt her by letting her see her mummy upset. Because we had been on the run, we had no food. All we could do was wait and hope that Stuart would help.

'I was trying to play with Jasmine and amuse her with the coins. As we were counting, I was teasing her – she didn't like to get teased – saying, "Come on, then. Let's see you count." She replied, "I can count, Mummy," and I said, "Let's pretend these are pound coins and see how many you've got here." She got up to eight or nine, and I said, "You're telling me that you can't count up to ten now?" She replied, "Of course I can." I said, "Go on, then," and she said that she would count up to 20 in that case.

142

She had reached 15 when we heard the door open and Stuart came in. He said, "What are you doing here? Marcus has been on the telephone to me. You've got to get out." All I could say in reply was, "Stuart, we've got nowhere to go," but he wasn't interested in us, only in protecting himself.'

Back in Austin, the four o'clock deadline had come and gone. When the Chapmans arrived to collect Jasmine and found that Morag's apartment was empty, they called Jake Harris, who confirmed that he had taken them to the airport and claimed that he thought their destination was Britain. The Chapmans immediately telephoned their son, who suspected that Morag might make for San Diego, thinking that she could seek sanctuary with her brother.

Later, Stuart told Flora and Morag exactly what he and Marcus had spoken about and why he had been so terrified to help his sister: 'The police are at this minute being notified, and they'll be issuing a warrant for her arrest. By crossing state lines, she's now made this a federal offence, and the FBI will in all probability be brought into it. If she comes to you for help, you'll land yourself in serious trouble by giving any assistance, and you'll probably end up doing seven or eight years in jail. She's very bad news, because she's failed a whole series of drug tests, and we're worried that Jasmine may have come into contact with drugs. We know you are hoping to get your green card to stay and work in the USA, but if you help in any way, you can wave goodbye to that. Have you seen her?'

'No.'

'Well, if you do, ring me right away. Remember, Stuart, if you give any assistance, even let her have something to eat or drink or let her use your telephone, you've broken the law.'

'What's the charge?'

'I don't know yet, but it will probably be along the lines of kidnapping.'

'Kidnapping? But Jasmine is her own daughter. How can you kidnap your own kid?'

'At the time she jumped, Jasmine was in the temporary custody of my folks. Now, remember, call me if she turns up.'

The truth was that Morag had taken seven random tests aimed at discovering traces of alcohol or drugs in her body and had successfully passed each one.

Morag remembers the meeting with her brother well: 'He just stood and looked at us, ordered Jasmine to put the dimes back in the bottle and said we'd have to leave. I told him we had nowhere to go, but he said that there was no way he was going to spend eight years in prison. I told him not to be silly and began telephoning people, such as Jake Harris, to let them know we had arrived OK. Stuart ordered me not to use the phone. He called my mum, and I heard him tell her, "She is using my phone. Has she not learned anything about America yet? She is in serious trouble, and I don't want her using my telephone. She's failed all her drugs tests." I gather my mum replied, "As far as the drugs tests are concerned, Marcus has told you a heap of lies. She passed all the tests. And as far as using your telephone, well, you tell her not to use it. She's with you, not me. What am I supposed to do about it? Don't bother ringing me back here. She's your own sister, and you're a grown-up. Handle it yourself. Be a man."

'He kept insisting we had to leave, and I asked him if he was going to throw us out onto the streets: "How will it look, a little girl of two and a half left to sleep on the pavement because her uncle is too scared to help?" He let us stay the night, and the next morning I started telephoning around again to ask if anyone in Austin had heard any news. Stuart began grumbling about my calling from his telephone, and he again rang my mum. I heard him complaining, but she told him it was his problem. So he unplugged the phone and went out, taking it with him. I was trying to trace a battered women's refuge and needed a telephone, so I just went to see the two girls who lived next door, told them who I was, said Stuart's phone wasn't working and asked if I could use theirs. They had a spare, which they gave to me, so I plugged it into the connection in Stuart's apartment and began making calls again. Stuart must have tried to ring his own number, and when he got the engaged tone he came home and gave the girls their receiver back.

'I was worried that Stuart would ring Marcus to tell him where we were, so Jasmine and I left. I said, "If you won't let me make a call, at least give me some dimes." We were trudging along the road with them clutched in my hand, carrying the bags and pushing the chair, when a man outside a garage must have noticed that I was crying and asked what was wrong and could he help. When I asked if he knew where I could find the refuge, he looked up the number, let me call it and then rang for a cab to take us there. It was odd to think that a complete stranger was happy to give us the little help that my own brother refused.'

15

Refuge

Arriving at the refuge for battered women, Morag was reminded of her brief stay at a similar house of sanctuary almost 18 months earlier in Austin. She had been shown kindness then, and she was again this time. She hoped that this episode would have a similarly happy ending with her reaching the safety of Britain. She remembered how Tony had come to her rescue by sending, at the touch of a button, £699 for air tickets soaring through the airwaves. Morag knew her father would willingly repeat his largesse, only now there was no way that she and Jasmine could board an international flight without genuine – or at least what would appear to be genuine – United Kingdom passports. Waltzing through the domestic checks at San Antonio had been one thing, fooling security-conscious specialists was another thing entirely.

Settling into the refuge, she listened to horror stories from women, some in their teens, who had suffered horrendous beatings from drugged and drunken men. There were those whose scars were visible, and others showed no humiliation in lifting a dress or sweater to reveal horrific markings. Her associates in sadness were anxious to hear what had brought this slim, beautiful foreigner to their midst, but she felt weak and ashamed at constantly breaking down in huge shuddering sobs that left her unable to speak of the past or a future which promised even worse. She was still not over the gruelling taking of her deposition just four days earlier in Texas. So much had happened in such a short space of time, and where had it got her? She had turned up at the home of a brother who refused to help, and now she was stranded with Jasmine in a refuge with little money and no means of making it home. It was depressing and desperate. There was more bad news to come when those running the home told her, with genuine regret, that the maximum permitted length of stay was just a week. So, no sooner had she arrived than she would need to seek somewhere else to stay.

Not all of the other women had children with them. Some were in a similar situation to Morag but others were being blackmailed into returning home and dropping their complaints to the police with promises of reconciliation with their children. If they did not, they would need to fight for access and expect, in the process, to suffer more of the punishment they had so far endured.

The women fussed around Jasmine but discovered Morag was heavily protective of this child for whom she was risking so much, even her very life. A federal warrant was in force for her arrest, and some American states carried the death sentence for kidnapping. California was one, Texas another.

She was desperately anxious to keep her daughter clean and neat, insisting on bathing her each day, but she was terrified at the thought of reaching the end of the week and not having anywhere else to go. That problem was solved on her second-last day when it was pointed out that with such a young child to protect she would in all likelihood be given a temporary bed at a shelter on Seventh Avenue run by the Salvation Army. Morag called and after explaining that she and her daughter had been made homeless by her husband was told she could come in for a few days.

It was pointed out that they would be expected to vacate their room each morning so that it could be cleaned, but there were, she was told, plenty of nearby parks and other facilities where Jasmine could be amused. Mother and daughter moved in on 30 November 1994. During the day, they wandered the streets of San Diego, gazing at shop windows already filling up with signs of Christmas: toys and clothes that Morag knew she could now no longer afford. She would have dearly loved to have been able to take Jasmine inside and kit her out with new outfits, but it was an impossible dream. She had little money left, and the strain of worrying about how they were going to survive was beginning to tell. Nevertheless, her obvious devotion to the child did not go unnoticed. Weeks later, an investigator employed by the San Diego County Department of the Public Defender, was commissioned to trace her movements in the city and interviewed Ms Cooper Jones, an official at the shelter. His report poured scorn on those in Austin who had sought to challenge her dedication as a mother:

> Ms Jones stated that Ms Dodds seemed like a caring mother, although she was quite distressed by her situation. She described the child as being well cared for. Jasmine wore clean clothes and her hygiene was good. The child's hair was a little disheveled [sic] but she seemed well taken care of and clean. Ms Dodds was attentive and responsible as a mother. She described Ms Dodds as being very upset about her situation. Ms Dodds did not know what to do about her custody problem.
>
> Ms Jones stated that she had never seen Ms Dodds drinking at all. Nor had she seen Ms Dodds under the influence of alcohol. Ms Jones further stated that she never told anyone else, including any other investigator, that she had seen Ms Dodds under the influence of alcohol at any time.
>
> Ms Jones stated that her observations of Ms Dodds were based on a very brief stay. However, she did recall one occasion in which Ms Dodds was concerned about whether there were towels so that she could bathe her child. Although Ms Dodds was very, very stressed during her stay, she still managed to take care of the child's needs. She made sure that her child was fed and made sure that she was bathed and clothed. Further, Ms Jones recalls seeing Ms Dodds rocking her child to sleep. Overall, Ms

Jones stated that Ms Dodds seemed caring and attentive and played with her daughter. She described Ms Dodds as a fit mother.

Ms Jones stated that Ms Dodds told her that she had left Texas out of fear of losing her daughter. Ms Dodds felt that the custody hearing in Texas was not going as it should. Ms Dodds became afraid when it seemed that the social worker in Texas was misconstruing her situation and she then fled Texas in order to keep her daughter.

Nevertheless, an arrest warrant had been issued by state prosecutors in Texas for this fit and caring mother who rocked her little girl to sleep. It had been sent to the FBI, whose agents were instructed to notify airports, railway stations, ports and bus depots throughout the USA that a national search was under way for a fair-haired woman with a strange accent and her blonde-haired daughter. It could be enforced, if necessary, by armed police, the warrant alleging that she had abducted Jasmine. Morag was, of course, unaware of these details.

Her immediate concern while in the kind hands of the Salvation Army was to find sufficient cheap food with which to feed her daughter. Jasmine was never a fussy eater, but even she did not take to the seemingly never-ending diet of burgers, crisp streaky bacon and home fries. So, during the daily banishment from her room, Morag scoured the streets in search of bargains. During one excursion, tired and tearful, she stopped outside a store boasting a sign that proclaimed that everything inside cost less than a dollar. 'We began using the store, which was run by an Irishman, because it was just about the only place I could afford. I was never too keen on Jasmine eating junk, but beggars can't be choosers, and we had to buy biscuits and crisps.

'The Irishman spotted us, because I was looking so unhappy, and took us outside, where he offered me a cigarette. We had a smoke while Jasmine sat in her pushchair, and he asked me what was going on and why I was upset. After I told him, he said, "You come in my store any time you wish. Any time you want something to eat, I will tell the staff that you can come in and pick up anything and do not have to pay for it." It was really sweet of him.

'At that time, I was very down and feeling extremely sorry for myself, desperate and worried about what the future held. I couldn't get a job, and I had a brother living in the same city who treated me as an outcast. At least the Celtic connection with the Irishman made me feel a wee bit closer to home.'

She was also missing Randy Berry. Not a day went by when she did not think about the lawyer. Despite their sparse contact, Morag knew she was in love with him, as did Flora. In conversations with her daughter, Randy's name was invariably raised by one or other of the women, usually Morag. Flora knew how hard it must be for Morag to find herself having to move from one place of refuge to another, not knowing what lay around the corner or what each new day would throw at her. Yet when Randy was mentioned, her tone became more confident, she would sound cheerful and there was a hint of hope in her voice. Morag spoke kindly of him but tried not to betray her true feelings to her mother. She did not know, and did not ask, how Flora would react to her confessing that while she was in the throes of a complex custody fight against one man she had already fallen for another. In fact, Flora would have admitted that she was thrilled by the development. She knew Randy was good for her daughter. He gave her stability and support.

Morag believed that Randy loved her. But neither had told the other of their feelings. The relationship would develop, but in the meantime Randy was in an awkward position. As a lawyer, he was looked upon as an official of the judicial system. If he had knowledge of a wrongdoing, he was duty bound to inform the authorities, as long as the suspect was not his client. And Morag was not on his books. Morag regularly placed reverse-charge calls to her mother to ask for news and find out whether she had had any luck persuading a fair-haired mother and child to part temporarily with their passports. She always enquired whether the kindly lawyer had been in touch. He had, of course, but avoided placing either of them in difficulty by refraining from asking if Flora knew the whereabouts of her daughter. But Randy did ask Flora to pass on his concerns and best wishes to Morag and Jasmine should they get in touch.

There was no pressure on her to leave the Salvation Army refuge, but one afternoon she got what seemed to be her first lucky break. Sitting on a park bench crying, she became aware that someone had joined her and looked up to see an elderly man. 'What's wrong?' he asked, and Morag immediately realised that he had a Scots accent. She told him about her predicament and how she expected to be asked in the near future to give up her room at the refuge for another victim. 'Why not come and stay with me?' the stranger suggested.

At first, she was somewhat alarmed by what appeared to be a wholly unsubtle attempt at a pickup. He then explained that his name was Sam Frazier and that he was a former university academic and professor from the Dundee area of Scotland who had moved to San Diego many years earlier. 'I live alone and need someone to clean my house,' he said. 'If you take the job, there's a room you can share with your daughter. I have a delightful garden in which she can run around, and in addition to your keep, I'll pay you some dollars. How about it?' The following day, Morag and Jasmine arrived with their possessions at Sam's home in Kantor Street. It was now December.

Morag enjoyed staying with Sam. His home was packed from floor to ceiling with books. There were thick books, thin books, old books and new books, and there were books about birds, bridges and almost every conceivable subject and in many languages. She found Sam to be a genuinely nice guy, and he treated her with respect and Jasmine with real fondness. His home, an apartment, simply needed to be tidied and the books put in place. In other words, it only lacked a woman's touch. Morag told him little about her own personal mess, and he did not ask, knowing that she would open up to him when she felt confident enough.

The professor had another helper, a Mexican who said that his name was Thomas Garcia. 'But you can call me Tommy,' he told her. Tommy worked around the house and garden and fancied his chances with most women, seeing them as little other than potential bed mates, the category into which he placed this beautiful young woman who had arrived with her little child. Tommy wasted no time in beginning his advances. One night while Morag prepared a late meal, he wandered into the kitchen, slouched on a chair and began boasting of his sexual prowess, even singing a Mexican love song, the words of which had evidently brought about the surrender of most women in the past. Tommy was astonished to find a kitchen knife pointing towards his throat. Morag said, 'Come near me once more, and you'll never sing again.' He was a proud man and stormed off vowing revenge. Later, he would taste victory.

Morag loved sitting on the patio with Sam and watching Jasmine run about, squealing with childish laughter. 'She dotes on you, Morag,' said the old man one evening as they chatted. 'You give her happiness and love few children experience. But she also needs a settled home where she can see the same friends each day and a wee dog that will show he needs her as much as she needs you.' She knew Sam was talking sense. He usually did, and she thought about what he had told her. The trouble was that she felt comfortable and secure in his home. But it could not go on for ever, and the longer she stayed with Sam the more difficult it would be to make a move.

One day, she picked out a slim red-backed volume from the shelves and saw that it was the wonderful story by Charles Dickens, *A Christmas Carol*. Opening the pages, she read about the sadness and joy of that season, and just as Scrooge had suffered an unpleasant taste of what his own future might be, so she began to ponder what would happen to her and more importantly to Jasmine. In the story, a child is given hope and happiness thanks to the determination of an adult to change the direction of his life, and Morag knew that there was a message in this for her. She also thought about the upcoming Christmas. When she replaced the book, she knew the time had come to act. She went to look for Sam. 'Jasmine and I have to go somewhere, Sam,' she said. 'It should only take a couple of days, but there's a chance we might not be back.'

16

Betrayed

Morag knew that the key to solving her dilemma lay in getting passports for her and Jasmine. Once those were in her hands, she would call Tony and ask him to bail them out. Then it would just be a matter of taking a flight to Scotland. She had decided that she wanted no more of England's legal system. It had cruelly let her down, casting her into the den of the enemy and leaving her to fight for herself.

Sam Frazier had shown kindness and generosity, giving affection and money. When he was not hidden among his books, he delighted in passing the time chatting with Jasmine, and the child obviously loved listening to his stories. He had never demanded that Morag tell him why she had turned up distressed and evidently abandoned in a San Diego park. Where she came from and what she was doing in America was not his business. Not long before she'd left the sanctuary of his home, she had asked him about getting passports, and he had said the nearest Consulate-General was in Los Angeles. 'Is that far?' she had asked.

'No, about 80 miles along the coast. You can get a bus and be there in a couple of hours.'

'And if I needed a passport for Jasmine, would I get one there?'

'I don't know about that, but I'm pretty sure anyone who turned up and told them that they had been robbed or had lost theirs would be able to get an emergency passport.'

And so she decided to seek help at the British Consulate-General. She had increasingly felt as though she was drowning in a sea of hopelessness. She knew that she had been badly advised, allowing herself to end up in a position in which she had effectively been forced to come to America to do battle over Jasmine. Having reached Austin filled with confidence, her self-assurance had waned as the matter dragged on and on. 'They are making a complete mockery of this case,' she'd told herself while still at Sam's. 'Jasmine is getting older, and instead of being able to play and have fun she's been tugged from one country to another and one continent to another. Where will it all end? We are up against people who are very rich, who can afford to let this continue indefinitely and who are on their home territory. They know the people who will decide Jasmine's future.'

The ruling that her daughter should be placed with the Chapmans had been unfair, giving them a distinct advantage when it came to deciding who should have her in the long term. As Christmas approached, she had also begun to feel homesick. There would be no presents, no tree, no steaming turkey and no pudding. It was true that Jack Reeves, after returning to Scotland, still smarting from his brush with the law, had continued to send her money, but it was barely enough to buy them food. She would, therefore, have to watch the faces of other people's children as they ran around the streets of San Diego clutching their new dolls and toys, riding their scooters and wearing their new clothes, knowing Jasmine had missed out. She had already endured seeing her little girl miserable and unable to understand why she could not play with the other children in the park opposite the bleak Austin apartment. Morag did not think she would be able to bear to see her daughter suffer much more.

She had taken only what they were able to carry, telling Sam that if she did not return to collect the rest of her belongings someone else would, although she did not know who that would be. She had also abandoned possessions in Austin but hoped Randy might care enough about her and Jasmine to one day rescue those for her. Sitting in the coach as the miles sped by, and with Jasmine safely at her side, she thought about what story she should tell the officials at the Consulate-General. She was pinning all her hopes on getting their assistance and wondered whether the truth might not be a wise option. Dared she walk in and tell them, 'I've defied a judge's ruling in Texas and run off with my daughter. Can you get us back to Britain, please?'

At the bus depot in Los Angeles, she was given directions to the British Consulate-General, and they set off, Morag humping cases and Jasmine pushing her own chair, barely able to see above the pile of toys and clothing. It seemed strange that this was the Christmas season with red-cloaked and white-bearded Santas bellowing invitations to enter shops while passers-by were sweltering in light tops and shorts. It was hard going for them both, especially Jasmine, who was determined not to add to the pain and worry on her mother's face by insisting on climbing into her chair and being pushed. They kept up one another's spirits with songs and stories, but Morag was becoming increasingly worried as they neared their destination on Wilshire Boulevard. However, the sight of the Union Jack lifted her. But what happened next brought no credit on those representing their country.

'We walked for about half an hour, but it seemed for ever,' Morag remembers. 'The noise was deafening, and people were pushing past, carrying great armfuls of packages – Christmas presents, presumably. We must have looked an odd couple, weighed down with cases and bags. Jasmine was tired but too stubborn to want to stop. Had anyone spoken to me, I would not have noticed, because I was too intent on getting to the consulate. I kept thinking, "These are my people. They'll give us some help."

'We expected the consulate to be busy, but there was hardly a soul about, and we had to wait around for nearly an hour in reception. Eventually, a woman came to see us, and I simply told her the truth: who we were, what I had done and why. She went off, then came back and said, "Did you know there's a warrant out for your arrest? A lot of people are looking for you." I told her I did not know that but was not surprised. I also said that it was all the more important that we got some help, but she simply said, "I'm sorry, but we're all off to a Christmas lunch. Can you come back tomorrow? I've booked an appointment for you at three in the afternoon, and we'll see then what we can do for you." I was appalled and tried to stress how urgent our needs were, but she was adamant. "Come back tomorrow," was all she would say. I said to myself, "You're fucking joking." But I actually said, "See you then."

'On the way in, we'd noticed that they had a huge Christmas tree, beautifully decorated, with an amazing automatic train going round and round it. Now I stopped beside it, not just because I needed to pull myself together but because Jasmine was so fascinated by it. Sam Frazier wouldn't have had room in his house for one. She looked so bonny sitting there, and as people walked past they looked and admired her. The delight on her face clearly passed to them and made them feel good. Many of them probably had little girls at home who would have been just as enthralled. She was even more mesmerised by the train. She made no effort to touch it, just sat there following it with her eyes.

'Jasmine was watching it so intently that I thought, "Well, at least she's taken some bit of Christmas for herself." At that moment, a security guard who had been watching her came up to me and said, "Take your child away from that train. I don't want her touching anything." I was surprised and angry, and said, "She's not touching anything. I'm here, and I wouldn't let her." But he insisted: "I want her away from the Christmas tree." I thought, "You sod. Why be so cruel to a little girl who has never really had a proper Christmas?"

'By that point, I was in tears. Everything I had hoped for had collapsed in a matter of minutes. There was no passport, no help, just a realisation that these people, my people, were going to hand me over to the police. I could imagine them on the telephone telling the police that we were in the city but advising them not to worry because if they came to the consulate the following afternoon we would walk right into their trap. We were even being told we couldn't look at their fucking Christmas tree. Jasmine was clinging to my arm, thinking that she had perhaps been the cause of my upset and telling me, "Sorry, Mummy. Mummy, please don't cry." I was wondering where the hell we'd stay that night, because apart from the bus ticket back to San Diego, a ticket I'd hoped never to have to use, and a few dollars, I was broke.

'Suddenly, the receptionist came over and asked what the trouble was. When I told him about our plight, he said, "I'm not having you in this state. I'll book you a hotel." I said, "Please don't. I haven't enough money to pay for it." He simply replied, "In that case, stop worrying. It's Christmas. How about if I make you and your little girl a present of a night in a hotel, and I'll even throw in a cab to take you there." He asked for nothing from us, just picked up the phone, booked us a room using his credit card, called a taxi, gave the driver some money and had us taken to a hotel, where we stayed the night. I never found out the name of this man, and I will never be able to thank him for what he did. I didn't ask him to help me, he just did. He didn't know me from Adam, yet he went to all that trouble and expense.

'The next morning, we carried all our belongings back to the bus depot. Every step of the way, I was nervous and looking about. Whenever a police car drove by, I expected it to stop, the officers to jump out and us to be hauled into the back seat at gunpoint. Jasmine was singing away, oblivious to all of this, and I tried joining in and was telling her stories about Santa and his workshops and how the elves and fairies helped make all the presents. She was very chirpy, and her happiness kept me going. But I was glad and relieved when we climbed on the bus and set off back to San Diego. At last I felt safe. However, I was bitter and disappointed that we were making the journey at all. I had imagined us at Los

Angeles airport showing our passports, picking up tickets paid for by my dad and flying home never to return.

'We arrived back at Sam's house at around the time when the police would have been preparing to head for the British Consulate-General to wait for us to turn up. I wondered if the security guard would object to them standing too near his precious Christmas tree.'

Morag called her mother in Scotland but broke down in tears. 'They are not going to take Jasmine from me,' she pledged with a mixture of fury and heartbreak. 'We'll have to start all over again.'

However, sly forces had been at work in her absence. Unknown to Morag, Tommy Garcia had pilfered through her handbag while she was at work cleaning Sam's house and had discovered Marcus's address and telephone number. He'd called the Texan, curious about the background of the young woman who had turned him down and been forced to defend herself with a knife. What were she and the beautiful little girl who was always at her side doing so far from home? Was there a mystery involved, and, more importantly, was there something in it for Tommy Garcia?

Marcus gave little away. Although Garcia had drawn up a list of questions to ask, he instead found himself being questioned. All Marcus wanted to know was where the woman and the child were, and when Garcia told him he instantly hung up and called the police in Austin. Within minutes, a call was being made to the FBI, and it was only a matter of moments before Morag and Jasmine were once more in the bag.

On the patio, sitting in his favourite chair, Sam Frazier was enjoying the sunshine and thinking of Scotland. Christmas was just six days off, and he remembered his own youth when he awoke to presents scattered at the foot of his bed and watched pine needles fall from the tree in the corner of the family living room. Morag sat beside him, quiet and no doubt thinking over the trip from which she had returned a couple of days earlier. He had not asked her where they had gone but assumed it to be Los

Angeles. Nor had he enquired about the purpose of the journey, although he had noticed that since they'd come back Morag had been quiet, contemplative and evidently, from her red eyes, crying. He guessed a broken romance lay somewhere in the mix and thought it was so tragic that someone who cared so much for her daughter had no one to care for her. He wondered whether they would stay for Christmas and was watching Jasmine run barefoot in the sunshine chasing a butterfly on the grass in front of them when he heard the sound of a car pulling up to his home. Next, two uniformed policemen came around the corner with their hands on their gun holsters as if they were anticipating a replay of the gunfight at the OK Corral. It was Morag's worst nightmare – one she had imagined a thousand times in her head.

'They asked if my name was Morag Dodds,' she remembers, 'and when I asked them what they wanted they simply took hold of me and began yelling in my ear that there was a warrant in force from Austin, Texas, for my arrest. I was trying to struggle free and kept demanding to know what I had done wrong, but I was pushed face down into the ground and my arms were forced up behind my back. Then I felt handcuffs on my wrists, and I was helpless. I could hear Sam protesting and demanding to know what was going on, but they ignored him and were joined by another couple of cops. I was terrified and in agony, and the police were obviously enjoying it.

'It all happened so quickly and suddenly. One moment, Sam and I were watching Jasmine, the next I felt as if my arms would break. Jasmine was just sitting there on the grass crying and saying, "Mummy, Mummy." I said, "Sweetheart, run into the house," and Sam was trying to console her, but one of the police officers just grabbed her and put her into the back of the first car. I was forced into the rear seat of the second and left there while the policemen went to talk with Sam, who was angry and insisting that he had a right to know what all the fuss was about. Through the front window of my car, I could see Jasmine kneeling on the back seat and waving to me. The policemen must have told her that we were playing a game and that she should wave and smile at me. Clearly, they thought she would calm me. I smiled back and was trying not to cry, because I didn't want her to see her mummy upset.

'I was taken to a downtown police station in San Diego, pushed into a cell and told that they would notify the police in Austin and ask what they wanted them to do with Jasmine and me. When I asked why I had been arrested, an officer said, "I guess they're saying you are being charged with interfering with the possession of a child." I said, "But she's my daughter." He said, "Your daughter! Well, that's what it said on the sheet: interfering with the possession of a child." I then said, "What does it mean?" He replied, "It means they say you've kidnapped her." He was shaking his head as he moved on.'

Later, another officer came to tell Morag that she was being taken to the Vista Detention Facility in the city. She begged to be told what was happening to Jasmine. 'Don't worry, ma'am,' the officer said, 'she is being well treated and cared for. Some people are coming over from Austin and will take her back there. She will then be returned to the temporary care of the Chapman family, but I promise no harm will come to her.' When she asked to see her daughter, she received only a blank look and silence. In fact, the following day, Jasmine was flown back to Texas and returned to the Chapmans, who whisked her off to their Woodville home after a judge formally gave them temporary custody until a full hearing that was scheduled to begin in Austin in mid-February.

At the detention centre, Morag was forced to undergo a humiliating introduction to the routine of what was effectively a prison. She was ordered to strip naked, bend over and hold on to her ankles while a female prison wardress poked inside her for signs of hidden contraband. Then she was given a white T-shirt and told to don the standard prison uniform: a blue V-neck boiler suit. She was then taken to a cell, where she found two other women: one white, one black and both friendly. They told her that they were being held for drug-related offences and were appalled when they heard her story.

The cell was sparse with only a toilet and three-tier bunk bed. She was allowed out to exercise in a high-walled yard for one hour a day. The rest of the time was spent reading or in a communal recreation room, where she could play board games. One of these was the classic time-passer Monopoly, and she joined in at the invitation of three other women. She had often played Monopoly in the past, but her first game in the detention centre brought cheers and howls of laughter when she picked up a card and turning it over read 'Get out of jail free'.

'The other girls in the detention centre were very kind to me,' Morag remembers. 'Most of them were in for very minor offences. The white girls' parents seemed to be able to put up bail for their daughters, but not the mums and dads of the black inmates. There was a lot of discrimination in there. One woman was in for killing her children and chopping them into pieces.'

She did not enjoy prison food and would complain of its 'tasting funny'. There was a bizarre reason for that, she was to discover. The prison authorities added a special additive to all meals, one that left traces in the inmates' bodies, making it easier for tracker dogs, in the event of an escape, to sniff out their quarry.

On the first night of Morag's capture, Sam Frazier wistfully reflected that his hopes of hearing the laughter of a child at Christmas had gone. He would miss them both. The following month, the investigator called to see him. Later, he included Sam's observations in his report:

> Frazier described Ms Dodds as a fine example of a mother. Frazier said that Ms Dodds did not tell him much about the situation in Texas that led her to be in San Diego. Frazier had numerous opportunities to observe Ms Dodds with her child. He stated that Jasmine had the run of the house. He described her as a happy and bright child. He stated that Ms Dodds was very attentive and very responsible as a parent. Frazier also said that

Ms Dodds kept Jasmine in clean clothes and kept her well fed. He described Ms Dodds as a good mother who loved her child. He said, 'You could tell that she really loved the little girl.'

Frazier stated that on the day Ms Dodds was arrested, he, Ms Dodds and Jasmine were out on the patio, because it was such a beautiful and warm day. She was not wearing shoes, because it was difficult to keep her clothed and she loved to run around without shoes or clothing.

The professor, a kindly, thoughtful man, had never failed to be moved by the care and love his young guest showered on her daughter. Saddened by Morag's arrest, he was concerned as to what would happen to her and Jasmine. He was not the only one.

17

A Little Piece of Home

Back in Austin, news of Morag's capture had been relayed to Randy Berry, who was saddened but not surprised. He had known it would be only a matter of time before she ran out of money, and not having a passport made her a virtual prisoner anyway. He rang Flora and said, 'I think you better seriously consider getting out here. It's becoming apparent that the Chapmans are going to abandon Marcus as their chief hope and go for her themselves. They already have temporary custody. We need to show that you're around and just as determined to look after Jasmine. At some stage, Morag will be moved back over to Austin, and unless we have somebody who's going to be looked on as a responsible guardian it's going to be a struggle to get her out of jail.'

Flora also decided that it was time to stir things up and rally support for her daughter's plight. She began making calls to local journalists, but some of them were initially worried in case the court in London had placed a ban on the reporting of the case because it concerned a child. She had to point out the ruling had been made in England, not Scotland.

As Christmas Day neared, it was evident that Morag was taking prison life badly. 'I could not eat because of worry about what was happening to Jasmine,' she remembers. 'All I had been told by a lawyer we'd hired was that she was back with the Chapmans. My heart sank when I heard that. I more or less lived on bread and water.'

The Austin authorities began moves to have Morag extradited from California to face trial for taking Jasmine. She also had to answer to the bouncing-cheque charge and prepare to fight for custody of her daughter. An extradition hearing was set for 30 December.

On Christmas Day, Flora rang the detention centre and asked to speak to Morag. A surly guard refused to put the call through. Morag, meantime, had been told that she was allowed to make one call. It was supposed to be within the state, but it was decided to turn a blind eye to the rule. 'I told the guards I'd like to put in a call to Woodville to Lawilda so I could speak with Jasmine,' Morag recalls. 'I told the other girl prisoners about the Chapmans, and they urged me not to bother, because I would get upset, but I was determined. I hadn't spoken with Jasmine for six days and wanted to wish her a happy Christmas. We'd been so close all her life, and when we'd been on the run had shared all the knockbacks and hardships together.

'The phone was answered by Lawilda, and I said, "Can I speak to Jasmine, please? I want to wish her Happy Christmas and to tell her her mummy loves her." But Lawilda just said, "I don't know what you hope to gain from this. She is outside playing with the dog, and she cannot come to the telephone." The other girls were waiting to find out what had happened and what Jasmine had said, and when I told them about the conversation they just said that Lawilda was an evil bitch.

'Stuart made no effort to visit me while I was in prison, and I didn't hear from him. No doubt he was scared in case Marcus got to hear. But an elderly lady, a Scot living in California who got to hear about me when the case began to be reported in the local newspapers around San Diego, turned up to visit. She said that she felt great sympathy for me and had been so moved by reading how I had gone on the run with Jasmine that every time she thought about us she started to cry. She had gone to great lengths to find a store that sold British goods and had brought me a tartan-coloured tin of Walkers shortbread. It was such a lovely gesture that I cried when she left. A complete stranger had gone to a lot of effort to bring me a little piece of home.'

In Scotland, news that Morag was in jail was broken on the front page of Aberdeen's *Press and Journal* on Monday, 26 December 1994, under the headline 'Snatch Mum in US Prison Nightmare'. The story quoted Randy Berry as saying, 'Under Texas law, she is in serious trouble. A judge has granted temporary custody of Jasmine to the paternal grandparents. In the circumstances, with the child's parents being unmarried, this is accepted under Texas law. That is why Mrs Dempster has to enter into the lawsuit.'

Flora realised that Randy was right. She needed to be on the spot. She was also quoted in the paper:

> 'This past week has been a nightmare. How can anyone keep a mother from being with her baby daughter, especially at Christmas time? Morag must be heartbroken, and I can't even get to speak to her on the telephone. It just does not bear thinking about. I only wish I had gone out to America earlier to give her moral support. She has been driven too far, and I am obviously concerned for her mental state. Now it appears that the only way my daughter will see her child again is if I raise an action for custody. Under Texas law, I have the right to do this.'

She also claimed that Marcus had said he would give Morag $22,000 if she would return to Scotland and leave Jasmine with him and his family. And the guardian *ad litem* had been a witness to the proposal. It might well have been the offer of a decent man who knew that he had the support and financial means to provide a comfortable future for his daughter and who was, at the same time, aware that fighting for custody had stretched to breaking point the reserves of Morag and her mother. But Flora was not impressed. 'It was insulting,' she said. 'There is not enough money in the whole world to persuade someone so dedicated as Morag to give up her daughter.'

So, the battle lines were being drawn up, and Marcus was determined not to be left out of the spotlight. Two days later, he too was quoted in a newspaper:

> 'Jasmine is doing real fine just now. She is looking good and is perfectly happy. Morag and I have split up. She has not proved to be a good mother. She has had her problems for a long time. The custody fight over Jasmine has been going on for a long time, and I just hope we are now coming to the end.'

The next day, it was Flora's turn:

> 'I telephoned the Vista detention centre and spoke to a nurse who promised to tell Morag that I sent all my love and hoped to see her soon. Just to know she has been made aware that we are all thinking about her back home has given me a wonderful feeling of relief. I was assured that she was in good spirits and in good health.'

In fact, there were deep worries about Morag's health. Tony, who was still receiving mail for his daughter, had telephoned Flora to say a letter had arrived indicating that a routine hospital check for ovarian cancer had revealed the possibility of serious infection and Morag needed immediate treatment. Flora managed to persuade the Vista nurse to organise an urgent examination. 'If my daughter dies, I'll hold you responsible,' she had threatened. Clearly, the message got through, because tests were carried out right away, and Morag was given the all clear. It later emerged that the letter had been intended for a girlfriend of Morag, who had wanted to know if she was pregnant and had not wanted the result to be sent to her own address. Morag recalls, 'My mother even faxed copies of the hospital letter, and suddenly I was lying on an examination couch with my legs up in the air telling myself, "Only my mother could have thought up this idea."'

She did not look in good spirits or healthy when she appeared in court in San Diego on 30 December to be officially told that she was to be extradited to Austin. Judge Harvey Hiber told her that she could expect to be jailed for three years for running off with Jasmine. Onlookers were shocked by her gaunt, tired appearance, but at least she had not lost her defiance or determination. She refused to give her name when called on to do so or even to answer to the question, 'Are you Morag Dodds?'

The next day, a journalist quoted Morag's thoughts on the so-called abduction:

'I would take Jasmine away again under the same circumstances. I was really scared when I did it, and I knew the consequences, but it was better than letting her suffer. I am worried about Jasmine and what this is doing to her psychologically. Jasmine cannot understand why she was taken away from her mummy. I tried to tell her that it was only for a holiday. But being only two and a half, she doesn't understand. She was clinging to me. She needs the security of a stable home environment. I would be happy to stay in jail if I thought my child was going to be with my mother in Scotland.'

Flora flew to America in early January. Going through a security check while switching flights in Amsterdam, she was asked, 'Is this trip business or pleasure?'

'I don't know,' she replied. 'I am going to try to get my daughter out of jail.'

In her handbag was a video she had shot of Forres and the surrounding countryside. Making the little movie had been Randy's idea. 'Let the jury see your home and the land around it,' he had said. 'Give them a taste of the life to which you want Jasmine to be a part: the town where she will grow up; the school she will attend; the places where she will play; the ponies she will ride. Make the jury really want to come and live there themselves.'

When she arrived in Austin, she was met by Randy, who said, 'The Chapmans will want to delay and delay. They imagine they can wear you down. Jimmy Ross carried out interrogations as an army officer, and this is a classic interrogator's technique: put off, put off, delay, delay, keep you hanging on and on until you become unsettled and perhaps even contemplate giving up. It's our job to persuade the courts not to allow this.'

Morag was still in California but was told she was being returned to Austin on 9 January 1995. 'They strip-searched me when I left the detention centre,' she remembers, 'and I was then taken to the airport and put into a sort of cage to await the arrival of the aircraft. When it came time to leave, they strip-searched me again, and I thought, "Maybe they've been watching too much television." On the plane, the two sheriff's officers sent out from Austin to take me back were going to handcuff me to one of the seats, and I objected. I said, "No way you're going to do that. I used to work in the North Sea, and I know that if we go down I'll have absolutely no chance fastened to a seat." The guards argued and said that they were only going along with the rules, so I asked them, "Is it the rules to kill somebody? You do this and I'll yell and scream the whole way." They asked, "Are you going to cause that amount of fuss?" I said, "Yes, because you're killing me." They replied, "In that case, we'll take one of the shackles off." I said, "Brilliant," and thought to myself, "Some freedom at last." They just cuffed me to one of them, and I thought, "Well, if I'm going down, you're going to go down with me."'

In Austin, a police car was waiting on the runway. Morag was taken to a police station and handcuffed to a radiator while officers searched for a suitable cell. She was then taken to prison, where she discovered that her cell was even more basic than the one she had been held in at the Vista Detention Facility in San Diego. She was ordered to change out of her San Diego blue prison uniform and into an orange boiler suit over a blue-green blouse. 'There were two three-tier bunks and a toilet without a seat,' she recalls, 'and you had to have a wee in front of the other girls. We came

170

to an arrangement not to look. There was no television, I wasn't allowed any books and when I asked if I could get a newspaper that too was refused. Basically, you were shoved in there and left until a judge decided he would see you. It was three days before I appeared in court, and by then I was in a terrible state, worrying whether I'd ever get to see Jasmine again. I was in such turmoil that I didn't even know what had happened at the hearing until it was all over and someone explained the proceedings to me.'

What upset her most was the sight of Marcus at court, his arm around the shoulder of a female with long blonde hair from the district attorney's office. 'I thought, "All is lost here," when I saw them together,' remembers Morag. '"I've got absolutely no chance." I'd come from jail at the end of a line of people all in shackles, and the first thing I saw was Marcus cuddling a woman.'

Her mother was there too. With the help of Randy, she had hired another lawyer, Ken Houp, to represent Morag in the abduction case, and his first objective was to get her out of jail. It would not be an easy task. Despite it being a Sunday, he agreed to meet Randy and Flora, and from there went on to call on Judge Jeanne Meurer, asking her to release Morag on bail to the custody of her mother in order that they could prepare their defence. The judge went along with the proposal. However, newspapers had got wind that Morag was back in Austin and interviewed her in prison. During the interviews, Morag hinted that her mother might have encouraged her to go on the run. The stories that subsequently appeared infuriated Houp and the judge. It had been hoped that the outcome of her court appearance would be her immediate release, but this did not look so promising as a result of her comments.

At least Flora was able to see her daughter again when the bus arrived carrying the day's flotsam from the Travis County Correctional Facility in Del Valle: 'I was anxious to discover what she looked like in the flesh and was standing in court. Just before the prisoners came in, a whistle blew and a line of about

171

ten big, hunky black guys entered. Right at the end of the line was this wee girl from Scotland. It was the first time I'd seen her since collecting her furniture at Killingworth before she set off to fight for Jasmine, and I thought, "Oh, my God, what are you doing to my daughter?" The prison warders pinned us against a wall until the line went past.

'The district attorney's office wasn't too pleased with me, because when Morag went on the run they telephoned to see if I could help them trace where she was, but I told them, "I'm not helping you. If she did go, then I would have encouraged her to do so."'

During Morag's spell on the run, Flora had also been accused by Lawilda of aiding her daughter. The telephone had rung in the bedroom of her home just before 6.30 a.m. one morning. When she picked up the receiver, a voice said, 'Is that Flora Macdonald?' She realised that it was Lawilda but decided not to counter this rudeness over her name and simply replied that it was. 'Well, this is Lawilda Chapman here. Morag, as you are well aware, has run away and has taken Jasmine. A man named Jake Harris has somehow got her the plane tickets, and we are concerned about Jasmine's welfare. Do you know where they are?'

Flora was furious. 'If you had been concerned about Jasmine's welfare, why did you make her mother leave her own home and drag a little child all the way over there for a custody case?' she asked.

Lawilda protested, 'Well, I didn't.'

'Yes, you did, and I don't want to speak to anybody who does that to a child.' Flora then slammed down the receiver.

At the hearing, Justice of the Peace Jade Meeker set Morag's bail at $120,000, but the sum demanded was way beyond what her family or friends could raise. Houp said to the judge, 'Her mother has come over from Scotland, and if you let her out on bail she will vouch for her good behaviour.'

Assistant District Attorney Melissa Douma took a very

different view, however, remembering the call for assistance to Flora in Scotland: 'She's already encouraged her daughter to go on the run. I don't believe she can be trusted. We have no guarantee that she holds this court in any higher regard than she did for Judge Meurer's court.'

Houp, to his immense credit, was firm: 'No way. That's wrong. She can't have said that and must have been misquoted.'

The next day, Meeker reduced the bail figure to $20,000. But it made no difference. In order to go free, Morag needed to hand over a bond for 10 per cent of the bail figure. Unable to find $2,000, she sadly went back to prison for another night. The following day, the money was lodged by the *Press and Journal*, meaning that Morag was at last able to get out of prison.

As Morag walked through the prison gates to freedom, journalists asked her what she was most looking forward to. 'Wearing my bra again,' she replied. 'They take your bra away in there in case you want to use it to hang yourself.'

There were major conditions attached to her freedom: she had to live in an apartment found for her by her mother; she was not allowed to attempt any contact with Jasmine; she was barred from leaving the apartment unless it was to get medical treatment or to see her lawyers; and she was even prevented from using a swimming pool in the apartment complex. And the judge also ordered Morag to be tagged. A metal bracelet around her ankle, which had to be worn continuously, would monitor her movements and warn the authorities if she went out of bounds. However, it needed to be operated in conjunction with a telephone so that the monitoring team could call to check on her if they suspected she had left the apartment. That mean installing a telephone, and until it was in place she had to stay in jail. Thankfully, the telephone company worked promptly and she was able to walk free at last.

'I discovered that any supermarket could organise the installation of a telephone, and it cost just $45,' Flora remembers. 'But no sooner were we connected than someone called the telephone company and claimed that we were making hundreds of international calls. This meant that they made me pay up to date instead of the normal system of getting charges on credit until a bill was sent. It was a cheap and nasty little trick.'

Next was the problem of finding furnishings for the flat in Apartment Chaparosa in Red River Street, Austin. Expats, among them businesswoman May Cherry, gave superb and selfless support. May had heard of Morag's plight from her sister Marlyn, who read about it in an Austin newspaper report. They were immediately sympathetic to her because they were originally from Aberdeen and called Randy to ask if they could help.

'Randy immediately said, "Yes,"' May remembers, 'telling us that Morag and Flora had no one in Austin. After telephoning to make sure we would be welcome, we took a bus from our home at Round Rock to look them up. We were horrified to find that they were living in very meagre circumstances. They had a couple of cups, one pot with which to heat water and cook, one knife which they shared and a couple of forks. Luckily, Flora had mentioned on the phone that she'd like to fix us a cup of tea when we visited but they only had two cups, and so she asked if we could bring a couple of cups. Needless to say, on our second visit to them a day or two later, we loaded the car with pots, pans, silverware, cooking utensils, towels and everything we could think of to make their lives a little easier. They were so appreciative. We had no idea just how involved we would become.'

18

Bad Dog Defence

If in Marcus Morag had discovered a Judas in disguise, in Terry Weeks she had found her Sir Galahad. So far, she had been represented by Richard Jones and other lawyers, all of them appointed by the Public Defender's Office, but the system, similar to our legal aid, meant she could not be guaranteed the same lawyer for any length of time. It was often a case of pot luck as to whom she was given. A highly skilled and respected attorney practising in Austin, Terry had been approached by his friend Randy, a law-school classmate, and asked to take on the task of representing Morag.

'Randy said he would do Flora if I would take a fling at Morag,' says Terry, a kindly, helpful man who had first heard about the case through the local media. He had handled many divorces and custody squabbles but was fascinated by this young woman who had risked so much for the love of her child. 'I'm one of the original family law specialists in the State of Texas. I have got a bit of experience, and so that's why he picked me up.' In fact, Randy had homed in on Terry because he was the best in the business. 'So, I said I would do it, and I finally got to meet her.'

Morag was still in jail at this point on the abduction charge, which was being handled by Ken Houp. Once Ken had rescued her from her prison cell, she was able to concentrate on fighting for custody of Jasmine, and so Terry rode into the fray. 'Morag was a rather mercurial girl,' he remembers. 'She was just as cute as could be. She had a wonderful wit about her, and this came out especially when she was required to take some psychological tests. They said she wasn't very bright, and they were clearly wrong, because she was just as clever as a pet coon. And it turned out she could outtalk most of the lawyers in the case. For example, at one point the psychologist giving her the IQ test said, "When is Thanksgiving Day?" She said, "Why do you want to know?" He said, "Well, it's one of the standard answers you are supposed to know." She replied, "Fine, when is Boxing Day?" He said, "I don't know, but you are supposed to answer the Thanksgiving Day question." She said, "I don't have any idea. We don't have that where I come from." She was very, very clever and thought well on her feet.

'I thought that her chances at the beginning of the case were pretty bad. It was one of those where you looked at it and said to yourself, "This isn't really a difficult case. This is a case that's gone right past being difficult, a case you are not going to make, not expected to win, so let's go for it and have some fun." It just didn't look like much of a winner. For a start, the judge who was going to hear her custody case, John Dietz, was very angry at her because she'd run away and hidden in darkest California somewhere. She had flouted the court's orders, and he was of a mind to punish her.

'With any case, you sit down with your client and talk to them and decide, "How am I going to take this? What route am I going down?" It was no different with Morag. When she first came in and started talking, I listened and interrupted a lot. She'd tell me about something and I'd say, "Wait, stop, tell me about this." But I knew all the time that my eye had to be on the day when we would stand in front of the court and say to the judge that we were ready. So, the entire process of interviewing and putting together evidence was about staying very focused on the day when we would face the judge and tell him, "We're ready." If you don't do that, don't stay focused on that day, you waste a whole lot of time looking and talking about the sort of crap that no one is ever going to think about. This might be about interesting things, but they won't bear on getting the result that you need.

'Once Morag was released from prison, she was tagged, but before the case we went to the judge, and he said, "I don't want that in my court." She first came to see me just after she had been set free. Randy went down to the jail and brought her to my office. She came in with all that electronic business on her legs, and we had our first interview. That was the first time I talked to her, and it was maybe a month or a little more before trial. Certainly, it was real close to trial. So, it was not one of those situations where you could sit around and scratch your head and think for six months. It was coming up quickly, and there was a lot of hard work to do.

'She was charged with a felony offence – the cheque – and then they were going to say that she had run away, invalidated laws, thumbed her nose at American jurisprudence and all the things you would expect them to say about a girl that's in a lot of trouble. She had been arrested by the federal authorities, and that was not good from her point of view. But that's just something you started with, and if you lost on that one, well, you were going to lose anyway. So you had to get in there. I'm a pretty big believer in not hiding your bad side when you're putting your case on. I wanted us to say what the bad things were about her and what she did, rather than having them drawn out of her. So, I started getting her ready to do that, and then I worked pretty hard on her about the "Bad Dog" defence, although it didn't work as well with Morag as it might have because she wouldn't bend much.

'I had a lawyer who worked for me, and I asked him how he was going to win some jury trial, what he was going to do about some bad criminal case, and he said, "I'm going to use the Bad Dog defence." I said, "What's that?" He said, "I had a dog once who'd be messing around in the trash when I got home. I'd spank him, put his nose in the trash and yell at him. Pretty soon, it got to the point that if I came home and he'd been in the trash, he'd hide under the bed, and I'd go get him and spank him. Finally, it got to the point where if he had been in the trash, he would meet me at the front door, roll over and pee on himself. When the dog is rolling over and peeing on himself, all you can really do is say, 'It's all right. We're going to work this out. Just stop doing that.'"

'And that works amazingly well with witnesses. It's the Bad Dog defence. You say, "So you're sorry?" And your witness says, "Yes, I am." You say, "OK, let's move on." But your witness says, "No, I really need to tell you that that was a really terrible thing I did." You reply, "OK, that's fine." But the witness continues, saying, "I don't know what got into me. I've risked my child. I've just done such a terrible thing. I don't know how I'll ever get over it." By that point, everybody is saying, "Just shut up. We forgive you." So we worked on that a bit.'

Persuading Terry to take on the case had not been difficult. For the top attorney, the challenge was intriguing. But attorneys, like the rest of us, have to live; they have bills to pay, staff to employ, offices to run. To hire him would normally have cost $10,000, money that Morag and her mother simply did not have. They already had the expense of renting the apartment in Red River Street, buying food and clothes, and paying telephone bills. Morag was penniless. She'd sold everything she had to go to America to fight for her daughter. Marcus was supposed to be taking care of her upkeep, but he had fallen behind with payments, letting her down, as usual. Flora was willing to sell one of her horses if it came to the crunch. But then Jack Reeves stepped in: 'Morag rang me to tell me that she was out of prison and had the opportunity to get the best lawyer around. He was her only chance of winning and coming home with Jasmine, but it would cost $10,000. She was breaking her heart during the call, because it was such a large amount, but I told her, "Stop worrying. Give me a couple of days. I'll see if I can sort something, and I'll call you back." What I did was for Jasmine, because she was my goddaughter, and I'd taken a vow to look after her and do my best for her. I went to my bank manager and asked him for a loan of £7,000. I had always been a steady earner, but he naturally wanted to know what the money was for. When I told him, he gave it the go-ahead. I rang Morag and told her, "Go and hire Terry Weeks." She was over the moon.'

At that first meeting in Terry's office in Nueces Street, Flora sat in while Morag's lawyer, and occasionally Randy, questioned her daughter. What she saw did not come as a total surprise: 'That day, I realised Randy was in love with Morag. As Terry asked her lots of questions, I was watching Randy and saw that he could not take his eyes from her. It was not a look you would expect a lawyer to give his witness. It was a loving look – one that said, "Trust us. We won't let you down, and when this is over I want us to be together." I knew Randy was married but that some years earlier he and his wife Kathleen had split up. Kathleen had left Randy and gone to live with another man, but when that didn't work out she had asked Randy if he would take her back, and he'd agreed.

'During the break-up, he had not looked for another partner or taken a mistress, simply throwing himself into his work instead. When she'd returned, they'd lived separate lives. Randy later admitted that they slept in separate bedrooms. So, the fact that they did not get on and had again discussed separating was not caused by Morag. The marriage had problems long before she came on the scene. And as time went by, it became plain that the feelings Morag had for Randy were not one sided. They were equally fond of one another, which was the best basis for a strong relationship.

'As much as Morag loved Randy, when she was released from prison she seemed more determined than ever on getting her mind focused on winning Jasmine back. She no longer wanted to smoke and would politely decline the offer of a drink, preferring juice or water. It was simply that she was angry. She was motivated by anger over her treatment, her jailing and having Jasmine kept from her. The Americans had handled the entire affair shockingly badly and had shown a callous indifference to the feelings of both Morag and Jasmine.'

Despite her anger, Morag was also relieved that her case now seemed to be making progress after the long and eventful months of waiting. But she was still on tenterhooks because of not being allowed to see or speak to Jasmine. And she was nervous, anxious and frustrated by the bail condition that kept her a prisoner in the apartment. Ken Houp had warned, in a newspaper interview, that getting bail was not the panacea it might have seemed:

> 'She will have to be willing to subject herself to round-the-clock electronic monitoring. She will be fitted with an ankle bracelet, which she will not be able to remove and which will monitor her movements at all times. She would not be able to move far from her house without this being detected.'

In reality, it was much worse than having to wear a bracelet. The monitor was a cumbersome plastic device, rather like a modern mobile telephone, and it was strapped permanently in place. She wore it when she slept, when she moved around and even when she went for a bath or shower. She had to try to wash in between the straps. She couldn't even get a pair of tights over it, which meant that she sometimes felt only half dressed.

This transatlantic tug of love was attracting increasing publicity in America. The *Austin American-Statesman* newspaper reported, 'Mother, grandparents fight for child's custody. Custody of girl puts mother at odds with paternal grandparents.' It quoted William Powers representing Jimmy and Lawilda as saying, 'Dodds should not have Jasmine permanently. They feel that Morag Dodds was not able to provide a safe and stable environment for Jasmine.' And Morag was quoted as saying, 'Jasmine is Scottish. It seems such a shame to leave her in a land that is not hers.' *The Dallas Morning News* wrote, 'If Mr Chapman does not win custody, he wants Jasmine to stay with his parents.' And San Antonio's *Express-News* reported, 'A two-year-old girl is at the centre of a custody battle spanning two continents.'

The result of so much newspaper coverage was that other expat

Scots joined May Cherry in offering help. But the bail curbs often meant that their good intentions backfired. Along with her mother, Morag was invited to the Austin Caledonian Society's annual Burns Supper. It would mean leaving the apartment for the evening, and she made a formal request for permission to do so. 'The authorities just laughed when I asked if I could go with mum,' Morag remembers. 'I don't think they had ever heard of a Burns Supper. The situation was desperate.'

Flora attended and found herself to be something of a celebrity. May Cherry took the lead and explained that Flora and her daughter had been dumped with little or no help in an apartment and that expectations of money and assistance from Marcus Chapman had not come to fruition. May told the Scots in exile that the women needed anything and everything, and before the night was out Flora found herself trying to remember the names of all those who'd come forward with offers of help and pledges of support. Among them was Christine Matyear, who lectured at the University of Texas in Austin and who would become friends with Flora and later Morag. 'I was very taken with the story, since I had been the subject of a custody battle when I was about three or four myself,' Christine says. 'It was similar in some respects – grandparents versus my father following the death of my mother. I was very young, but I remember the anxiety of being separated from my beloved parents. In light of this emotional response, I felt very sympathetic towards Jasmine and began following the developments of the case. Morag had been under a great deal of stress and was largely without resources. I think that hearts went out to her from many people in Austin because of that. It was her passionate concern for little Jasmine that won me over. When she spoke about her, the maternal distress showed very plainly.'

The tagging restrictions forced Morag to spend another lonely and disappointing night in the apartment while her mother was at the Burns Supper. That she had to spend so much time cooped up became so dispiriting that ultimately she felt she was going out of her mind. In prison, both in California and in Austin, she had at least had some freedom, albeit limited, to move about and mingle. She rang Ken Houp and pleaded, 'This is too much. I need some fresh air. I must get out and walk somewhere.'

Houp went to Jade Meeker, who agreed to relax her conditions and allow Morag out for an hour each day. Eventually, Terry Weeks would point out that her inability to have freedom of movement was interfering with her right to work on her defence and the restrictions would be dropped.

Friends such as May and Christine wondered what went through Morag's mind as the trial date in February grew nearer. Morag's thoughts simply revolved around her daughter: 'I was worried about her. Naturally, I wanted to know how she was feeling emotionally. I knew how I was feeling, but she was more important. I knew she would be wondering what had happened to me since we'd been ripped apart in Sam Frazier's garden, because after being together 24 hours a day I was suddenly no longer around. I had always been with her. I would take her to nursery at Killingworth and then pick her up and bring her home. When I took her off to play with her friends, I was always there to meet her when it was time to go home. I would be outside watching when she was playing with her friends.

'She had been with me constantly, from the moment she woke up to when she went to sleep. I kept thinking, "My God, she hasn't got me, she hasn't got her friends, she hasn't got our house. Nobody will be telling her anything. Poor wee thing." It might have been OK had they let me speak to her on the telephone to reassure her that everything was all right, even though that would have meant telling her a lie. But, being her mum, I would have lied if it would have helped her.'

Because Morag was prevented from being with her daughter, Randy was anxious that Flora should see Jasmine. Flora's name would be put forward as a potential custodian of the child, and he needed to show a court that she bonded well with her granddaughter. After an initial request was rejected, Flora was finally allowed to meet the youngster at the end of January. She still finds it difficult to speak about that day: 'Randy arranged everything, and when I did get permission to see her it was to be in a play park in Austin. Morag was breaking her heart knowing that Jasmine was to be so near. She gave me a Barbie doll and a little green dragon that had been favourites of Jasmine's, and Morag sprayed the dragon with the perfume that she normally wore – it was Coco – so that Jasmine would recognise the scent. It was a sort of code. Randy drove me there but remained in his car doing paperwork. It was like the gathering of the 5,000. The guardian *ad litem*, Lawilda, Jimmy Ross Chapman and even a security guard were all there for half an hour's play in the park with a two-year-old kiddie.

'Jimmy Ross carried Jasmine everywhere, as though he was afraid that if he put her down she would somehow be spirited away. When I first saw her, I began crying because she looked so sad, depressed and quiet, and they'd even cut her blonde curls short. There was a sort of stream running through the park, and I got her down to the little creek at one point and said, "Come and play stones." They all stood and watched, and that was the only time I got to be on my own with her. I could not have gone anywhere anyway. While we were together, I said quietly, "Your mummy loves you. She told me to tell you that she really loves you and misses you." At that, her little eyes lit up. I had been told I could not say to Jasmine that I was with her mummy, but there was no way I wasn't going to tell someone of that age that her own mother thought about her and cared for her. It would have been inhuman.

'Of course, I hadn't seen Jasmine for a while, because she had been living in Killingworth, so it was difficult for us both, and she began to cry too. She went up a chute to slide down and cried all the way. Then, she was put on a swing, but she continued to cry the whole time she was on it. There were so many people standing around watching our grief, which made it seem even worse. It must have been such a sad scene, and they created the appearance that Jasmine was some sort of hostage.

'When she was at home in Scotland, we had taken her horse riding around Forres, and she'd been free to run around picking hazelnuts and chestnuts. Now, they were holding her like a baby when she wasn't a baby but a child perfectly capable of walking on her own.

'No wonder Morag had told me during our telephone conversation before she ran off to California that her daughter had gone back to crawling around on the floor. I wanted to scream out, "Get real. Give the kid her freedom." Did they think I was going to pick her up and sprint off, or did they imagine I had an army of Scottish gangsters hiding around a street corner with pistols who would suddenly emerge and snatch her at gunpoint? The sheer theatre of the situation, the unreality of it all, made it impossible for Jasmine not to wonder what it was all about and even to think that it was her granny Flora who had caused all this. I was so angry and upset that I wanted to walk up to Lawilda, grab her, march her down to the creek and throw her in.

'I had a camera, and I took photographs to take back to Morag. The visit was only for half an hour, and when it was over and Jimmy Ross had picked her up and carried her off once more, I asked Randy to drive me to a supermarket where they offered an instant developing service. We waited around, but when we saw the photos I wondered if I'd done the right thing. They didn't show a happy, smiling child but a waif. It was only then that I grasped just how unhappy Jasmine was.

'Outside the store, I turned to Randy and said, "I know it will be possible to get more visits, but don't arrange anything, please." When he asked why, I simply said, "I am not going back to put the child through that again. She's like a little animal who's dying, a little girl that has simply been left somewhere. She was so sad, just so sad." I think Randy understood, but he had a job to do and needed to make sure that this wasn't just a knee-jerk reaction on my part. "You've got further visits," he said. "You cannot not go again." But I said, "No, Randy. She will end up hating me, because she'll believe I'm responsible for sending her to live with the Chapmans. And, in any case, I just couldn't put myself through it again either.'''

Reluctantly, Flora took the photographs back to Morag, who remembers opening up the coloured envelope in which the shop assistant had stored the prints and negatives: 'Seeing them just got me even more upset. It was obvious that this wasn't the same little girl I'd looked after. Every photograph taken in the past showed her grinning like a Cheshire cat, happy as could be. But when I saw those photos it looked like somebody had stuck a golf ball in her mouth. She looked so upset and that distressed me. I went into my bedroom and burst into tears.'

Her sorrow made Flora angry: 'All of us around Morag had been looking forward to the thought that she would be allowed to visit Jasmine. For her to be told that she could not see her own daughter was a cruel, despicable and heartless thing to do. I told myself, "Lawilda is a mother herself. How can she be party to destroying not just my daughter but Jasmine too? Because this is harming Jasmine. For a child who has been so close to her mother from birth to be suddenly parted from her is not right."

'One of the lowest points in my life was having to look at the photographs I'd taken of Jasmine. The child looked so full of sorrow. It was awful seeing her in tears. In the end, I wished I'd never taken the camera.

'I had taken a card from a local supermarket and written on it, "Mummy Loves You". It was for Jasmine, but the guardian *ad litem* refused to let me hand it over. The Chapmans could have intervened and said that there was no problem, but they didn't. As far as I was concerned, this was just one more ploy by them to wear Morag down.'

The custody trial was now just two weeks away. Morag had at least some good news when Ken Houp called her: 'Try putting the abduction at the back of your mind for a little while. The decision whether to proceed with the charge has been put off by the grand jury until after the future of Jasmine is decided.'

'What does that mean?' Morag asked.

'It means that if you are awarded custody of Jasmine, it will be unlikely that they will want to prosecute you for taking away someone who has been legally given to you. Don't go thinking you're out of the woods yet, though. They might still go ahead and charge you with contempt for defying the temporary custody order, but for the time being at least it's looking good.'

19

Good Guy, Bad Guy

B efore the trial could get under way, lawyers representing Marcus and his parents wanted to know what evidence Morag and her witnesses were likely to give. She had already gone through the unnerving experience of making a deposition, one that had contributed to her going on the run with Jasmine. Now it was Flora's turn.

It was a strict rule that witnesses were not to be coached by their lawyers in what evidence they would give at a deposition. Of course, it is inevitable that clients, inexperienced in the ways of the law and unfamiliar with courtroom procedures especially, will seek advice from their legal representatives about what is probably going to take place. So, one day before giving her deposition, Flora, accompanied by Morag, went to lunch with Randy at his home and began quizzing him about what might be expected of her. He explained the format and in doing so tried to give an indication of what she would be asked at the deposition and in court by taking her through a mini question-and-answer session. Naturally, to preserve the proper procedures and avoid embarrassment, Terry was not told about the little tête-à-tête.

And so the day after her meeting in the park with Jasmine, still bristling from that nightmare reunion, Flora arrived at the offices of William Powers on Lake Austin Boulevard. With her were Randy and Morag. This time an extra lawyer was present.

Andrew Hathcock, who taught law at the Children's Rights Clinic at the University of Texas at Austin had been appointed attorney *ad litem* – in other words, Jasmine's lawyer.

An account of the deposition, taken under oath, suggests hostility to Flora, and it soon became apparent that she was suspected of knowing considerably more than she was prepared to admit about the absconding of her daughter and granddaughter to California.

To begin with, Powers asked, 'Ms Dempster, you've intervened in this lawsuit to ask for custody of Jasmine. Would you tell me and the court why you think you should have custody of Jasmine at this time?'

The answer, when it came, was predictable, and she left Powers in no doubt. Her response was simple and direct. She said, 'Because she's a Scottish child – my grandchild's Scottish. She was born in Scotland, and I think she should come back and stay in her own country with her mother.'

The questioning continued and she was asked to list in order of preference which of the various claimants she thought should have custody. Eventually, she settled for herself and Morag in the first two places followed by Lawilda and Jimmy Ross, with Marcus being the least satisfactory option. From that point onwards, the questions became more barbed. Powers asked her what type of access Marcus and his parents ought to have, and Flora, tempted to retort that they had been part of an arrangement that prevented her own daughter seeing Jasmine, had to remain calm. In the case of Marcus, she stated that he should be allowed supervised access and Jimmy and Lawilda should initially be given the chance to visit their granddaughter in Britain during school holidays. Later, Jasmine should perhaps be allowed to visit them in America.

Of course, Flora had anticipated questions about any role she might have had in the disappearance to California of Morag and Jasmine, and it was not long before Powers broached the topic. Flora also realised that if she acknowledged that she'd encouraged Morag, it would show her in a bad light and thus throw doubt over her suitability, should it be sought, to have custody of the infant. She recounted the conversation in which Stuart informed her that the runaways had arrived, knowing that she had done nothing wrong by merely listening to what her son had to say. She also recalled that Jack Reeves had called her some days later to tell her that Morag had contacted him. Flora told the lawyer that Jack had said that Morag seemed to be in fairly good spirits. Powers then asked if she had given money to Jack Reeves to pass on to Morag. It was a simple but clever question, because Flora was on a loser no matter what answer she gave. She knew the natural reaction of any mother hearing her daughter was in need and in trouble would have been to help her out. By denying financial aid, she could face criticism on moral grounds, especially from other parents who might think her hard-hearted and indifferent. But, harsh though it was, the law maintained that no matter how bereft Morag and Jasmine became, how desperate, hungry or cold, it was a crime to aid them. Thus Flora could not admit to have given encouragement of any sort, and so she had to answer in the negative. She said that she hadn't known where Morag was, apart from her brief visit to Stuart, until she'd discovered that she was in jail.

Powers then turned to how the press in Scotland had latched on to the fact that Morag had fled and been arrested. His aim was to show that Flora had encouraged Morag to run off and to demonstrate that she knew what was going on well enough to be able to brief local journalists. 'Do you know how they became aware of the story?' he asked.

'No idea,' Flora replied.

Before the taking of the deposition, Powers had also requested telephone records to see who Flora had been speaking to. The intention was to show that she had been plotting to get her daughter and Jasmine back to Scotland. A call made by her to Jake Harris had been logged. Powers wanted to know why she had called him. Flora explained that it was to ask if he knew anything and whether Morag was safe. Powers then wanted to know what reason had been given by Morag for leaving with Jasmine when Flora was finally able to speak to her daughter after her arrest. 'She said that the child was distressed at having been parted from her mother,' Flora replied. 'She was mostly in tears when she was speaking to me.'

After asking her what she knew about the night that Jack Reeves and Morag had been arrested, the attorney suddenly switched back to the decision by Morag to flee. Had Flora known that by doing so Morag was violating a court order or that she had travelled under an assumed name, the lawyer wondered. Flora might have thought that the sudden change in subject was an attempt to catch her with her guard down, expecting another question instead about Jack Reeves. If it was, it did not work. She said she had not known that her daughter was doing anything wrong or had been using another identity.

The telephone records clearly showed a conversation had taken place with Marcus, and Powers wanted to know what had been said. 'He was just full of cheek,' Flora said, 'and was shouting down the phone at me: "She's disappeared with my child and she's going to do this; this is going to happen to her and that's going to happen to her; this is what she's been like and what she hasn't been like." I hung up on him in the end, I think.' Flora then denied telling Marcus that she and Jack were arranging for money to be sent to America so that Morag and Jasmine could get safely home to Britain or that there were other ways for them to get out of America without a passport.

She also recounted a one-minute-long telephone conversation with Lawilda: 'She phoned to tell me that Morag had disappeared with Jasmine, and I said that I didn't think what had happened to Morag was fair.' Then Flora explained that she'd hung up.

Next, she went through her recollections of her visit to Woodville: 'Marcus kept leaving Morag on her own for long periods and going off and not coming back until late at night. He left on Boxing Day at seven o'clock in the morning with Stuart, my son. Neither of them came back that night, because they'd gone out on the town in Austin. When they came back late the following night, there was some argument, because he hadn't taken us with them and Morag had already been left for long periods on her own. Marcus put Morag into a hotel that night, I think. She was banging on my bedroom window as he tried to lift her into the pickup because she didn't want to go. There's nothing much I could do. I was in someone else's house. She never appeared back again. He didn't tell me where she was.'

Asked how Lawilda and Jimmy Ross had behaved to Morag, Flora recounted the conversation in which Marcus's mother had 'upset Morag by saying she was going to take their child away when it was born. That was just the gist of it. There was an argument going on, and Lawilda made the statement, which upset Morag. Morag had been describing what Marcus was like to live with back in Scotland, and they had been disagreeing as to whether he was a good guy or a bad guy.'

These were hardly responses that could aid Lawilda and Jimmy Ross's cause, should they be put forward as potential custodians of Jasmine. And there was more to come from Flora. The lawyer reminded her that she had spoken about Morag running away with Jasmine after saying that the child had been upset. He wanted to know the nature of her distress. Flora said, 'Whenever Morag went to the bathroom, Jasmine would be banging on the door, wanting to go in with her. She wouldn't let her mother out of her sight, and she wasn't doing things that she normally would. She seemed depressed, and she was crawling to people instead of walking and generally just going backwards from the normal child that she'd been before. She wouldn't let her mother go anywhere or do anything.' This behaviour, she said, had emerged after Jasmine had been sent away from her mother to stay with the Chapmans in Woodville.

Flora was relieved when the questioning was over. Powers had come remarkably close to the truth that it was she who had motivated her daughter to get out of Austin. And it was in fact true that there had been discussions with Jack Reeves and Tony about getting money to mother and daughter in San Diego. An escape plot had been discussed in considerable detail, and even Randy, sick at heart at not having Morag near, had been brought into the discussions.

One possibility had been for mother and daughter to make their way into Canada, head for one of the ports there and throw themselves on the mercy of the crew of an English merchant vessel, effectively returning home as stowaways. Normally, a crossing at one of the major border checkpoints would have been relatively straightforward. All that would have been needed would have been for them to produce their borrowed passports. But they would not have been able to take the chance that the subterfuge involving Jake Harris had gone uncovered. If the authorities had realised that Jake had given Morag his wife's passport, all crossing points would surely have been warned to watch out for documentation bearing Caroline's name.

If they were to use one of the principal cross-country routes, they would have required new passports, yet another reason for the decision to visit Los Angeles and the British Consulate-General. If for some reason it transpired that it was not possible or advisable to fly out of the country once they were armed with their new passports, they could have reverted to the road and an admittedly long journey north. But this would have led to the second huge hurdle: lack of money. A journey of around 1,200 miles to Vancouver, for example, would have cost several hundred dollars, a sum beyond Morag's purse.

Crossing the border without passports would have always been difficult, but there were, Morag had been assured, back ways that avoided checkpoints. Morag hadn't known whether this was true but had been sufficiently desperate to try anything, provided she could have got money to ensure their survival. The ideal solution had always been to secure real passports but in other names, and Flora had continued to ring her friends for many weeks before discovering her daughter had been caught and was in jail.

It would have been a heartless mother indeed who spurned pleas for help from her own flesh and blood. Following Powers' line of questioning at the deposition, Flora knew that the Chapmans intended to destroy her as a potential guardian for Jasmine, but she had the mettle for the forthcoming clash of wills. Terry Weeks, who was briefed later that day by Randy on how the interrogation had gone, already knew that they had an uphill task if they were to rescue Jasmine from Marcus and his family. But a saviour was in the offing.

20

Uphill Fight

The trial at which the future of so many lives was to be decided began as scheduled on 14 February 1995 in the Travis County Courthouse. A report in the *Press and Journal* hinted that the opening round might have gone to the young Scot, whose photograph accompanying the article showed her looking grim and stressed:

> 'It is like having a prisoner in prison clothes in my court. I don't want that,' said Judge John Dietz, who will be presiding at the week-long custody case in Austin, Texas, which will determine the future of Morag's two-year-old daughter, Jasmine. 'She does not have the child with her, and there is no way she is going to abscond,' he said. 'She has every incentive in the world to stay right here in Texas.'
>
> Last night a delighted Morag said, 'I will be glad to see the back of that bracelet. It is the one piece of jewellery I can do without.'
>
> Earlier, Judge Dietz warned lawyers involved in the case, 'There had better not be any goddam hot potatoes in this courtroom this week. If there is, I am going to hurt you all a little bit.'
>
> His decision to allow Morag (31) to shed the electronic ankle bracelet she had had to wear since being freed on bail last month came after a request from her lawyer Terry Weeks. The device had restricted her to the confines of

her tiny apartment, where she was monitored regularly by the court authorities after being brought back from California following her abduction of Jasmine.

A 12-strong jury will be asked to decide later this week whether Aberdeen-born Jasmine returns home to Scotland with her mother or remains in Texas with her father Marcus Chapman (35), Morag's former boyfriend.

Both Morag and Marcus were in the Travis County Courthouse building in the heart of downtown Houston yesterday but they did not meet. Proceedings were confined to a legal debate.

In a no-holds-barred three-hour session with the five lawyers involved in the case [Terry, Randy, Neal Pfeiffer, William Powers and Andrew Hathcock], Judge Dietz discarded his official robes, picked up a red felt-tip pen and walked to a display board in the court to map out proceedings. He made it clear that he wanted the case to be resolved by the end of the week. 'I am going to scare you, and you are all going to start screaming, but I am going to limit you all to a total of four hours' questioning each,' he said.

He has introduced a stop-watch to enforce his ruling. 'I think we are all going to have problems with this case – and I don't want any horsing around.'

In exchanges that would not happen in a staid Scottish courtroom, the judge told the lawyers, 'I hope you will all be able to be sweet to one another.'

Mr Weeks replied, 'I think we all know how not to get on your corns.'

The jury will be selected this morning and evidence in the case will get under way later in the day. Texas is the only state in America where juries are involved in child-custody cases.

Don recalls what happened on the first day of the hearing: 'The judge was as sharp as a razor. Before the trial began, Morag appeared in court with the tag on her ankle, and Dietz said, "I don't want people in this court with a uniform on. To my mind, that tag is a uniform. I don't want that in court. Are there any objections?" Of course, all the Chapman side objected to having it removed, as did the guardian *ad litem*, interestingly enough, because I thought he would have kept out of that argument.

'It was fascinating when the judge said, "OK, who says she's going to boogie? Why are you objecting? You think she's going to boogie? She boogies, she loses the child. Is that right? She boogies, she's lost her case." He scribbled out an instruction and said, "Get that off." The man was right: why object? She wasn't going to run away, because if she did she'd lost her case.

'And the selection of the jury was an extensive process. I remember the judge asking one potential juror, "Do you have any car stickers on your car?" He simply wanted to know whether he was the sort of person who felt strongly about things.'

Terry Weeks knew he had an uphill fight on his hands, the equivalent of trying to roller skate up a mountainside. He needed to make sure that the jurors who were selected would be able to sympathise with Morag and even with the problems created for her by Jack Reeves. He also knew that he needed a good start to the case, an early goal. He laid the ground for the first by showing Morag as a good mother and by pointing out that Scots such as Jack Reeves enjoyed a drink from time to time. The second was provided by Don Evans.

Terry questioned potential jurors carefully. One man was ordered to stand down after admitting that he had been one of the policemen who arrested Morag over the bounced cheque. The man's mother had also been called for jury service but was allowed to remain. Another prospective male juror told Terry, 'I went for custody of my daughter when my marriage broke up, but my daughter missed her mother so much that I had to return the child to her.' He was a potential gold nugget to Morag's case. 'Where on earth did you find him?' asked Judge Dietz. Unsurprisingly, Terry had no objections to the man remaining. But lawyers for the Chapmans were able to get him to stand down.

It was by accident that Don became the goal scorer Terry needed. Don had flown over before the case began, against the wishes of his employers, to support his then partner Flora and do whatever he could for Morag and Jasmine. He was fond of the little girl and she of him. Whenever he saw her, she would say, 'Come on, Jammy, tell me what you've been doing today.' His knowledge of social work and child-custody cases could, Terry knew, make Don a vital witness for Morag, because he was in the unique position of being able to offer both expert and personal testimony.

Lawyers acting for the Chapmans had been told that Morag would be producing an expert witness but not who that witness would be. Terry wanted to keep Don up his sleeve so that the opposition would not have the chance to take a deposition from him, thus learning what his evidence was likely to be. It was essential, therefore, to keep Don hidden away, and this involved organising some remarkable diversionary tactics, strategies of which Vietnam veteran Jimmy Ross Chapman would have been proud. For instance, when Don wanted to hire a car, Terry and Randy realised that this might be a giveaway. If a prying private detective employed by the Chapman camp was to spot a hire car outside the Red River Street apartment, ownership could easily be traced, which could in turn lead to the identity of the hirer. The solution was for Jake Harris, who worked for a car-hire business, to hire a car himself and then let Don have the use of his own car. It was deceptions of this nature that enabled Don's evidence to come as a crucial but total surprise.

Terry asked Don to swot up on the very latest research into child care and psychology, and the Scot headed for the magnificent Perry-Castañeda Library at the University of Texas at Austin. 'It was an incredible place,' Don recalls. 'Terry instructed me to get genned up, and I spent about a week in the library with my head in books and papers. It was a phenomenal, massive place and a researcher's dream.'

But it looked as though all the hard work might have been for nothing when the start of the hearing was delayed. Don had his return flight already booked. He was in an awkward personal position and could not extend his sojourn in Texas for a variety of reasons. The previous year, his employers, Grampian Regional Council's social-work department, had suspended him after he was charged with resetting stolen property – the Scottish equivalent of handling stolen goods in England. At issue lay the antiques business that he was running from his home in a former inn near Forres. He had bought paintings and silverware, including a teapot, two milk jugs, sugar bowls, napkin holders and a condiment set, from two men. It later emerged that his suppliers had not bothered to tell him that the property was stolen. Months after the end of the custody hearing in Austin, he faced his own court ordeal when he was convicted of reset and fined £750, despite his protestations of innocence. It would mean the end of his social-work career – he subsequently resigned – and by that time his relationship with Flora had also collapsed.

The effect of the hold up was that Don would be back in Scotland by the time it was his turn to give evidence. Terry had to act quickly. He explained his difficulty to Judge Dietz, and with his agreement, and that of the other lawyers, Don was allowed to go first, out of turn. It was to be a decisive move.

His week of studying had made him a knowledgeable and superb witness. He spoke with authority, and attempts to challenge him were met with a confidence that shook the Chapman camps. It was clear that he was more at home with the very latest child-care techniques than the professionals from the Travis County domestic-relations department, which had been given special responsibility for investigating the rights and wrongs of the Jasmine case.

Don spoke of why it was best for Jasmine that she should be allowed to stay with her mother in a settled and happy environment in Scotland, of the distress the constant moving about was having on her, and of how being forced to live with strangers in a strange land, eating strange food and without the comfort of her mother and friends was potentially disastrous for her future happiness. He qualified each of his pronouncements with evidence from a leading and highly regarded authority. It was a masterpiece of logic and intelligence. The jury sat mesmerised and were obviously impressed. Hours after he completed his evidence, Don was on his way back to Forres, the thanks of Terry Weeks, Randy and their legal teams ringing in his ears.

'Flora's boyfriend was over here, Don Evans,' Terry remembers. 'Old Don happened to be a social worker, and he knew all about all of the issues involved in this case. He had to leave early, and the case got delayed a little bit, so when we finally convened half a day or a day late I asked everybody if we could put him on before he left, and everybody said yes. So, the first witness was called not by them but by us, and it was Don. They just thought that he was going to say, "I am Flora's boyfriend, and I'm over from Scotland, and this is a fine little girl." But by the time that they saw what we were doing, we were way ahead of them, and there wasn't much of a way to stop us. The jury were sitting there listening, and he was saying, "You've got to be careful. This is a child." I thought, "Oh, that's marvellous."

'And there were no limits on what Don could say, because they had not asked us if we had experts, so I qualified old Don as an expert witness in the field of child development. We had a little chinwag in court about what effect it would have to take this little child away from her mother and what effect it would have to break her attachments. And we talked about some great paper on child development prepared for the World Health Organization in 1948 and about attachment disorders, and on and on and on. It was brutal.

'Don was a marvellous witness, and he sounded real smart. And, of course, they didn't know that he had some problems back home, so the effect of it all was that we started out on a real upbeat note. Quite simply, Don did a marvellous job. He was as good an expert witness on child development as I have ever put on the stand. I don't know if he knew more than the rest of them, but he said it well. If they threw him the fast pitch, he would hit it right over the fence.

'Judge Dietz was so mad, because it was pretty clear that we had stolen the case and were running early on. When the hearing adjourned for the day, I went back to the office and said, "We beat those bastards already, and they haven't put on a witness." I thought that we maybe broke their back with Don, who did such a marvellous job that I thought it was one of the great tactical victories of my entire career and all because somebody started court half a day late.'

There was a feeling that Terry had pulled a fast one on the opposition. Lawyers representing Marcus and his parents would need to work hard to take away the advantage Don Evans had clearly won for Morag and Flora. Morag's attorney was now confident that he had the high ground and that the jury might well be with him, but he still needed to be careful. However, he watched as the battle lines shifted from Morag and Flora versus Marcus and his parents to near infighting among the Chapmans.

'Marcus did not do well,' Terry recalls. 'He was sullen, and I got the impression that Lawilda was just a million-candle-power bitch. His daddy was sort of the best of the lot, a retired air force colonel, a bit of a gentleman. He was under the thumb of Lawilda, but if he had been given the freedom to run the case, it would have been settled, and these two young people could have found some peace and wouldn't have had to spend all that money. But he wasn't free to do that.

'I gave Marcus some rope to get back on the boat, wanting to make it a clear choice between the parents, because we didn't want the grandparents to raise the kid. I said, "Everybody is jumping on Marcus and saying what an awful man he is, but he has an engineering degree, and he owns a couple of nice pieces of real estate here. He's not a monster. He's really a great daddy." I left it at that, which confused them. They couldn't figure out why I was doing it. I wanted him to look a little bit better and take away from all the nasty things and have him compared with Morag as a parent, because she was going to beat him on that ground. I said, "The worst thing she ever did was run away from the cops, and that was wrong."'

In this way, Terry accepted and answered an accusation that he knew would form the foundation of the Chapmans' case. It was a problem from which there was no escape, so he had attempted to diffuse it in advance. Now he braced himself to deal with another.

21

Poison Pen

Jack Reeves had arrived back in America to lend a helping hand. He would never live down his first trip to Austin the previous year, so it took a brave decision to put him on the stand, where he would advocate that his goddaughter should come home to Scotland. He would be open to keen and probably hostile cross-examination. What would the jury make of the judgement of a man who had, according to the police, been discovered half-naked standing over the little girl's cot?

'It was a difficult decision to use Jack as one of the witnesses,' remembers Terry. 'But if you are surrounded by Indians and you have a couple of small bullets, you are going to go ahead and shoot. It wasn't like we could have said, "No, let's not use the cavalry. Let's use the air force." We didn't have anything. All we had was a lot of pictures of Forres and Scotland, a charming girl and a very nice mother.'

Even though he was encircled by the opposition and needed every weapon he could lay his hands on, Terry had to be convinced that bringing Jack into the fray was a wise move. Morag twisted her attorney's arm. 'My mother was surprised when I told Jack to come back over,' she recalls. 'She thought it might not be the best idea. He was a bag of nerves and needed a drink to calm himself but was dressed very smartly and looked good. Terry told me, "I don't want to risk him." But I said, "Look, Jack will do what I tell him. What I want him to say, he will say." All the same, we didn't want the Chapman representatives to get to Jack before it was his turn on the stand and get a deposition from him, so we took him to the top of the courthouse building and hid him in an empty court until he was needed. Nobody knew he was there. I was really pretty confident about him, and he came over very well.'

Jack told the seven women and five men on the jury, 'I would make a better father for Jasmine than Marcus Chapman. I will do everything I can for that child. It's true I was arrested in Austin, but I wasn't causing trouble, and I was only trying to protect Jasmine. I had been up for more than 36 hours, and I had been drinking.'

By the time Flora came to give evidence, the progress of the case was the subject of considerable gossip in Forres. Someone had decided that it was time to settle old scores. Over time, Flora had allowed homeless friends to temporarily park their caravans on her land. During the court case, an anonymous letter was sent to the court, which included a number of photocopied cuttings. One of these featured a short item from a local newspaper, reporting the case of a twenty-five-year-old man who had been fined £100 after six cannabis plants were discovered growing in his home. The headline read 'Caught with Cannabis in Caravan'. The man's address was given as the bungalow. Scrawled in shaky capital letters around the article, someone had written a message:

> ONE OF DEMPSTER'S TENANTS. COULD ONLY FIND THIS ONE. THERE HAVE BEEN OTHERS. SOME OF DEMPSTER'S TENANTS LIVE IN CARAVANS ON GROUNDS, OTHERS LIVE IN HER ACTUAL HOME WHERE JASMINE IS. WAS THIS INCIDENT ON FLO'S VIDEO??? HA, HA!

The same anonymous writer had gone to considerable trouble to collect and copy other newspaper items concerning court appearances in which the accused had given their address as a caravan site on land occupied by Don Evans's antiques centre. There was no connection between Don and the miscreants, one a young woman fined for committing a breach of the peace and for possessing amphetamines, another relating to a man selling to a second-hand dealer a video recorder that he had rented from a shop in the area.

Another letter, naturally unsigned, copies of which were evidently sent to George Bush, then Governor of Texas, to Lawilda Chapman and to the Mayor of Austin, had been postmarked 'Elgin', a small town a short distance from Forres. The letter included vicious allegations about the private lives of Don Evans and Flora, and the suspicion was that it came from a woman who was jealous of their relationship. A copy of this letter had somehow made its way into the case file, which was open, under Texas law, to anyone with an interest.

Flora was used to being the recipient of correspondence from someone whom she imagined to be a jilted admirer. A valentine card – unsealed – had once been sent to Don at her home. She had also received, through the mail, what purported to be one of his brown stockings with a note attached, reading, 'He's not half the man he used to be. Maybe he's spreading himself too far.' The sender of one of these unpleasant missives had cleverly stuck see-through tape over the stamps, thus ensuring the postmark would not show.

There were suspicions as to the identity of the sender of at least one of these malicious letters, which were clearly aimed at ensuring Jasmine stayed in America. As it would turn out, the writer, or writers, could have saved the cost of postage. None was admissible in evidence, because the allegations were uncorroborated, and the writer had opted to remain anonymous, thus making him or her impossible to contact.

A different letter writer had been in touch to allege that Jasmine had been taken onto a deep lake near her home in Killingworth. One of the boat's passengers had supposedly begun to rock it, and Jasmine had screamed in fear. In fact, Jasmine, who loved water, whether it be to bathe or swim in, had not been on the little craft – it had been another child.

The letters were just one more bizarre turn in a case that fascinated and at time beguiled Terry Weeks. He recalls another strange incident, this time in court: 'A funny thing happened with Morag and lip gloss. The opposition was continually maintaining that she couldn't quit drinking. So to make sure that they couldn't accuse her of stepping out of line, I was with her all day, starting at 8.30 in the morning. By the time it was 2.30 in the afternoon, I had only been out of her presence two times when she had gone to the bathroom. I ate breakfast with her, we were in court all day, we went to lunch and she was beside me all the time.

'At one point, she whispered something in my ear. I turned around and looked at her and said, "You're drinking." She said, "No, I'm not." And I said, "Yes, you are. I mean, by God, I can smell it. What else could that be?" She said, "Well, I just put some lip gloss on. It's a thing you can't buy here."

'So, I was left dumb. Then she was called back up to the stand for something, and I got the little lip gloss thing marked "Respondent's exhibit 15" and went over towards her and said, "You know, I just asked you if you were drinking. What did you say?" She replied, "I said no." I asked, "Is there any reason why you might smell like you've been drinking?" She said, "Well, I'm using some lip gloss." I said, "Is this it?"

'At that point, Dietz said, "Stop. Come up here. Weeks, you're not getting that exhibit into evidence." I said, "Yes, I think I am." He said, "No, you're not." I thought, "I goddam am." He went on, "And don't you dare offer it." I said, "You won't even let us get it properly identified so I can't offer it?" He said, "Don't bring that up any more." And I said, "Well, I'm going to keep trying until you put me in jail. I have a job to do, and I can't sit here and do nothing if you're going to be like that." So I put it down on the reporters' desk. Everybody was looking at it, and I went on to something else and passed the witness.

'Billy Powers went over and picked up old Respondent's exhibit 15 off the court reporters' desk, opened it and said to Morag, "Why don't you put some of this on your lips and walk by the jury?" I didn't say anything, and she agreed. He said, "Walk back, and they'll know if they can smell alcohol or not." Even the judge had to say to her, "Leave the witness box, apply the lip seal and get as close as you can to kissing the members of the jury." After she did, I stood up and said, "I offer exhibit 15." It had to be admitted because it had been displayed to the jury in a demonstration. So that was that.

'The lip gloss was full when it was entered as evidence. When the jury came back after their deliberation, the damn thing was half-empty, so we knew they had been walking around breathing on each other. The judge was so mad at me. But I was just doing my job.'

Morag spent nearly seven hours in the witness box. She described her first meeting with the guardian *ad litem*, which had ended in a bitter row and threats. He had arranged to pick up Morag and Jasmine and take them to the Kids' Exchange, an organisation with a local drop-in centre to which children could be taken, allowing estranged parents who did not want to – or were officially not allowed to – have contact with each other to see their children. Morag told the jury that she had complained about the guardian *ad litem*'s car not having a baby seat in the back, as was the rule in Britain, and that she had not been prepared to risk the safety of Jasmine by travelling in the vehicle. 'I'm not getting into your car,' Morag had said. 'You come back when you have a baby seat.' The guardian *ad litem* had claimed that by rejecting the lift Morag had defied a court ruling that Jasmine had to be taken to the Kids' Exchange. The effect of this, said Morag, was that the guardian *ad litem* worried her into believing that this might be grounds for having her daughter taken away from her.

Newspaper reports of the custody hearing reported that Morag said she had taken Jasmine to California to get her away from Lawilda and Jimmy Ross:

'They do not love Jasmine. In the early days when I was weaning Jasmine, Lawilda used to stare at me like I was the Devil. She did not like me breastfeeding my baby. I haven't even thought of what I would do were custody given to the Chapmans, because nobody in their right mind would do that to a child.'

Terry remembers what happened to the guardian *ad litem* when it was his turn to take the stand: 'Marcus couldn't have adopted a cat in the pound, because he just didn't have any background and hadn't been a very good parent. But the guardian *ad litem* got so close to all of the Chapmans.

'The judge conducted an experiment during the hearing. After everybody was finished with a witness, we would stop and the jurors would hand in their own questions. We would go up to the bench, the judge would read them to us and we would agree on which ones could be asked. But it quickly turned out that you didn't give any the thumbs down, because then the jurors would know you had rejected their question.

'It was a kind of free-fire zone, and one of the questions they asked the guardian *ad litem* after I cross-examined him thoroughly was, "Do you feel bad cashing your government cheque considering what kind of work you do?" Another one was, "Are you ashamed of yourself when you think of how many lives you've ruined?" It was just fucking brutal, and he promptly resigned after the case. The jury was just awful to him. I'd been pretty mean to him, but I didn't come near to what they did. That made me understand that we had pretty much won the case. At that point, I was trying not to lose it, because I could still screw up and throw it away.

'We called one of Marcus Chapman's former American girlfriends, who was a trashy little thing. She talked about him as an angry man. But she was so damn trashy, and she just wouldn't leave. We couldn't get rid of her. She hung around wanting a drink. She was like a damn stray dog in my office. We didn't want her to really get mad and recant her testimony, but we were as sure as hell tired of feeding her. Her appearance and demeanour, and the way she spoke and dressed, took a lot away from Marcus and made Morag look good. Because whatever Morag's flaws, they were not apparent to the jury. She was dressed very nicely and was fairly demure. When they saw the other woman, they thought, "Well, my goodness, he married that."'

A *Press and Journal* reporter was in the courtroom to follow the proceedings for his newspaper. It soon became plain that the Chapman family were moving the emphasis on who should look after Jasmine from Marcus to his parents. On Thursday, 23 February 1995, the newspaper reported that the hearing was almost at a climax:

> Texas child-care authorities want Aberdeen-born tug-of-love toddler Jasmine Dodds to remain in America. They claim this is the only way the two year old will be guaranteed a stable and secure future. But Jasmine's grandmother, Forres horse breeder Flora Dempster, told the child-custody trial in the Texas state capital of Austin, 'If Jasmine is allowed back home to Scotland, she will get all the support she needs.'
>
> The claim that Jasmine would be better off in Texas was made by . . . the court-appointed child welfare officer who has been monitoring the case since last September. She told the jury that neither of Jasmine's parents – Morag Dodds (31) from Forres and her American former boyfriend Marcus Chapman (35) – were fit to look after the youngster.
>
> 'They are both very immature and lack judgement,' she said. 'I don't think they have the ability to put Jasmine's needs before their own.'
>
> [The court-appointed child welfare officer] said that, in his opinion, Jasmine's future should be with Marcus's parents – retired US Army colonel Jimmy Chapman and his wife Lawilda, who live in the small town of Woodville, 200 miles south of Austin. Both are full-time school teachers.

Marcus's parents – who have had temporary custody of Jasmine since mid-December – assured the jury they would provide the youngster with a secure home and that there would be no financial problems. Mr Chapman said he and his wife would be willing to travel to Scotland on occasions so Jasmine could be reunited for short spells with her mother. And he said he would be prepared to contribute financially towards Morag coming to the US when she wanted to take advantage of any access visits. Lawilda Chapman (57) said, 'I just want Jasmine to become the young lady she wants to be.'

[The child welfare officer] told the court that Morag was obviously a loving and caring mother, but in his opinion had shown signs of having a serious drinking problem. Marcus, he said, had a very impulsive nature, a quick temper and was easily upset and angered.

In fact, Marcus had come over very badly. He had been accused by Morag of being violent to her and had bitterly clashed at one point with Terry Weeks, telling the attorney, 'I know where you live,' causing the judge to intervene and order him to stay well away from Terry's home. The lawyer was even given authority by the judge to shoot at Marcus should he come close to his home.

Don thought Marcus's behaviour was extremely odd: 'Marcus Chapman is a strange guy – a screwball. When Terry was cross-examining him, he actually said, "I know where you live." It wasn't the brightest thing to say. Terry said, "Your Honour, permission to speak." They adjourned to Judge Dietz's chambers. In America, you don't get an interdict to keep somebody away from you, and the judge said to Terry that he could shoot Marcus if he came within 200 metres of his home. After that, we were trying to work out ways of getting Marcus near the house!'

Claims that Morag was not a good mother were destroyed by the statements made to the investigator by Sam Frazier and Lana Cooper Jones. One more independent voice backed their views. It was that of a nurse employed by the child-protection department of North Tyneside Health Care in England. She had been asked to routinely examine Jasmine shortly after the youngster's second birthday. The nurse had put the youngster through a series of tests that involved running, squatting and rising, climbing up and down stairs, getting on and off a chair, chatting, playing and singing. Her conclusion was extremely positive: 'I found the assessment to be very satisfactory and was pleased to note Morag and Jasmine seemed to have a busy life attending local groups for mothers and toddlers, which they clearly enjoyed and an activity which I am constantly recommending to parents of children at this age. I did not find any cause for concerns regarding Jasmine's overall development at this time.'

Yet another bizarre claim was made during this sad saga. On the day the custody case opened, Lawilda told the guardian *ad litem* that Jasmine had been jumping on a four-poster bed, licking the posts and saying the word 'penis'. The claim caused immense distress, and Dietz ordered Terry Weeks not to refer to it. But to the fury of the judge, he did, pointing out that what the little girl had been saying was 'peanuts', because there were acorns carved onto the posts. Almost before she could walk, she had loved nuts, and Jasmine assumed the carvings had nuts inside them.

The judge's decision to let jury members put forward their own questions also dented Lawinda's chances. One juror asked Marcus's mother, 'What have you told Jasmine about her mother?'

She replied, 'She's never mentioned her mother.'

'That was absolute rubbish,' Morag says, 'and it was obvious from the expressions on the faces of the jury that they thought, "That's not right. It can't be true, because a little girl would have been asking for her mother all the time." She was only two and a half, and was bound to have been saying, "Where's my mummy? What's happening to my mummy?" Yet Lawilda was trying to convince everyone that my child wasn't bothering to ask about me.'

Morag hoped exchanges such as this between Lawilda and the

jury would damage the Chapman case. But at the same time she realised that what was needed to sink the opposition was a full-scale broadside. Morag was confident that Terry was the right man to apply the *coup de grâce*.

22

'The Kid Got Hurt'

On the big desk in his office in Austin, Terry Weeks keeps a bundle of papers. They have been there since not long after the day in February 1995 when he told a jury why Morag Dodds should be reunited with her daughter Jasmine. The bundle includes a copy of his closing address, a crucial off-the-cuff speech intended to summarise the arguments in her favour and comment on the cases put forward by the other claimants.

Very often, juries are swayed more by final addresses than by what they hear from witnesses. During his, Terry was frequently interrupted by Judge Dietz, who at one stage even threatened to jail Morag's lawyer for making statements considered to be unfair to the opposition.

He opened by tearing into the ruling that the custody hearing should have been held in Texas in the first place. Jasmine, he said, had needed protection from the court system, and Morag had been forced to live through a nightmare: 'This little girl was healthy and doing all right until she was ordered by some court to come over here on the basis of a lying declaration that Mrs Chapman had lived in this country for six months. From that time on, this woman [Morag] has lived a life of turmoil and hell.'

Morag, pointed out the attorney, had been left in Austin, a town where she knew nobody and did not have a car, and was put up in a cheap apartment with nothing to do. Then she had been told to wait until a court got around to giving her some attention and trying her case nearly seven months later. 'Can you imagine being in her position?' he asked the jury. 'Goodness gracious. What did our helping professionals do? They went right in there and messed up the child and mother's lives in a way that perhaps can't be fixed.'

Terry was especially critical of the guardian *ad litem*, who was in court to hear his summing up. He reminded the jury of the incident in which Morag had objected to getting into the guardian *ad litem*'s car with Jasmine because it did not have a child-safety seat. His response to that, on the first day they had met, had been to warn Morag that he would take her child from her. The outcome, Terry explained, was that Morag had 'got in the guy's face and never had a chance after that'.

His savaging of the guardian *ad litem* continued. Terry said that he had carried out his threat to have Jasmine taken away, instead of providing stability and security for the child. Mature decisions by the official had been required. 'We need some exercise of empathy by the guardian,' he said, 'and we need an ability to put Jasmine's needs first, right. We need all of those things. Jasmine's needs first.'

Were, he wondered, the little girl's needs put first by taking her from the home she shared with Morag, breaking the bond between mother and daughter and putting her with Lawilda and Jimmy Ross Chapman? It was, of course, a rhetorical question, and he gave the jury the answer to which he had guided them. 'No,' said Terry. 'We were punishing the mother.' Instead of the attention being focused on Jasmine and what was best for her, the fact that Morag did not get along with the guardian *ad litem* resulted in life being made difficult for her. The victim of the personal differences between the two of them was neither of the adults, but Jasmine, who was taken away from her mother as a result of the dispute, even though records showed that she had been well raised and lovingly cared for.

In England, Jasmine had been carefully checked. 'They are pretty intensive about child care over there,' Terry explained, 'and they think that mothers ought to stay home until the child is five or six. This child was developmentally OK. Nobody had any problems with her. Everybody thought she was doing just fine. Her mother had trained as a nurse and held certificates in child-care work and in training other mothers how to raise their children. Her mother had a good job. There wasn't any problem in this little girl's life. She was on target until we started helping her, and our help has hurt this little girl.'

He pointed out that while she lived with her mother, Jasmine loved water and enjoyed swimming in streams, being bathed and having her hair washed. But when she returned from living with the Chapmans in Woodville things had changed. 'The kid didn't want to take a bath,' Terry told the jury. 'And they had to cut her hair because it was matted.' The Chapmans, he said, were not bad people. But having a granddaughter and daughter-in-law from Scotland had been unexpected. Terry also softened the jury's opinion of Marcus: 'People keep saying bad stuff about Marcus. But wait a minute. Let's look at Marcus. Marcus went to college. Marcus got a job. Marcus bought a house. He now has two or three properties and has a house on Lake Austin. He is not the best guy in the world . . . He has got problems, but Marcus is by no means some piece of dirt that you need to sweep under the rug. He is apparently a pretty upstanding citizen who works and wants to be here in court to talk about the welfare of his daughter. It is not at all reasonable or fair for us to sit here and dump dirt on Marcus. He has got his shortcomings, of course, and he didn't participate as much as he could have in the upbringing of Jasmine, but we all know that. You know, he was busy working. He is rough, but he is not somebody you just need to put right out of existence. He has showed up here. He has hired lawyers. He has tried to do something about his kid. He has had a lot of help from his mother and father. But Marcus hasn't been a monster, by any stretch of the imagination. He has stayed involved with the child, and he should continue to have involvement.

'Perhaps his mother had wanted a daughter. The testimony is that before Jasmine was even born she said, "I will take this child from you." Do you have any reason to doubt that she would really like to raise the child?'

Terry then told the jury that instead of there being a close bond between Jasmine and her grandmother, the youngster had actually been closer to Jimmy Ross, who seemed to be a warmer person: 'Is he a monster? No. He went off to war for the United States and rose to the rank of lieutenant-colonel, flew his helicopter, did his job, got hurt, got out, went home to his home town, established a life and goes to work every day.' The Chapmans were 'pretty regular people', Terry said, and Lawilda was no monster either. However, he left the jury in no doubt as to her intentions: 'She wants this kid.'

As the case had progressed and it had become evident that the Chapman family were favouring Lawilda and Jimmy Ross as custodians of Jasmine rather than Marcus, the question of whether they were young enough to raise a toddler had been raised. Terry told the jury that the couple were about the same age as him: 'If you placed a three-year-old kid in my care, you would probably be on thin ice. They are kind of old. People that age don't have three-year-old children unless it is by accident or one just kind of drops in the way this one did. They are too old, they are too busy and they have their own work. They have their own jobs. They are ready to retire. They are tired. But they stepped in and are involved in the drama.'

The result of the Chapmans becoming involved in the custody battle, Terry argued, had been Jasmine and Morag's relationship being adversely affected: 'Jasmine's relationship with her mother is being destroyed, and it is being intentionally destroyed. They don't want Morag here. They want her to have to post a $250,000 bond to see her own child. They want her to go back to England and come over here whenever she can. What will happen to

Jasmine and her relationship with her mother? She won't have a mother. She will have somebody that drops in once or twice or three times a year.'

Terry then described what would happen if the jury gave custody of Jasmine to Morag and she took her daughter back to Britain: 'First of all, Jasmine will be with her mother and Flora. She will be in a nice small town with a sense of community and friendship, and she will have her family around her. If her mother has custody, will it significantly impair her physical health or her emotional development? It hasn't in the past. She has been on target physically and emotionally, right up to the day that she started being injured by our help. Is she injured today? Yes, she is showing signs of distress. She is on a bottle at almost three years old. If that isn't a regression, I don't know what is.'

Terry then said that the members of the jury should put themselves in Morag's position and try to appreciate how vulnerable and alone she felt when she realised that the future of Jasmine might well be determined by the guardian *ad litem*. There had been numerous meetings to discuss Jasmine's future, sometimes with Marcus present, but mostly just between Morag and the guardian. Terry explained to the jury why these had worried Morag so much: 'She didn't trust the guardian, and she was suspicious and frightened of him. She found him to be arbitrary and dangerous. And imagine what went through her mind when she found out that her child was to be taken away. I bet that's never happened to any of you. Think about it. You can't see your kid for two weeks. What would you do? She got scared, so her friend bought her airline tickets. He helped her, and she ran off. Would you have? You sure might have.'

The evidence of Don Evans, he said, had not been challenged. And Don had said studies showed that breaking the attachment between a mother and a daughter of Jasmine's age meant 'running a giddy and senseless risk of injuring the child for life. That broken attachment has been well researched and has been the subject of the basic studies in the field of child placement. The breaking of

217

that attachment indicates that the child may have difficulties with interpersonal relationships for the rest of her life. You don't place her with someone who will broker her into a day-care facility. You place her with somebody who will take care of her all day every day. You re-establish the bond between the mother and child or you run the risk of damaging the child's personality for life. Nobody has quarrelled with that. He said it the first day we started, and nobody has quarrelled with it.'

Terry also said that Don Evans had warned that after she was taken from Morag, Jasmine needed to be given a full explanation of what had happened to her mother, but this had not happened: 'Instead, she was told only that her mother "had to go somewhere". What kind of care is that to give this little girl?'

Terry said that during the two months she had been separated from Morag, Jasmine had been told nothing and had not even been allowed to receive a card from her mother. The result had been that both Morag and Jasmine had been hurt: 'The best interests of the child count, and the kid got hurt. I submit to you that you need to look at the evidence carefully and decide for yourself whether or not this case has been handled responsibly by your county officials. And look at the history. Look at the pictures. Is that a happy kid? Is that a kid that's got a good mother? Think about the issues and who should be appointed guardian.'

Terry said that the jury had a choice of who they could appoint to take custody of Jasmine. Then, turning towards Morag and pointing to her, he said, 'This woman has done a good job. When this case is over and when Morag has her child back with her in Scotland, Jasmine still needs these people [the Chapmans]. She has got to have them or she will not be whole. She will need her extended family on both sides. The complicated arrangements for Jimmy Ross and Lawilda to see this child will have to be made. The child needs to be given the opportunity to have two citizenships and to spend summers in the United States and in Scotland.'

The Chapmans, he said, were wealthy and able to afford to travel between Texas and Scotland to see Jasmine. But legal bills had drained Morag and Flora's savings. He added, 'That little girl will not have a mother on a regular basis if she isn't in Scotland. And there is no danger for her to be in Scotland. She has been well raised there. She was a normal happy little kid until we started helping her. We are asking that you award custody to Morag.'

23

Motherhood and Apple Pie

Travis County, named after William Barret Travis, who commanded the heroic Texan forces at the battle of the Alamo in 1836, and home to the city of Austin, had seen many skirmishes during its growth. But few can have matched the bitterness of the Jasmine custody case. There had been vicious allegations and counterclaims, and while those on the periphery did not believe that the jury's decision – whatever it might be – would signal a lessening of the dislike between the two sides they might have expected an easing of hostilities. Only time would tell whether their hopes would be met, but they would not have long to wait for the outcome that would mark the end of one chapter in the story and the beginning of another.

Judge Dietz sent the jury out in the morning of Thursday, 23 February, after giving them his final instructions. Then he, like everyone else, waited around. Morag and Terry decided to relax by having a smoke – a cigarette for her and a pipe for him – and stepped out to their favourite smoking haunt: an enclosed fire escape within the courthouse. They were there when the door opened and the judge popped his head around. 'You may as well go home,' he said. 'There's no point in hanging around. It could be some time. We'll telephone you when the jury are ready to come back with a decision.'

Morag and Flora headed back to their cheerless apartment in Red River Street, where they paced around nervously, trying to make the time pass more quickly by occupying themselves with trivial household chores. They had, in fact, not been there long when the telephone rang. It was the judge's secretary, who said, 'Please come back to the courthouse. We have a verdict.'

Minutes later, they heard the outcome of the long struggle. By ten votes to two, joint custody of Jasmine had been awarded to Morag and Flora.

Morag was too numb to cry and unable even to grasp that she had won. Terry turned around to see Flora sitting behind him sobbing quietly into a handkerchief. Around them there were gasps and murmurs: some of relief, some of disappointment, some of astonishment, some of hate. Randy hugged Morag and tried to explain that although her ordeal was at an end, a full judgment would be issued by Dietz later. When the courtroom had calmed down, the judge said, 'Our legal system has let you down badly.'

Of course, Morag was not free to leave Texas until the abduction case was settled. And while there was occasion for rejoicing, she had to remind herself she might yet be imprisoned once again. Even without that problem to contend with, she would need to stay on until a maintenance agreement had been hammered out with Marcus.

Her immediate priority was to see Jasmine. While the Chapmans had been attending court, the youngster had been looked after by relatives near Austin – it was they who owned the four-poster bed. Flora recalls, 'The allegation that Jasmine had been using the word "penis" was a particularly vicious one, intended to suggest that Morag had loads of boyfriends who paraded around naked in front of the child. It was a pretty sick thing to come up with, and despite the judge's wish that it should not be discussed it was brought into the open so that the truth could be revealed.

'At one stage, the Chapmans had been close to getting custody, and when the jury decision was announced they were absolutely gobsmacked. Lawilda came up to me, waved a finger in my face and said, "That child is doomed, doomed. You better look after that child, Flora." I couldn't believe it. In the circumstances, I would have at least shown some dignity, probably by keeping quiet and just leaving. But Lawilda had probably never lost anything in her life and did not know how to handle defeat.

'When the case was over, they didn't go near Jasmine but drove off. They didn't even say, "Cheerio, Jasmine. We'll see you on holiday." Nothing. Not a word. Instead, someone appointed by the court had to drive to the home of their relatives and bring Jasmine back to Terry's office for a huge reunion. Everyone was there, including Jake Harris's children, because Jasmine loved playing with them. Terry had a giant oak-topped table, which was polished to perfection, and suddenly kids were throwing chips and crisps all over it. He went ballistic, and no wonder when all he probably wanted was to relax with a drink.'

Christine Matyear sat in court throughout the hearing and was there when the verdict was announced. 'At the trial, I saw the Chapmans for the first time,' she remembers. 'The senior Chapmans gave the impression of cold superiority and stern self-righteousness. Their case was based on showing Morag to be an unfit mother and offering to provide Jasmine with more material benefits than Morag. Then their son testified, and I wondered to myself, "If that's how they reared their son, what will they do with their granddaughter?" Unlike Morag, he did not give the impression that he wanted responsibility for the child and seemed pleased to have his parents take charge. During the trial, I also met Flora. Her warmth, genuineness and down-to-earth common sense seemed to impress the court. I think she won the case for Morag.

'If I had been on the jury, I would have made the same decision. Flora offered stability and affection, and I think the judge and jury were comfortable in entrusting Morag and Jasmine to her care. In the days after the trial when I had occasion to visit with Flora, Morag and Jasmine, I saw a totally new Morag. She was relaxed, happy, optimistic and not really as bitter toward the Chapmans as one might have expected. Jasmine was evidently very happy to be with her. I thought the entire case had a very satisfactory conclusion.'

The following day, Morag and Flora insisted that Jasmine be taken for a check-up. They needed to know if, during her lengthy absence from her mother, she had developed problems that could be resolved before her long journey back to Scotland. Additionally, both feared that if something was amiss, the blame could be put at Morag's door and used as a lever to prise her daughter from her once more.

A friend took all three to a local hospital. 'Jasmine became desperately upset when the doctor tried to undress her,' says Flora. 'She was screaming, "No, Mummy," and even tried to hide beneath a wooden chair. Morag told the doctor, "This isn't like her. Normally she would happily go along with being examined. What has happened to make her change?" The doctor asked Morag whether she wanted the check to continue, and she insisted it go ahead. After Morag managed to soothe Jasmine, the doctor was able to examine her, and he said that there was nothing to be concerned about.'

The Chapmans were not to know about the examination. Had they found out, it would have only added to their shock and anger at losing Jasmine. A few days later, Marcus was quoted in a local newspaper:

> 'It's all motherhood and apple pie. This country's got that shit all mixed up. Justice ain't justice in America. I gave up a $100,000 a year job in Syria to come back to Austin and try to make a family. I didn't do that because I didn't care. I cared about my daughter, and I cared about Morag then, too. This case isn't about Jasmine. It's about hurting me, and she's done it.'

His mother was no less forthright:

> 'The decision is no good for that child. When you pull 12 people off the streets who are nothing but labourers,

they don't know anything. They come in with biases. They had a momma, and maybe she was loving and kind. They made their decision before they even came in that courtroom. The case should never have been heard by a jury. It should have been a judge. The jury's decision was based on motherhood and apple pie. That's this nation. But what they don't realise is motherhood and apple pie ain't what it used to be.'

The Chapmans would soon transform their rage and disappointment into a more tangible form.

Terry Weeks had been confident from the moment Don Evans took the stand, but experience warned him not to take a win for granted: 'I thought we were going to win when I got them pointing at one another and Lawilda said, "Well, we are very good grandparents and she's awful and Marcus isn't any good." They had ganged up on Marcus, because of our attacks on him, and they were trying to distance themselves from him rather than saying, "He ain't much, but he's the only father we've got." It was a bad decision. I was pleased when we won the case, but I can't say I was surprised. We had beaten them so damn bad by that point.'

The lawyer had broken with his own golden rule to charge clients on an hourly basis by taking on Morag for a flat fee of $10,000. 'If I'd been running up a bill, it probably would have been another $10,000 or so,' Terry says. 'But it was the kind of case which was very easy to do, because all you had to do was to try the lawsuit rather than do all the getting ready and all the shuffling of paperwork. And I got in late, so it wasn't my fault if we lost. I got to have a helluva lot of fun and would have done it for nothing if I had to, because it was so much fun.'

Attorney *ad litem* Andrew Hathcock, now an associate judge hearing a variety of child-support, child-custody, divorce and adoption cases, says, 'It was a very colourful case, factually, and it was a very complex case with a complex procedural history. To be honest, my personal view in retrospect is that I think the case probably should have been tried in Great Britain and not in Texas, because I think there was probably more information about Jasmine and her life and what had been happening there than there was in Texas. One of the challenges was getting information from overseas in front of the jury.

'My job was to represent the child's interests. She was two and a half at the time, and children of that age cannot really form an attorney–client relationship like an adult can with a lawyer. That's where the guardian *ad litem* comes in. The guardian is the sort of substitute decision maker on behalf of the child and gets to direct the representation of the child's lawyer.

'I think the guardian *ad litem* made a very thorough investigation. We spent a lot of time discussing the case, and I know his recommendation was that it was in Jasmine's best interests to be placed with the paternal grandparents, which was the position we advocated at trial. And talking to the jurors after the trial, I think they felt that the grandmother kind of supervising the situation would help keep Jasmine safe, even though I think they agreed Morag needed some help.

'When I was first appointed, I went and checked out the court file. It was a pretty extensive file. Buried in the back of it was an anonymous letter, mailed from Scotland and addressed to the Mayor of Austin. I thought it was pretty remarkable that that letter managed to find its way into the right case file. I guess you would call it a poison-pen letter, and it was very critical of the grandmother and the mother's family. It was probably written by somebody who lived in their town and knew them. But it was inadmissible in evidence. There was no way to authenticate it or get it before the jury, but it was an interesting phenomenon.'

After winning custody, Morag was in no doubt as to where she would head. She was determined not to risk her daughter coming within the clutches of the English justice system again. First, though, she was determined to make sure that Judge Dietz knew how grateful she was for the fair way he had handled the case. 'We knew when he usually stopped for a lunch break and wanted to speak to him,' Flora recalls. 'It meant being screened for guns and knives by security guards at the courthouse, who asked "Aren't you off back to Scotland yet?" Morag wanted the judge to meet Jasmine and was allowed into his room. He presented her with a plastic magic wand. Terry was amazed that she'd just breezed in and asked to see Dietz and that he had agreed.'

Flora flew back to Forres happy in the knowledge that the abduction charge was being dropped. Morag had received the good news the day after the custody hearing had ended. The Texas authorities clearly had no taste for trying to delay her from leaving the USA. However, Morag was unable to head home until the conclusion of another hearing at which access and how much Marcus would be expected to pay towards his daughter's upkeep would be determined.

As much as Morag wanted to be back in Scotland, her heart remained in Austin with the kindly Randy Berry, another Vietnam veteran whose legal career had been slow to get off the ground because of his service in that theatre of so much death and misery. She had always looked forward to visiting the offices of Richard Jones, knowing that there was every likelihood she would see Randy there. As time went on, Randy would often be waiting for her and would invite her out for a coffee when her consultations with Richard had ended. She found herself increasingly drawn to the tall American and would invariably invite him in when he drove her home to the Georgian Apartments. It was there that they kissed for the first time, she standing on tip-toes and he lowering his head to meet her lips. Randy's appointment as Flora's lawyer inevitably meant that they saw one another even more regularly, and he frequently called on her to pore over statements and reports. During these meetings, often late into the night, they told each other about their lives and marriages, and their hopes destroyed and dreams shattered. She felt comfortable and safe with him, but at that stage a kiss was as far as it went.

When she fled to California with Jasmine, she would often lie at night with Jasmine in her arms wishing Randy was there. When she was finally freed from prison, they became lovers. Morag recalls making love in Randy's office, and on occasional nights when Flora was out of their apartment visiting expats Randy would call and she would take him into her bed. 'I loved this guy, and I knew I wanted Jasmine and me to spend our futures with him,' Morag remembers. 'I knew his family owned a farm in Alaska, and Randy said that maybe Jasmine and I would like to visit it with him some time. But he would never discuss whether we would be together after the case. If I raised the subject, he would simply say, "Let's get Jasmine home first, honey."'

Randy had given his own closing speech to the jury. He had been the last to speak, and his whole body had shaken with emotion because of the feelings he had for Morag and the realisation that her happiness might become his own. She noticed that the stitching up the seam of his trouser leg had become undone and told herself, 'I could be a good wife to Randy.'

In fact, he had already made plans for a new life with Morag, although he had kept his hopes to himself. Following the death of his parents, the family's Alaskan farm had passed to Randy and his brother. He had a choice: settle on the farm, an idea encouraged by his brother, or begin a business as a legal liaison, probably based in Scotland, for cases of the sort that had just been completed in which lawyers in America needed representation in Europe. His role in Jasmine's case had already attracted interest, and there had been approaches from legal firms offering him work in mainland Europe. This would, of course, mean his leaving Kathleen. However, in private, he had vowed not to split from his wife until both had sorted out their respective futures. Kathleen was diabetic and badly needed a hip-replacement operation. When that was successfully over and she was back on her feet, he would tell her that he felt the time had come for him to move on, and move on with Morag and Jasmine.

The reason that Randy did not share any of this with Morag was that he felt she needed time and space to get her life back together. He would stay in contact with Flora, and when each thought the time was right he would head to Scotland to find out whether Morag still carried a torch for him. In the meantime, when some of her personal possessions, including clothing and skiing equipment, were returned by Marcus, Randy sent them to his farm in Alaska, where they were stored in the hope that one day in the not too distant future their owner would be reunited with them.

While Morag remained in Texas, he could meet her on a more relaxed, informal basis. However, he was aware that she was not wholly comfortable with having to remain so close to the Chapman family. Morag suspected that Marcus would seek a court order forcing her to stay on the grounds that the child was receiving treatment for an ear infection. The former oilman turned property entrepreneur failed to appreciate the humiliation and terror she had suffered because of his actions: misleading judges in London about the duration of Morag and Jasmine's stay in Austin, which in turn led to them wrongly sending Morag and her daughter to Texas for a custody hearing; causing her to be thrown into a police cell as a result of his emptying their bank account; and frightening her into absconding with Jasmine, resulting in her having to spend three humiliating weeks in prisons and detention centres.

However, an inability to understand the depth of emotion in the other was in all likelihood partly to blame for the course the Jasmine story took from that point onwards. Marcus, maybe spurred on by his mother, was hell-bent on getting his daughter at all costs. Morag failed to defend against his attacks and did not realise that even in her moment of triumph the danger was at its greatest. The Chapmans would never abandon their claim, never concede defeat, never give up.

She poured salt into the wound by dismissing a request by Lawilda and Jimmy Ross to take care of Jasmine in Woodville at weekends. 'My lawyers advised me against this,' says Morag. 'If they wanted to see Jasmine, they had to come to Austin. All I wanted was to get back to Scotland. Jasmine was asking, "When are we going home, Mummy?" I knew how she felt.'

It was clear by their actions that Lawilda and Jimmy Ross had no conception of the distress Morag had been caused by the decision to place Jasmine with them in the run-up to the hearing. They might well have argued, with some justification, that they were hardly to blame for the action of a judge. But they still did not understand the hurt Morag had experienced or that it was only natural her enmity would be directed at them. This was a case about feelings – or the lack of appreciation of them.

Marcus's feelings were made apparent during a hearing at the end of March. Terry, on behalf of Morag, demanded that Judge Dietz grant a temporary order for $3,000 a month from Marcus to support Morag and Jasmine until a full agreement could be worked out. The lawyer pointed out that Morag was unable to work and living in housing she could not afford. Indeed, at one stage her landlord had threatened to take her to court for falling behind with rent payments.

What happened at that hearing shocked onlookers. It was clear that the judge was becoming exasperated at what he saw as delaying tactics by Marcus in coming up with an offer of money. 'You will take care of your child,' he warned. 'There is no society in the world that allows a child to be abandoned by his parents.' Finally, he told him to empty his pockets, at which two $1 bills were produced. The judge said, 'You are going to see what our jail looks like.' He then made a white-faced Marcus follow him out of the courtroom to the adjoining Travis County jailhouse. In the meantime, the hearing had to be scrapped.

When Morag heard about the incident, she was convinced that it was a deliberate ploy by the Chapmans to leave her so bereft of support that she would ultimately have to throw herself on their mercy and in doing so hand back Jasmine. She saw the unwillingness of Marcus to provide for his daughter as a form of blackmail and was determined it would not work.

Suddenly, in mid-April, she appeared at her mother's home in Forres with Jasmine. 'I told Marcus I had an appointment with a doctor but instead went to the airport,' she says. 'It meant leaving everything behind.' She had had enough and had simply run off with Jasmine once again – and with good cause. Flora had also been dreading a repeat of the entire saga, with Morag and Jasmine being forced to wait an interminable time in Austin. Morag's friends in Texas envisaged mother and daughter being forced onto a legal merry-go-round. They encouraged Morag to leave, pointing out that this time there would be no warrant issued for her return, no police hunting her, no door slammed in her face by a timid brother. But there would be a pursuit, although she did not know it then, with the intention of forcing her to crack.

Once again, the Chapmans were furious at her disappearance, and this time their spleen was vented on Judge Dietz, as they demanded that he be removed from having any further dealings with the case. They were still smarting from his public humiliation of Marcus when he had shown him the inside of the jailhouse.

When it was finally confirmed, the court judgment did not go as the Chapmans hoped, although there were many supporters of Morag who felt that they had come out of it remarkably well, given that they had been awarded generous visiting rights. The main gist of it was that mother and daughter could settle in Britain. Marcus, Lawilda and Jimmy could have Jasmine for up to two weeks and take her to any country in Europe that was a signatory to the Hague Convention. And during the summer of 1995, Jasmine would be allowed to spend up to three weeks with the Chapmans in America. In future years, the youngster would be flown to Texas for six weeks each summer, with the Chapmans footing the bill for her flight and a ticket for Morag if she wanted to accompany her daughter. Marcus was ordered to pay $924 a month in child support from 1 August 1995 and to hand over $22,176 to the court authorities in Austin as a guarantee that two years' maintenance would be available should anything untoward happen to him. In addition, he had to pay Morag $7,250, half the value of a Ford Explorer vehicle they had jointly owned. He was told to cough up $385.87 to cover the cheque that had bounced after he had cleaned out their account, resulting in Morag's arrest, plus $225 court and administrative costs as well as $326.92 for their flight home to Scotland. Finally, Marcus was told that he must complete an anger-management course.

Although the Chapmans moved against Dietz directly after he delivered his pronouncement, their strategy was, in fact, an indirect attack on Morag's right to have custody of Jasmine. Effectively, they wanted a rerun of the whole case, and if it was not evident to Morag that they would not give up their relentless pursuit of the little girl, now aged three, it was to Terry Weeks, who vowed to resist them.

Lawyers acting for Lawilda lodged papers alleging that Dietz showed bias in favour of Morag, had broken court rules to get the case finished on time and had let her go home before the maintenance issue was settled. But the appeal process had not begun when Morag left, so the judge had not been duty bound to insist that Morag stay in the country. Lawilda even paraded outside the Austin courthouse carrying a placard declaring 'Judge Dietz violates father's Texas Constitutional Rights'. Marcus had also thrown his hat into the ring, insisting that there were grounds for a retrial because Morag had encouraged some members of the jury to become 'unduly friendly and sympathetic towards her' by chatting to them in a room in the courthouse set aside for smokers.

Because of the effect that a successful claim would have on Morag, Terry Weeks formally opposed the Chapmans. It was an odd situation. Repeatedly at odds with Dietz during the hearing and especially as he made his final speech, Terry now found himself defending the judge. He hit back by claiming Lawilda's action was 'frivolous and scurrilous'. He put forward formal documents, which read:

> All of these acts by Mrs Chapman are, of course, to an extent understandable, in that she is attempting to help her son. But in doing so, she is using the judicial process in an inappropriate way and is causing expense for her former daughter-in-law. The importing of judges from out of the county in order to give a hearing on pleading that

is inappropriate is not covered by the rules and amounts only to meddling as a matter of law. The pleading, on its face, is frivolous, and Morag Dodds should be awarded her attorney's fees for attending the hearing, preparing this motion and for studying the motion filed by Mrs Chapman. Reasonable attorney's fees for the above necessary acts are $200 per hour at the moment.

Lawilda had also set out her stall in an interview with a newspaper after she was told Morag was back in Scotland:

'We are going to fight this custody case. We were surprised to discover Jasmine had been taken away. All we want is a relationship with Jasmine, but Morag does not want us to know her. I was delighted when my son brought Morag home and said she was pregnant, but Morag disliked me for some reason. I tried everything to get along with her. I bought her clothes, and I bought her furniture, but there is only so much you can do. She is a very unusual person.'

At her grandmother's, Jasmine set about adjusting to life back in Scotland while the adults tried to accustom themselves to having her around again. Shortly after arriving back, she caught a minor eye infection. She arrived for breakfast one morning, rubbing her face and complaining. 'Mummy, my eyes aren't working,' she said. Everybody knew then that she at least was back to normal.

24

Love Lost

With mother and daughter safely ensconced in their homeland and the Chapmans still at war with the legal system on the other side of the Atlantic, the story ought to have ended. However, it was, in a sense, only just beginning. If there had been tragedy and sadness so far, it was nothing compared to what was to follow. The shock of the entire American experience was about to kick in – with devastating consequences.

'We were totally let down by the social-work department of Moray Council,' says Flora. 'After all that had happened in Texas, we thought we might be offered support, but no one came near. Of course, they knew all about Jasmine and what had gone on in her life. It was the sort of situation in which you expected to at least be offered help from your own people.

'Jasmine was home with us in Forres for her third birthday. It was such a happy time, and we'd got her a pony called Pip. How she loved Pip, and how fearless she was. Morag was also looking good when she arrived back and even began talking about going back to work offshore to build a life for them both. "If I get a job, would you look after Jasmine?" she asked me, and of course I agreed. "I need to get back on my feet," she said.

'Not for one minute did I think she would go under because of the pressure of what had happened to her in America. But she didn't like herself after the court case, because she's quite a private person, and had endured so much publicity, most of it bad, revolving around the Chapmans' allegations in court that she was drunk much of the time and including photographs of her in jail.

'While she waited for the maintenance issue to be resolved, she got very close to Randy. He took her away, made her feel better, asked her to help out with some of the paperwork in the other cases he was handling and generally tried to rebuild her confidence. She learned to trust people again and even allowed Marcus to take Jasmine away for a day. It was all because Randy made her feel better.

'But back in Forres, she was under a sort of microscope. People watched her. They would say to me, "I saw your daughter on the phone down by the river. Jasmine was playing about, and she wasn't watching her." She couldn't do anything right. If she walked along the street, people would be staring at her, and I said, "I couldn't cope with that." But she just said, "Well, I get it all the time."

'Some of Morag's old school friends stopped speaking to her, perhaps because of all the publicity. While we were out in America during the trial, friends faxed Scottish newspaper cuttings back to us. One story, based on an allegation made in court, carried a headline saying that Morag was a drunk. It didn't go on to say the claim had been strenuously refuted, but the 'drunk' tag stuck. The reporting had initially been very favourable, so I wondered why nasty things like that appeared. It must have been a case of the journalists thinking that there was no smoke without fire. And those are the sorts of things people remember, headlines like that, even though the drink problem had been alleged by the other side who were out to discredit Morag and were prepared to say anything to bring her down.

'People would say to me that they had seen Morag shopping. They would watch everything she bought, and they'd say, "Jasmine wanted a sweetie, and Morag wouldn't let her have one, while she had a bottle of wine in her shopping trolley." I'd say, "Well, she doesn't usually give her sweeties. Usually she just gets a treat such as a carrot or some celery – things that aren't bad for her teeth."

'The strain of the case seemed to get to her very quickly after she came back. It was as though all the tension she had been under was relaxed too soon. She won a long, hard fight and allowed her defences to drop. This was when she ought to have been offered professional help from the social-work department. I considered making an appointment for Morag with a psychiatrist but then decided that there was no point. The social-work department were used to handling situations like Morag's and should have offered her advice and support, but they were nowhere to be seen until things began going wrong.

'I became aware that there was something not quite right when Morag got a bit careless about Jasmine's safety in some things, but I had to keep asking myself if I was just a grandmother being overly concerned. Morag had been a very careful and protective mother, but she appeared to take it for granted that now she had won the case everything would be OK – that nothing else could go wrong for her or Jasmine. One day, Jasmine walked into one of the fields where there were four horses milling around, and I said, "You want to get her out of there." But Morag simply replied, "Oh, she'll be OK." I said, "Those are big horses, and she's a little girl."

'On another occasion, I had a stallion in one of the fields. Morag just wanted to sit and talk, but Jasmine wanted to go out and play. Jasmine went out to pick up a bucket when the stallion got hold of her by her arm and lifted her right up in the air. If I hadn't gone on an errand to the adjoining stable block, Jasmine might not be here today. It was incidents such as that when she wasn't watching or keeping an eye on her, almost wanting just to switch off, that made me realise how the whole experience had affected her mentally.

'Morag did not have a drink problem until the case was over. The Chapmans tried to make out that she did, but it simply wasn't true. Once she returned to Scotland with Jasmine, she changed. Perhaps she relaxed too much, and she began to have a drink, even getting drunk on occasions. But she had gone through a very bad time, especially when she'd been with Marcus, who'd treated her so badly. She'd always enjoyed a drink, but enjoying a drink and having a drink problem are very separate issues. Now she seemed to use drink to help her wind down after the pressures of the custody case in Austin and all that had gone with it: her jailing, having Jasmine taken from her and the tension of the case itself. When pressure continues for some time and doesn't ease off, it becomes increasingly difficult to counter. And the pressure on her had started almost from the day Jasmine had been born. If we thought winning custody was the end of it, we were wrong. It was only the beginning. And Morag had to handle it and face bringing up a daughter knowing that there were powerful and wealthy people who wanted to take her away. Now she had won, the pressures were different, but they were there all the same. Perhaps by having a drink she found it easier to cope with these different tensions.'

On their return from America, Morag had initially moved in with Flora and Don Evans, who were still together at that time. But she was ultimately given a flat in Forres, the first of a series of homes, all of which were unsuitable to house a small child. What she really needed was help up the emotional ladder of life. But this was not forthcoming from social workers, and, sadly, Randy would delay too long in travelling to Scotland to provide her with the confidence his presence seemed to give to her. Instead of an upward climb, she was doomed to a downward spiral.

Matters came to a head in June 1995 when Flora visited Stuart in San Diego. She was still angry with him for not having stood up to Marcus. 'Morag is your own flesh and blood, and Jasmine your niece,' she said. 'What sort of man kicks a little girl out into the streets?'

While Flora was away, Morag got herself increasingly agitated by the poison-pen letters that had cast aspersions about her mother and Don Evans. It had not been difficult to work out the identity of the writer of one, a woman who had once been infatuated with Don. In an impulsive fit of anger, Morag set off one day to drive to the woman's home to confront her. She was spotted by the police and was discovered not just to have been drinking but to have omitted to secure Jasmine, who was sitting in the back of the car, with a seat belt. Morag was ultimately fined and banned from driving but worse still was the report that was routinely sent to the Moray Council Social Work department alleging that she might 'wilfully neglect or expose Jasmine in a manner likely to cause unnecessary suffering or injury to health'. The dogs scented prey.

'Morag's heart was over in America with Randy,' Flora says. 'He had been a helluva support to her. He made her feel better and was almost a father figure to her. She needed the stability of someone like that and was hanging on waiting for him to come to her. In the end, he was too late, and she began to go downhill.'

Over in Texas, things were not going brilliantly for Marcus. Having already been shown the inside of a prison, he was given more time to study the interior of one in January 1996 when he was jailed for not paying Morag and Jasmine their maintenance. More than $3,000 behind in support payments and still not having handed over the $22,000 bond, he had appeared in court in December 1995, charged with contempt. When he was told to fork out $25,000, he disappeared but was eventually tracked down by sheriff officers to an office block in Austin and imprisoned, although he was soon released after intervention by his mother, who coughed up the outstanding amount.

The experience did little to mellow his anger towards Morag, an anger that deepened in the summer of 1996 when it was her turn to refuse to comply with the custody-hearing judgment. The Chapmans wanted to exercise their right to have Jasmine stay with them for six weeks and bought airline tickets for Morag so she could bring Jasmine to them. But Morag ripped them up and announced that she would not be going. 'There was no way I was going to go back to Texas after my experience there the previous year,' says Morag. 'I had travelled there expecting it to be more or less a formality that I'd quickly be back with Jasmine, but look what had happened. Now I was again being promised that all I had to do was to turn up and after six weeks we'd be on our way home. No way. I believed I was being lured into a trap – that they'd find some excuse, including the business of the seat belt, to have me back in court with them, complaining that I was not looking after Jasmine properly and as a result was breaking the terms of the custody order. Next would be the retrial they wanted.'

Lawilda was quoted in a newspaper as saying, 'We love Jasmine with all our hearts, and she is being denied her legal visitation rights to us. That cannot be called justice.'

Marcus said, 'I love my daughter, and I am going to get her back.' Once again, the battle lines were being drawn.

The pressure was back on, and it was clear Morag was handling it increasingly badly. 'Had she not fallen in love with Randy and come back to Scotland without an emotional tie over there, she might have managed to get on her feet a bit better, but she just seemed to go through one more emotional hiding than she could stand, than she could handle,' says Flora. 'There was pressure. She was put under the microscope and couldn't handle it. The absence of backing from social workers was also glaringly obvious.'

That is, in fact, a feature of the entire story. Numerous reports were compiled about Morag, most of them directly by or at the request of social workers. However, there is no evidence that they made an attempt to investigate the cause of her deterioration after she returned from America. Her friends and family thought that it was quite incredible that this woman, who so dedicated herself to the welfare of her daughter that she took flight in a strange land and suffered imprisonment as a result, was not offered help.

At the end of 1996, Lawilda and Jimmy Ross Chapman visited Scotland to see Jasmine. Social workers supervised their sessions with her. But if they came seeking evidence with which to launch yet another attempt to wrest the child from her mother's grip, they found themselves with a considerable amount of ammunition. At least one anonymous caller had told the social-work department that they had heard Morag shouting at Jasmine while drinking. In July 1996, she was back in a police cell after being arrested and charged with a breach of the peace and with possessing cannabis. In an attempt to cure her of her booze habit, she spent two weeks in a drying-out clinic. But it did little good. Three months later, kindly neighbours again contacted social workers to say that Morag was back on the bottle. If the Chapmans were interested, they could also have picked up on – and almost certainly did – a bizarre story of Jasmine and the cocaine lollipop.

Desperately unhappy at the absence of Randy, Morag began a relationship with a local businessman who had invited mother and child to join him for a holiday in Spain. The host enjoyed going out at night to clubs, but it was impossible for Morag to leave Jasmine behind, so she remained at their hotel with the child. One evening while he was out, Morag decided to take her daughter for a short stroll. It was a chilly night, and she borrowed a jacket belonging to her new boyfriend that had been hanging in a wardrobe in their room. As they sauntered past shops and bars, Jasmine spotted a stall selling gaily coloured lollipops and, as a special treat, was bought one. Deciding to save some for the following day, she gave the lollipop to her mother, who took a scrap of paper from the jacket and used it to wrap around the sweet. When she later handed the lollipop back to Jasmine, she noticed, after removing the paper wrapping, that it was coated in white powder. It transpired that the man was a cocaine user, and the paper had contained the residue from a recent fix. Back in Scotland, Morag confided the story to a friend, but it was soon the talk of the town. She also told Flora, who was furious that Jasmine had come so close to being harmed.

Soon after the Chapmans left to return to Texas, strangers began hanging about Forres. 'On one occasion, a car was sitting outside Morag's home. We took the registration number and

through friends found out that it belonged to a private detective,'
Flora remembers. 'When we managed to make contact with him,
he refused to say who had commissioned him to check up on her.
And she suddenly seemed to be befriended by a lot of oddballs
who wanted to paint and decorate and help and who for some
reason began writing letters to the social-work department and
elsewhere to tell them what they had seen at Morag's home or
what they knew of her. We later found out that some of these
people were in touch with the Chapmans. In some cases, these
people were being paid for information about Morag, although
we could never prove by whom that was. For instance, Morag
called round to the home of an individual who had been spotted
talking to Jimmy Ross at the hotel in Forres where the Texans
were staying. This man was little better than a down and out, who
rarely had money, yet there on his table was a pile of banknotes,
which he hurriedly covered up.'

A stranger began wandering about and constantly bumping
into Morag until the meetings became too much of a coincidence.
He somehow persuaded her to go to a strange sauna event held
in a nearby town, at which everyone was expected to strip off
and share some profound experience in the steam. Flora did not
approve when Morag announced that she and Jasmine had taken
part. The stranger vanished soon after.

Throughout these sad and degenerative times, Randy
Berry was a constant telephone caller. During one of their
conversations, Flora told him that Morag had a new boyfriend
and said, 'She's got the wrong person, Randy. If you love her,
come now. She's missed you so much that she's got herself
involved with somebody who is not good for her.' He flew to
Scotland in the spring of 1997, and Flora met him in Aberdeen.
On the journey to Forres, he explained that Kathleen had driven
him to the airport, where he had pecked her on the cheek and
said, 'I'm going to see Morag.' Sensing his tension and emotion,
Flora tried distracting him by telling him about the incident with
the cocaine lollipop.

When they arrived at Flora's home, Randy was instantly struck by the wonderful panorama before him and was shocked but delighted to discover Morag there. Morag, on the other hand, 'freaked out', according to Flora. Her new boyfriend was also there. 'You can't be here, Randy,' she told him, terrified that the meeting of the two men would lead to blows. She and her boyfriend left before trouble could erupt. Sitting with Flora in the kitchen of her home, Randy said, 'I've left it too late, haven't I?' Seeking consolation from a whisky bottle, he burst into tears, saying, 'I can't believe she's gone and picked somebody like that. I could have handled it maybe if she'd picked somebody nice, but this has really destroyed me.' He went home four days later to Kathleen and unhappiness, promising to come back, but Flora doubted that he would. She says, 'Poor Randy. I knew that he would be sitting in his home in Texas, sad at all the love and fun he was missing with her here. He would have loved to have been with her, but he just took too long. He was so supportive and loved her to bits. If he had been around, she would have come back to Scotland with Jasmine, and the three of them could have happily settled down and lived as a normal family.'

After arriving back in Austin, Randy rang Flora to tell her that he had returned safely. He said, 'I was so down that on the way over I felt like jumping out of the aircraft at 30,000 feet. When Kathleen met me, I wished I had.'

25

Downhill Journey

After the visit by the Chapmans, no one was in any doubt as to their intentions. They launched an all-out attack to gain custody of Jasmine. In this, they had two principal allies: Moray Council Social Work Department and Morag herself. Morag and her mother were bewildered by the apparent willingness of the local authority to bow down to the Chapmans. After all, Lawilda and Jimmy Ross had no claim on the child. An American jury had seen to that, and they had no legal standing in Scotland.

At the same time, Morag was finding it increasingly difficult to cope with the basic everyday task of looking after herself and her daughter. Flora was so concerned and distressed at the speed with which Morag was deteriorating that she contacted Tony on Tyneside. 'I think we have to try and get her into a clinic where she can be sorted out,' she said, and he readily agreed to pay for whatever treatment was necessary. Flora would look after Jasmine in the meantime. But Morag refused to attend a consultation with a psychiatrist. 'I can't see anything wrong with the way I'm acting,' she told her mother. The fact that she was unable to accept that she needed help simply added to the concerns of her family and friends. Flora told Tony, 'The stress of winning is causing her to lose.'

Watching her decline was heartbreaking for those who loved her. They prayed for the day when she would raise her hand and admit, 'I have a problem and I have to resolve it.' Eventually, Flora called on Don Evans. 'Don, somebody has to do something with this girl,' she said. 'She needs help.'

Don telephoned a local doctor and said, 'This girl is so far down that if you don't see her now, she won't be alive tomorrow.' The warning produced the desired effect. Morag was immediately admitted to a clinic, while Jasmine went to stay in the bungalow with Flora. After a short period of treatment, Morag returned home to be reunited with her daughter.

Before long, Morag's inability to cope was again evident. After the seat-belt incident, social workers had placed the child under a Compulsory Supervision Order, which greatly enhanced their powers to regularly check on mother and daughter. It meant that Morag had to inform them if she moved home, changed circumstances or even went on holiday. In all probability she was kept in deliberate ignorance of the growing relationship between the social work unit and the Chapmans.

There is a belief among those who sympathise with Morag's appalling treatment that it was with the encouragement of that unit or certainly one member of it that Marcus obtained an interim interdict in early 1997, barring the removal of Jasmine from Scotland. In April that year, he asked the Court of Session in Edinburgh to order Morag to send Jasmine to Texas for a two-month holiday. It was the development that she had most feared. She realised that if Marcus had his way, Jasmine would be back in America, and it was almost certain that the Chapmans would seek to keep her there. The entire sad circus would begin all over again, only this time she knew that she did not have the money, the strength or the ability to fight. She had given her all and saw little chance of getting off the floor again if she was knocked down. Morag is adamant that she ought to have been warned that unless she got her act together Marcus would be given the opportunity to benefit from her increasing troubles. She maintains that she was, in fact, left to rot.

'Things have been very difficult for me over the past two years, but I love my daughter. She is all I have, and I am determined to keep her,' she said on hearing of her former lover's latest legal move. 'I am not going to let Jasmine go. I just couldn't risk it.'

But the downhill journey continued. In April, Morag was found guilty of the breach-of-the-peace and cannabis-possession charges after her arrest the previous July. They were hardly the gravest of offences. The cannabis was worth £1.50, and the breach of the peace was a bust-up with a former friend over who should look after a dog named Tinkerbell. But they were offences and would be recorded on a criminal record that would, in all probability, be scrutinised by a court assessing her suitability to look after Jasmine.

In May, the Glasgow-based *Herald* newspaper reported:

> A Scotswoman who won a bitter transatlantic tug of love for her baby daughter was yesterday put on probation for neglecting the child. A court heard that Morag Dodds lay sleeping while the four-year-old child in her care went into the street to play.
>
> When police and social workers arrived at the house, they found 33-year-old Dodds in her bed. A bottle of pills and an empty vodka bottle were found lying in the next room. Dodds of Strathcona Road, Forres, was placed on probation for 18 months when she admitted a charge of wilfully neglecting the child.
>
> Elgin Sheriff Court heard how, in March this year, a neighbour had become worried about the welfare of the child in Dodds' care, who cannot be identified for legal reasons. Police tried knocking at Dodds' door, but when there was no reply they walked in and found her lying in bed. Dodds thought the young girl was in another room watching television, but when police could find no trace of her in the house Dodds admitted she had no idea where the child was.

By May, a social worker suggested that her department should be urging more contact through telephone calls and letters between Marcus and Jasmine. Morag's grip on her daughter was loosening.

Anonymous letters were sent to the social-work department and the little girl's school, alleging that her mother had been seen drunk, and early in July Jasmine was found wandering alone in the street after Morag had asked a neighbour to keep an eye on her while she went to a nearby shop.

Her choice of acquaintances did not help her cause. On one occasion, Flora went to Morag's home to collect Jasmine and was horrified to discover a young man eating the child's tea. Three days later, Morag locked herself out of her flat but was so ashamed of its untidiness that when a window cleaner offered to clamber up his ladder to get in through an upstairs window, she climbed up in his place, rather than have him report to his friends what he had found.

What many people considered to be the final straw came in the middle of the month, but there are conflicting versions as to what actually happened. Morag had been invited to dinner by a respected businessman and left Jasmine in the care of a boyfriend, giving him, as she says, 'a couple of cans'. When she returned, she was appalled to find the boyfriend in a distressed state, his clothing ripped and his leg badly cut. He said that a neighbour had called the police to allege that he was drunk. The police had arrived and had put Jasmine in the back of their van. When she'd screamed for her mother, the police had hunted for a neighbour who would sit with the youngster on the way to the police station, where the next move would be considered. But no one was willing to get involved, so the officers simply locked the door and drove off with the terrified child. The boyfriend, in a vain attempt to stop them, clung on to the door of the van but was dragged along the street before falling under one of the vehicle's wheels.

The official account is simply that the babysitter was spotted on the street – drunk – with Jasmine. This version of events is strenuously denied by the babysitter, by Morag and her companion that evening, and by other witnesses. Nevertheless, a sheriff signed a Child Protection Order, and Jasmine was handed over to foster parents. Morag would never again have her daughter to herself.

From then on, others would control the child's destiny. Flora and Morag might be legal custodians of Jasmine, but neither would have any say in her future.

Flora had been given joint custody of Jasmine by a court in Austin, which three English judges had ruled should be the ultimate decision makers. Why, therefore, was the child not placed with her that night? She was at home only half a mile away, but Jasmine was not brought to her, and she has never found out why. In fact, Flora was ignored in all the discussions that decided her granddaughter's fate. The judgment by the court in Austin was, to all intents and purposes, being dismissed by the Moray Council, which seemed to be ignoring Flora's legal guardianship of Jasmine. There were some who contended that Flora's position had no standing in Scotland on the grounds that a grandparent has no legal bearing in a custody hearing. But that was to effectively steamroller the terms under which the case had begun.

The social-work department found itself with a major problem: what to do with Jasmine. Having seemingly discounted Flora as an option, the possibility of Jasmine being placed permanently with foster parents was discussed. This would have been an expensive alternative, because she was only five and would require care for a considerable number of years if Morag was unable to recover and prove herself a fit mother once again. The ratepayers of Moray would hardly be overjoyed with that decision.

Of course, there were other possibilities. One was to allow Jasmine to be sent to Texas to live with a family more than happy to pay for her upkeep. That occasionally a social worker might need to make the trip to the States to check up on the youngster was purely coincidental. Another option, which seemed blindingly obvious, was to use resources to help Morag get back on her feet, instead of devoting them to the child being sent to America. Morag was of the opinion that a major part of the problem was that she did not bond with her allocated social worker and asked for a change in personnel. Her request was ignored.

Jasmine had by this time been moved from temporary to more permanent foster parents. A report on her situation stated, 'Jasmine remains very loyal to her mother and prefers to say that her mummy is not well.' It described the five year old as 'delightful and lively, interested in almost everything around her, confident but needing a lot of affection'. The report also made it plain that Tony was not in favour of his granddaughter being sent to live in America, despite Marcus's claims to the contrary. But Tony's preference would prove expensive to Moray Council, so it came as no surprise when it was rejected.

Flora, legally awarded joint custody of Jasmine in America, wondered why it was that she was not allowed to attend meetings about the youngster's future. The response was that under Scottish law grandparents could not be granted custody. Her protestations about the apparent moving of the goalposts to accommodate Lawilda and Jimmy Ross were ignored. Instead, she was sent an extract from a report into Jasmine's future. It was heavily critical of Morag's lifestyle and said, in effect, that time had run out for her. According to the report, which Flora has always insisted was unfair and failed to take into account the numerous pressures placed on her daughter as a result of the case in America, Morag was not acting as the mother of a five-year-old girl was expected to act. In particular, she drank too much and seemed to have lost either the will or the ability to change her behaviour.

Flora wondered why more had not been done to help her daughter to achieve her plans to change her behaviour. The more she thought about it, the further away she got to an answer. In fact, she failed to recall any help from the social-work unit.

The upshot was that Marcus was invited to come to Forres to get to know his daughter better and to seek full custody. That he had failed in his support obligations, had not bothered to send her birthday or Christmas cards and had been made to undergo a course on how to control his temper seemed not to matter.

In January 1998, at the Court of Session in Edinburgh, Lord Nimmo Smith said Marcus could take his daughter back to

Texas, adding that he would only need to bring her back if Morag mastered her problems. 'It's the best Christmas present we could have had,' said Lawilda. 'We've been praying for this and are particularly delighted for our son.'

The judge said, 'Going to America will be a big move for Jasmine and is bound to cause her some emotional stress, because she plainly loves her mother. However, she is a bright and resilient child. She has already been able to cope and care for her mother when her mother has been drunk. If she is resilient enough to cope with that, then she is resilient enough to cope with a move to Texas.'

In Forres, Flora said, 'People are coming up to me in the street and asking me why I did not do anything about it, but I have tried. Others ignore me, only speaking to me if they have to. They just don't understand. I am emotionally drained. I just cannot take any more. All the authorities here want to do is destroy two people: Jasmine and her mother.'

Within two days, Marcus had boarded a flight to Texas. Morag did not see her daughter nor kiss her goodbye. No social worker, concerned that she might be distressed, called to see her and explain what had taken place. She was given the news that Jasmine had gone by a journalist. 'I can hardly take any more of this,' she said. 'It has been going on for five years. I'm tired.'

26

Last Sighting

Two and a half years after her granddaughter left for Texas, Flora decided to visit her. She did not give the Chapmans warning that she was coming, anticipating that if she did so then some excuse would be found to stop her. She knew that Marcus lived in the town of Killeen, Texas, which had grown up around the giant US Army training camp at Fort Hood. With a population of around 100,000 it was a giant compared with Woodville, which was almost 200 miles away.

Flora had kept in contact with May Cherry, who had been so generous during the custody saga. Before leaving for the States, Flora called May to tell her what she was proposing to do. May's advice was to find Jasmine's school and ask to sit in on one of her classes. Flora also took with her a copy of a reference given to Marcus by Tim Driggers, associate pastor of the Memorial Baptist Church, 'Ministering Boldly for Christ' in Trimmier Road, Killeen, so that she could track him down in case he was able to arrange a meeting with Jasmine.

This is Flora's account of her visit: 'First, I went to Jasmine's school, only to find that I couldn't get in because it was on a military base and I didn't have the necessary authorisation. The Scots accent did not go down too well with the school receptionist, who said I would need permission from Jasmine's parents to sit in on the class. I pointed out that her mother was in Scotland and

I was her grandmother, but that made no difference. It made me think of the difference in attitude between the Texas authorities, which put obstacles in the way of Jasmine's joint custodian seeing her, and the Moray social services, which bent over backwards to facilitate the Chapmans.

'There was nothing for it but find somewhere to stay, and after booking into a motel I went to the church, where I explained who I was. Eventually, an older woman was brought in who said that she knew Jasmine because she looked after her when Marcus was working. I left a card saying where I was, and Marcus turned up at the motel that night in his working clothes.

'He said, "You want to see Jasmine? I'll ask her. I'll talk to her and ask her if she wants to see you." A child of seven and a half was being asked if she wanted to see her grandmother. He said, "I'll give you a ring and see if we can arrange something." He rang the next morning and said that they were going to go ten-pin bowling that evening. "We'll be around to pick you up," he said. I'd brought out her favourite hazelnuts and bramble jelly.

'When they turned up at the hotel, I looked out of the door, and all I could see in Marcus's 4x4 was the top of her nose. I could hardly see Jasmine because she was still quite small. She said, "I thought that red car was your one, Granny." She sat and cracked nuts all the way and was even more interested in them than the ten-pin bowling. She remembered her pony Pip. I was with her for about two hours that evening.

'We couldn't get a lane, so she played the one-armed bandits and at one point ran out of coins. I said, "Can I go out and get some more money?" Marcus replied, "Yes, but not the two of you together." It was unbelievable that he thought I was going to abscond with her from a ten-pin bowling alley. I went out to the car and got some more money so that we could play some more. Jasmine was delighted, jumping about like nothing on earth. She was full of herself.

'Marcus asked for my address and said, before I left Killeen, that he would keep in touch, sending school reports and photographs. But he never did. We have had nothing.

'I was leaving the next day, and the lady I'd met at the church brought Jasmine to see me. I wanted to buy her a Christmas present before returning to Scotland. Eventually, after changing her mind many times, she chose a set of horses in a box. We then went for lunch to a pizza parlour. Something happened there that struck me as quite funny. The parlour had a line of slot machines, which Jasmine began to play. When she came back, she sat and watched a little girl who didn't have any money to play with. When Jasmine was little, Morag had taught her to share everything, and she walked over to the girl and gave her some of her money. She had studied this little girl, and I couldn't understand what it was that she was staring at, but then realised she must have noticed she had no money. Then I left and drove back to Austin. That was the last time I saw Jasmine.'

Some months after her granddaughter was taken to Texas, Flora, distressed and depressed by the decline in her daughter, bought Morag air tickets so that she could visit the States, in the hope that a meeting with Jasmine might somehow kick-start an improvement in her deteriorating state of health. Marcus agreed to mother and daughter seeing one another, but only if Jasmine wanted to. Randy met Morag at Houston and contacted the Chapmans to say that she had arrived, only to be told that Jasmine had said she did not want to go ahead.

Morag's version of events was that she missed the appointment, but Randy rang Flora and speculated that there was another reason for Jasmine's decision: 'Perhaps Jasmine didn't want to see Morag because she was worried that the Chapmans would disapprove of her retaining contact with her mum. Maybe she was scared that they would throw her out, leaving her with nowhere to stay. She's only a child and probably thinks she must comply with what the Chapmans want her to do and say. So, being a clever girl, she said she wanted to stay there rather than meet her mum.'

It was typical of Randy to try and ease the blow by being kind.

Kindness ran in his blood. He had refused to take money for representing Flora during the tug of war over Jasmine, saying, 'What the Chapmans are doing is wrong.' And this generous man had to give up his plans to move to Alaska. He died from heart trouble, his dream of sharing his life with her destroyed. Within three months, Kathleen had also died.

Flora remains bitter about the lies told by Marcus Chapman to gain control of Jasmine, pointing out that his untruthful claim that they had lived in America for six months resulted in the case being sent to Austin to be decided. She is adamant that it was lies such as that one that have left Morag in her present, pitiable state. She also wonders why it was that when Morag asked for the return of her Labrador Dillon on her return to Scotland, she was told by Marcus that it could not be found. Yet he used Jasmine's affection for the dog as an incentive for her to be reunited with him when he sought full custody in Edinburgh.

And Flora is also angry about the way in which her rights were ignored when the child was taken into care: 'The impression given was that they were looking for any opportunity to take the child from her mother and that was it. There had been a few hiccups in the arrangement since Morag had returned from the States but nothing to justify Jasmine being taken away. It was the next day before we could find out where she had been taken. The people with whom she was placed by the social-work department were kind and allowed us to telephone Jasmine and see her. But when we arrived, she screamed and begged me, "Granny, you have saved me twice before. Come and save me again."' Even one so young remembered the role her grandmother had played in rescuing her from America and from the stallion.

Flora says that after Jasmine finally left for Texas, a television crew asked to interview Morag, who became so distressed a doctor had to be called. 'My lawyer asked, "Why the hell did you let her go on, considering the state she was in?"' Flora remembers. 'It was then that I realised just how dreadful she must have looked to anyone who had not seen her. The doctor said, "I don't know whether she will take her own life. Perhaps she still loves her daughter so much that we'll take a chance she'll not do anything to herself.'"

Morag blames social workers for the loss of her daughter: 'I have been betrayed by these people who ought to have protected us instead of destroying us. I was particularly upset because I bought her new Clarks shoes every three months, and every night she got a story and a wee singsong and a cuddle. When they took her into care, they never asked about what she liked when she went to bed or what kind of clothes she liked, their sizes, her favourite colours.

'After she was taken into care, I used to see her for an hour at a time. One afternoon, I was helping with her homework when I was told my time was up. I was preparing to go, but Jasmine insisted that I help her finish, which I did. It meant the visit overran by a few minutes, which was held against me. I was warned that if it happened again, my visits could be stopped.

'This was around the time that I was in a relationship with a businessman who had children of his own. His kids liked Jasmine and one day spotted her in town with the foster mother. Naturally, they went across to see her, but the foster carer said, "You must not speak to Jasmine." They were upset and wondered if they'd done something wrong. It was as if they had committed some crime, because I then received a call from a social worker, who said, "Look, we don't want this guy's children trying to talk to Jasmine."

'When Jasmine was at school, I would go and visit her. There was a fence around the playground, but I'd wave to her and she'd come over to see me. I'd kiss her through the bars and say, "Sweetheart, Mummy loves you." But one of the supervisors evidently saw me and reported the matter. The social-work people then got in touch to say that I must not do it again. I thought, "What are you going to do to? Shoot me?" I pointed out that I hadn't been in the school grounds, but they threatened to call the police. All the other mums could go to see their children but not me. It was horrendous, especially because Jasmine was always proud to be with me.

'I hope those who stopped this are proud of themselves. Maybe they have children. Well, no doubt they are pleased at ensuring I'm no longer with mine. Maybe there will come a day when they are no longer with their children. Then they'll know what I go through every minute of every day.

'That kiss was the last one I was ever able to give my daughter. One day, she was no longer there. When a reporter came to see me to say that she had been taken to America, I kept asking him, "How could they have done that without telling me?" I didn't even get the chance to say goodbye to her. I didn't even get the chance to reassure her. Nothing. She was just taken away. She didn't know what was going on, and I didn't know what was going on. Poor wee girl. She was taken by a man who was little more than a stranger in an aeroplane, and Mummy, who had brought her up for nearly six years, wasn't even around to give her an explanation.

'Now, there isn't a day when I don't think about her, but I seem to have fallen into an abyss of despair. I drink a lot and have health problems, but they are all because of not having Jasmine.

'I've tried overdosing three times but stop because I tell myself that if I go ahead I won't ever get to see her again. Then I look in the mirror to see just how much I seem to have aged and say, "I don't want you to see me like this, Jasmine. This isn't the mummy you knew. Maybe you wouldn't even recognise me." My hair is falling out, I faint and I have epileptic fits that make me fall down wherever I happen to be – in the house, in the street. I wake up in hospital with my head stitched, or my arm or leg or face. Nothing seems to go right. My dad bought me a house, but it burned down. Then I was given a council house, but I was surrounded by drug addicts who kept breaking in, and I was helpless to stop them.

'I know that there will be many people who say the condition I'm in now is all my own fault. Well, maybe part of it is, but when Jasmine and I were together things were fine. It was only when Marcus came on the scene and started throwing money around to take Jasmine away that my life began going wrong. All I ever wanted was to be with children, and now the only child I have I can't see.

'Without Jasmine, there doesn't seem to be much of an incentive for anything. I used to have some good times, like when I persuaded one of my pals to play Lady Godiva in a procession through Forres for charity. She needed a few stiff ones in the pub beforehand but kept falling off the horse, and in the end the police gave her a lift back to the pub. I used to laugh in those days, but not any more, and most of my friends have gone anyway.

'Christmases are a nightmare, and nobody speaks to me on Jasmine's birthday because they don't know what to say. I've spoken to her twice in ten years on the telephone. I knew Marcus liked a long lie in the morning, so I tried calling early when I reckoned he would still be asleep and Jasmine would pick up the telephone. When I spoke to her, I said, "Sweetheart, you know Mummy loves you." She said, "And I love you too, Mummy." On the second occasion, I said, "I would try to see you, but that man keeps stopping me." I don't call him her dad. She said, "That person you call that man has got up." Then the line went dead.

'I want help to get back on my feet. Some day, Jasmine will be old enough to travel on her own, and I so desperately want her to come back to see me. But not like this.'

In 2002, a package arrived for Morag from America. Inside was a Bible and leaflets suggesting that she should ask herself whether the life she had lived would get her to heaven. There was an accompanying letter, purportedly from Jasmine. It mentioned her schooling and extra-curricular activities and described her going to church. It concluded by stating that Morag should read the enclosed Bible and as a result change her life for the better.

27

Wrong Guys

The case of Morag Dodds is a classic example of the system failing the individual. Everyone has their own view of her. Some sympathise, others say she has deserved her fate. But the fact is that Morag and Marcus Chapman tried to create a family life. Was it the fault of these young people that it went wrong? There was certainly interference in their affairs, and Marcus's family in Texas was too dominant. The interest he showed in his daughter at first did not hint at the stubborn persistence of his subsequent campaign to take custody of Jasmine and suggests that he was perhaps pushed. Also, Marcus had a temper and was immature, something borne out by a court insisting that he do something to curb his lively temperament.

There is evidence of support from social workers in England on Morag's first return from Texas, but none in Scotland after she won custody of her daughter. That is a system failing. A system failing a mother who went to prison for her belief that her daughter's future lay with her. It is easy to condemn her for succumbing to the bottle, but those who have fed her vices must also examine their own culpability.

Terry Weeks, an attorney who has spent a career striving to untangle domestic mess, says Don Evans was probably the difference between winning and losing his battle. This is Don's perspective of the case:

'I went to America because I felt quite strongly that Morag had been buggered about by her husband, which was unfair, and I felt quite strongly that she should be given the opportunity to care for her child. I met my own expenses because I felt strongly enough about the whole business.

'The social-work department at Grampian Regional Council tried to stop me from going. From their headquarters in Aberdeen, they told me that I could not go, and I said they had no right to stop me. They said, "You are not going as a Grampian Regional Council employee." I replied, "I am going as a private individual. The qualifications are mine; the experience is mine. If I choose to do that in my own time, it is no concern of yours."

'There was no involvement of social work prior to the court case. It was only upon the return of the child to Scotland that social workers became involved. But when Morag came back, she was, of course, as high as a kite with all the local and international publicity, and she coped poorly with that. At that time, I felt that there should have been support given to both mother and child, especially when Morag gave them reason by going to visit the woman whom she was convinced had written one of the fairly damning anonymous letters. Morag went to remonstrate with her for the trouble she had caused, and, of course, the woman telephoned the police and Morag found herself in trouble. But there has always been a suspicion that information was leaked to the court in Texas and possibly the Chapmans by the social-work department, which was wrong.

'When she was arrested, another social worker called me, and I went to collect Jasmine and looked after her that night until Morag was released the next day. The police did not want to leave Jasmine with Morag, and I spent some time with her at the police station. I had Jasmine with me for a couple of days, but if social work had seen me they would have removed her, because I had her swimming in the River Findhorn with my two Alsatian dogs. It was a completely natural and safe environment. She loved that:

splashing about in water that was clean and not very deep. She thoroughly enjoyed it.

'It was at that point that social work had good reason to be involved: to offer Morag support, advice, guidance and to monitor the well-being of Jasmine. But I rather fancy, and it's an extremely difficult thing to quantify or to prove, that Morag was disadvantaged because of her acquaintance with me. The social-work department were not in love with me, and I think she suffered as a result.

'Quite honestly, the best thing that ever happened to me was getting out of social work. Had I been a social worker and the director had said, "Go and take charge of this case," I'm not sure what I would have done.

'In any case like this where there is an individual who has coping mechanisms that are suspect – and Morag was coping badly with the aftermath of the publicity and all the hype when she was back living an ordinary life as a single parent in Forres – the first thing I would have tried to do was to establish a good relationship with the mother and, secondly, with the child.

'The main concern is the child, but you have to establish a relationship with the mother too. I would have offered support and advice, and let her know that there was an understanding of what she had been through in her recent past, encouraging her to cope better with the present and to build for the future. It takes time, but the key thing in working with any individual or family is that relationship, which has to be positive.

'I don't know if that ever happened with Morag, because in any conversations I've ever had with her my interpretation has been that what the social-work department was doing was really quite negative. Negative checking – negative spying, if you like – rather than establishing a positive, caring and meaningful relationship. It was just upside down – wrong. And the effect of this was that Morag did not see the social workers as people. She didn't see them as coming from a helping, caring department. Instead, she saw them as coming from a department that was involved in social control, watching to see what mistakes she made. Sadly, there are some social workers like that. In Morag's case, they ignored or forgot or didn't bother to find out that she was a trained nursery nurse.

'The contribution of one social worker who came to visit was to say, "You've got a goldfish in a bowl on top of the television. That's dangerous." Morag replied, "We'll soon sort that out," and tipped the lot down the toilet. That was her concept of the social-work department: people who told her where to put her goldfish bowl. It brought out that bloody-minded reaction.

'She could be a difficult lassie to work with. I would have said that what was needed to begin with was a male social worker: somebody who was strong and sturdy; somebody who'd lived a fair bit; somebody who'd been knocked about in life himself; somebody who could understand some of the pressures she'd been through.

'She went through the mill in America, especially when she was jailed in San Diego. But when she arrived in Texas after her spell in prison, she was beautiful. She had been fed regularly, she had been given a routine and she had slept a lot. She looked like a movie star. I am full of regrets when I think of the lassie that came out of prison and then I look at the Morag now. There was certainly an absence of meaningful positive support. And I make no apology for repeating myself. I am pretty certain that she was disadvantaged because she was a friend of mine.

'Of course, she picked the wrong guys when she came back. I remember Flora saying, "Don, come and look at this." Morag had black eyes and a split lip, and her back was black and blue and yellow. Wrong guys.

'My job in Austin was to oppose the guardian *ad litem*, who was 100 per cent behind the Chapmans. It was fascinating, because he positioned himself with the Chapmans any time he was in the courtroom. The guardian *ad litem* should be an independent servant of the court who reports and makes recommendations regarding what's in the best interests of the child – should it be the father, mother, grandparents or whatever. But he was very much in favour of Jasmine being with the father, and it was my job to undermine what he was saying.

'The equivalent here is the same: curator *ad litem* or guardian *ad litem*. But in this country there is a fairly significant difference in that any reports produced have to be extremely well-researched and carefully worded. In Texas, they simply give a verbal report, which is surprising. I was instructed by Terry to get genned up on the very latest research, and after a week of that I sat in the witness box and spoke with great authority about the modern research, particularly Texas research. The guardian *ad litem* had never heard of any of this, even fundamental child-care research that he should have known about. I remember Terry saying, "Don, he's a three-ulcer man in a ten-ulcer job." But he was so dogmatic that the child should be with the Chapmans.

'Social work is about providing opportunities and encouraging the client and individual to make use of those opportunities, so I felt strongly that Morag should be given the chance to look after her daughter, and I was as disappointed as anyone when it did not work out. But at least she had the opportunity. All I feel now is sadness. It is literally a tragedy. What happened to Morag is a tragedy, but she is more sinned against than sinning.

'The key time in Morag's life was when she returned from Texas after winning custody. Once all the initial excitement had died down, that was the time to get working with her – the time to establish that relationship I spoke of and to guide her. Once there is a relationship established, you can say to her, "That's not on." You can be firm once you've earned that respect.

'Texas was a very traumatic experience for Morag, and I wonder how many medical professionals or social workers actually understood what that wee lassie went through. She went over to a completely alien culture and had to face a foreign court. Morag did not know that if you cross a state boundary in America it becomes a major crime. She spent time in San Diego in amongst the hard nuts, and that in itself must have been traumatic. But the court case was extremely trying and demanding for her.

'Randy was such a nice, likeable, caring guy, but he wasn't strong enough for Morag. He needed to be a strong social-worker type who would say, "Morag, no." There would be no discussion on the discussion. But there was a distinct absence of that in her life, and she kept picking the wrong guys. And things happened to her because she kept picking the wrong guys and having her teeth knocked out and stuff like that.

'I remember meeting an English guy – he was terribly English – who said, "If I saw a woman walking towards me in the High Street in Forres with a pickaxe sticking out of her head, I'd wager good money it was Morag Dodds." That summed her up.

'Before the custody in Texas was actually decided, social work had its mind made up, because it was passing information to Texas. Certainly, my association with Morag did not help her, and what the hell does that tell you about the social-work department?

'When she came back with Jasmine, I felt quite strongly that she should be given the opportunity to look after her. I thought that once she got over all the hype and the excitement and the buzz and celebrations of victory, she would settle down and get on with the job of looking after her special daughter, but it never worked out that way. She was searching for somebody to care for her and to look after her.

'When she is older, Jasmine will get her own life in order and make her own mind up. She might even tell her mother to get her life in order. A good social worker would help Morag to regain some hope for the future. But they've taken so much away from Morag that all she has now is drink. Her recovery begins with getting off the booze. There's an old saying in the navy: "If you want to stop drinking, it's hard; if you don't want to, it's impossible."

'I wonder what the future holds for her. If she wants to put her life in order, she needs to begin by getting rid of all her drinking pals and stick with sober people. If she can do that, then there is hope. There could still be a happy ending. But now it is a sad, sad story.'

Appendix

Daily Record, 30 October 1998:

Morag Dodds fought back tears as she read how Paula Yates had lost custody of her daughters to ex-husband Bob Geldof. Morag, too, has faced the anguish of handing over her child to a man she no longer loves.

Her most treasured possession is a faded photograph of herself and her daughter together. But the happy times they once shared now seem a million miles away. And her greatest fear is that, with every passing day, she is becoming a stranger to her daughter, Jasmine, now six.

Morag, 34, a former nursery nurse of Forres, Morayshire, has not been able to speak to her little girl for months, despite repeated attempts to make contact. Her estranged boyfriend, American Marcus Chapman, took Jasmine to live with him in Killeen, Texas, last January after a court ruled he should care for her until custody is settled. Still Morag refuses to give up and is planning to take her fight to the European Court of Human Rights.

No one could have blamed her if she had admitted defeat a long time ago. Her custody battle has taken her back and forth across the Atlantic, it has seen her thrown into a Texas jail for child abduction and brought her entire life under scrutiny. And she is no nearer bringing her daughter home. All the battle has brought her is a tarnished reputation and a bill for legal expenses.

Yet the advice Morag offers Paula Yates is, 'Never give up. No matter what they say about you, you never stop being a mother.'

The Herald, 6 March 1999:

> A missing mother involved in a custody row was found
> safe and well yesterday after a police search. Ms Morag
> Dodds, 35, from Forres, Moray, was reported missing on
> Wednesday night, and there were fears for her safety
> after she walked out of a Moray hospital. She was jailed
> four years ago after going on the run to defy a US court
> ordering her to return custody of her then infant daughter
> to her father in Texas. Police had issued an appeal for
> information on her whereabouts and yesterday she was
> spotted in Elgin High Street. A police spokesman said,
> 'There does not appear to be anything suspicious about
> her disappearance.'

Aberdeen Evening Express, 30 December 2006:

> A mum who lost custody of her daughter in a
> transatlantic tug of love has gone missing. Morag Dodds,
> 42, disappeared from her Fraserburgh home on Boxing
> Day after spending Christmas Day with her mum Flora
> Dempster. Mrs Dempster of Forres said Morag was still
> devastated by the loss of her child.

Within hours of this report appearing, Morag turned up, having
gone to stay with friends. Christmas Day and memories of Jasmine
staring at the tree in the offices of the British Consulate-General
had distressed and disorientated her. Thoughts of Jasmine still
overwhelm her now as she divides her time between a home
in the north-east of Scotland and visits to the bungalow, where
Flora continues her battle to avoid having to sell up and move
as the result of an action by her son. Morag's determination to
win Jasmine back is undiminished. But the most likely scenario
is that Jasmine will one day visit Scotland when she is older and
free to travel where she wants.